LOST VAN GOGH

The lost, the rare, the stolen, the obscure, the destroyed, the beautiful.

By JÉANPAUL FERRO

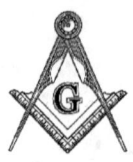

Thomas Winston & Company
South Ocean Drive
Hallandale, FL 33009

Text set in Sabon

LOST VAN GOGH

First Edition 2024

Manufactured in the United States of America

Kindle & Paperback ISBN: 9798884955578

INTRODUCTION

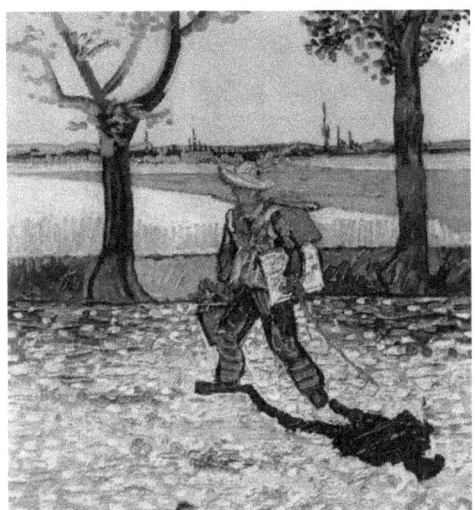

Painter on the Road to Tarascon, August 1888
(destroyed by fire in a German salt mine during WWII)

Vincent Willem van Gogh was born March 30th, 1853 to an upper-middle-class Dutch family in the municipality of Groot-Zundert, a small village in the south of the Netherlands that borders nearby Belgium. The eldest of six children, Vincent was known as a reserve and quiet child during his childhood; not someone who would one day become one of the most famous human beings to ever live.

Apt at art and drawing from a very young age, he often wandered the nearby countryside to soak up the magnificent sights of multi-colored songbirds, kingfishers, solitary woods and trees, fields, flowers, and streams, which he often rushed home to draw with pencil on paper. Shy, handsome, and altogether thoughtful, it was evident to others while still quite young that the young Vincent expressed signs of mental instability—"mental or nervous fever or madness, I do not know quite what to say or how to name it" he later described his bouts with madness in one letter to a friend. Unbeknownst to him he suffered from what we now know as bi-polar, or severe acute depression. He would spend his adulthood living through mad waves of highs and lows, institutionalized multiple times yet still able to spend weeks and months on end writing, drawing, and painting hundreds of letters, drawings, and landscapes.

In just over a decade Vincent van Gogh created over 2,100 works of art, including 860 known oil paintings, most of which were painted in a short frantic span that lasted during the last two years of his life at age 36 and 37.

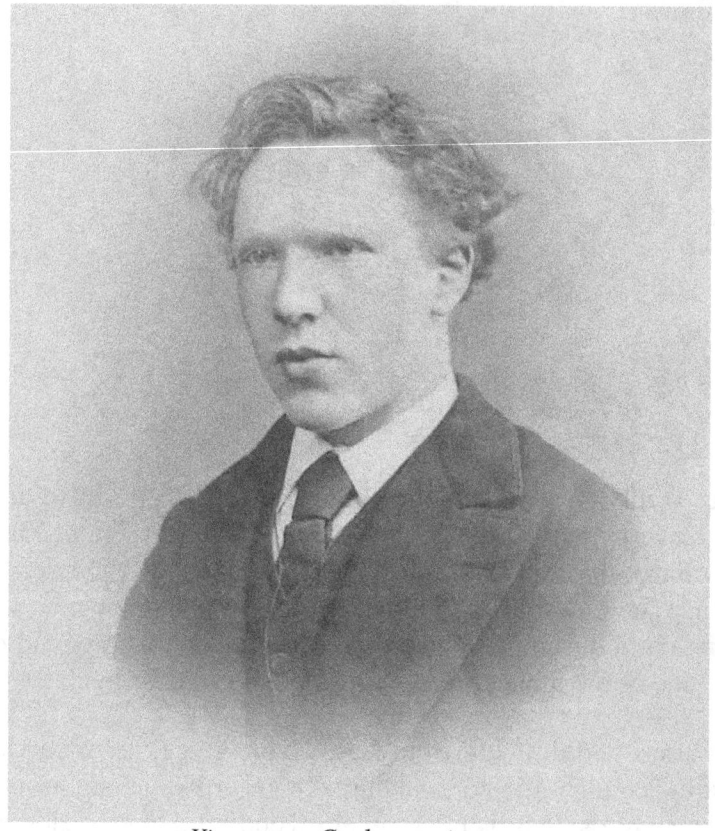

Vincent van Gogh, age nineteen

Although his works were once exhibited by André Antoine alongside the works of fellow masters, Georges Seurat and Paul Signac, at the Théâtre Libre in Paris, recognition and fortune eluded van Gogh. The more desperate and unknown he remained the more his output increased, which now is almost heartbreaking and pitiful. Almost completely unrecognized for his genius during his lifetime, he sold absolutely zero paintings to buyers not directly related to him. His Uncle Cor, a Dutch art dealer, tried to help Vincent get off the ground in the artworld by buying 19 cityscapes in the realism style of the municipality of The Hauge. His brother Theo talked the Parisian art dealer, Julien Tanguy, into buying one single painting. And after

Vincent painted the dramatically colored *The Red Vineyard* it was purchased for a mere 400 Francs (about $2000 by today's standards) by Anna Boch, the sister of Vincent's close friend Eugène Boch. Yet for all his lack of success while alive the hand of Vincent van Gogh's unique brushstrokes can be recognized today by mere three and four-year-old children from Berlin to Mozambique. His dramatic use of color, his skies, his stars, his wind rushing through the cypress and olive trees is unlike any other artist who was ever alive. One can almost taste his pain, anguish, and loneliness in the very foundation of each landscape and portrait he produced.

Van Gogh's early work done in the traditional realism style was quite flat, stoic, almost indistinguishable from other painters with his use of a darkened palette that is not altogether attractive. One might even say that it is depressing.

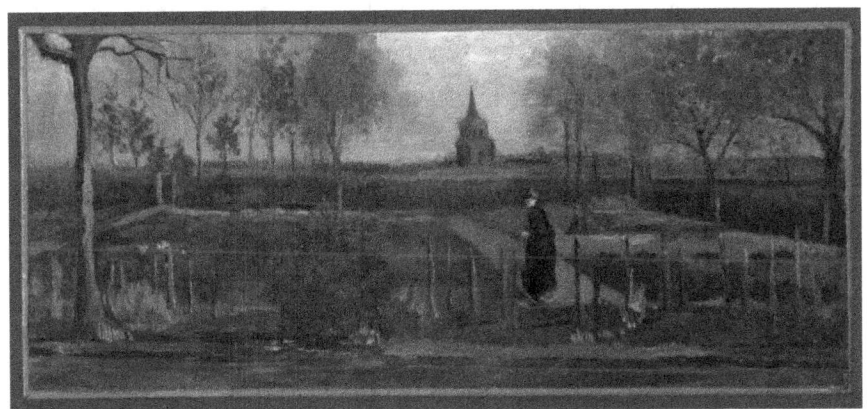

The Spring Garden, painted in Neunen circa 1883 – 1885.

It was after visiting Paris and leaving the city of light for the French Countryside of Arles, France that his use of pure colors and his vivid style of broken brushwork came into being, like sunlight from out of a dark bellowing cloud, where he became the artist of the iconic works that we all recognize today as "a van Gogh."

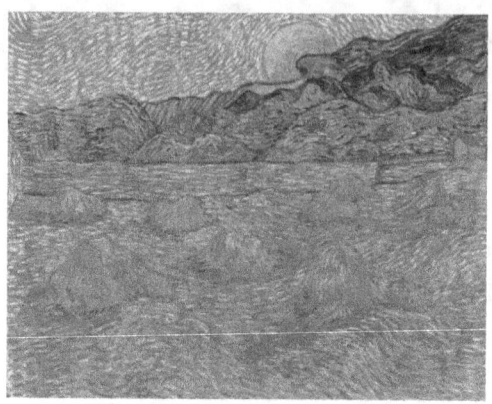

Wheat Fields, early June 1889.

During the 20th Century the works of Vincent van Gogh slowly began to be exhibited and recognized by fellow artists and connoisseurs alike thanks to the foundation that his brother Theo built for him back when they were both alive in Holland and France, otherwise there would have been no landscapes and painting at all to save.

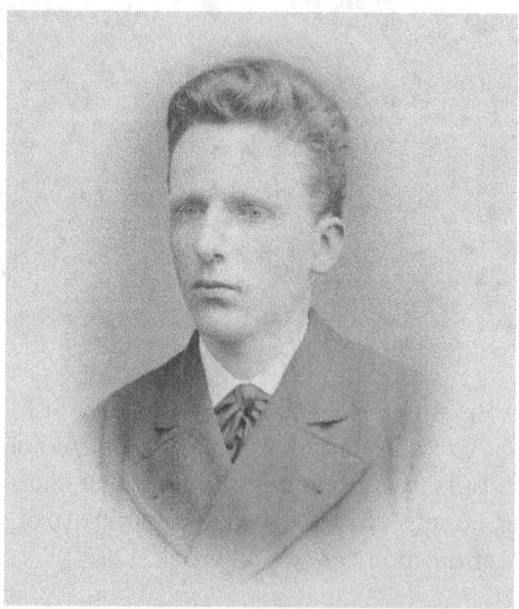

Theo van Gogh, age twenty-one

The following is an exhibit of a whole host of van Gogh works: some well-known and iconic, some obscure, some lost to Nazi raids throughout Europe during of WWII in Adolph Hitler's futile attempt to steal the greatest art works in the world to build the greatest art museum ever known to mankind: the Fuhrer-Museum (English: Leader's Museum), also known as the Linz art gallery in his birthplace of Austria; and other more van Gogh's that are simply rarely seen or locked away in private collections. I hope this travel through time brings you as much joy in viewing and learning about each peace as it brought me putting this retrospective together.

Je vous en prie!

Jéanpaul Ferro, March 2024

The Only Known Photo of Vincent van Gogh as an Adult taken at the Parisian art academy, February 1888.

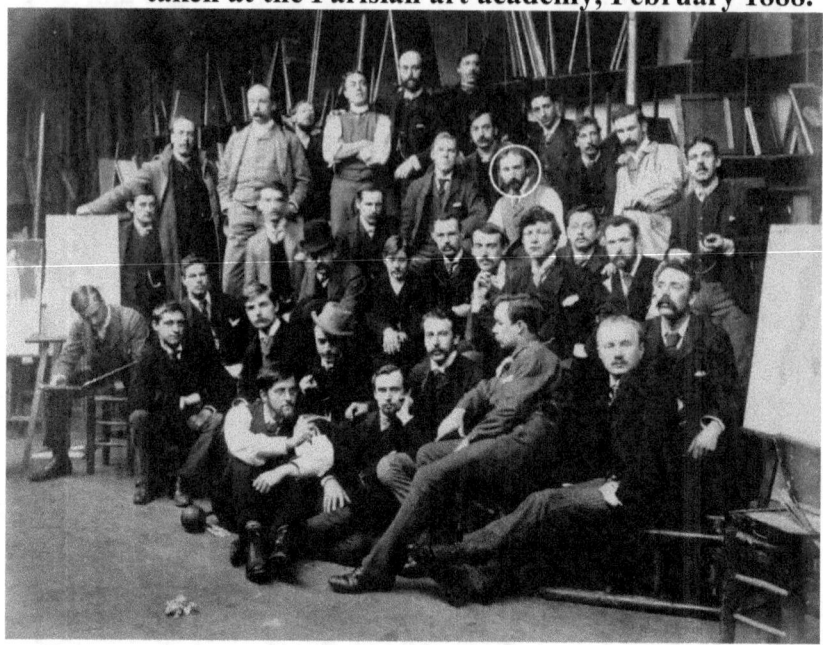

Charles W. Bartlett; Horace Mann Livens; Edouard Vuillard; D. Howard Hitchcock; Paul Sérusier; Paul Gauguin, Arthur Haytorne Studd; Akseli Gallen-Kallela; Paul Peel; Robert Bevan; William Laurel Harris, **Vincent van Gogh**; Georges Lacombe; Pierre Bonnard; Paul Ranson; Jéan de Francqueville; Eeero Jamesfelt; Albert Edelfelt; Eduard Frankfort; Hobbe Smith; John Peter Russel; Arthur Briet; Armand Seguin; Ker Xavier Roussel; Walter Whiters; Emil Wikström; Alfred Garth Jones; Oralando Guy Rose; Henry Ryland; Archibald Standish; Ferdinand Hart Nibbrig; Hal Waugh; Kenyon Cox; and Dodge MacKnight.

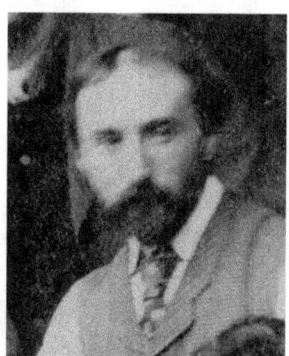

Vincent van Gogh, 1888

Six Sunflowers, destroyed 1945

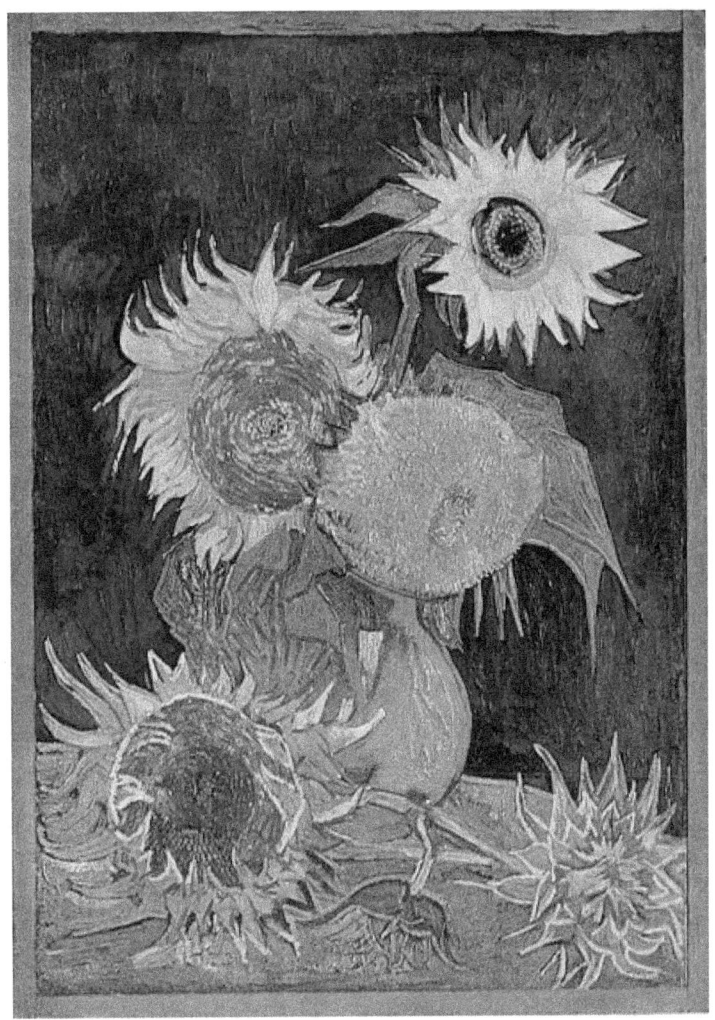

The magnificent *Six Sunflowers*, circa 1888, oil on canvas is known to have been destroyed in an American bombing raid on Imperial Japan during the waning days of WWII. It was painted in the span of six days with three other sunflower portraits in Arles, France when the models van Gogh hired, probably from one of the local brothels, failed to show up due on a day that turned out to be extremely humid, uncomfortable, and scorching hot. The painting met its doom on the same day the city of Hiroshima was destroyed by the payload of the 393rd Bombardment Squadron B-29 *Enola Gay* when it dropped the atomic bomb named Little Boy from overhead. In a separate bombing raid on Ashiya, Japan

Six Sunflowers hung in an elaborate gilt frame above a silk sofa in the timber with a tile roof home of wealthy Japanese art collector, Koyata Yamamoto, who absolutely was in love with this particular portrait. As fire engulfed Yamamoto's burning house, the heavy gilt frame that hung so beautifully upon his wall for so many years made the picture too heavy to rescue and he was forced to live it to ruin in the flames as he ran for his while *Six Sunflowers* fell into the ash-heap that is history.

Prisoners' Round (after Gustave Doré), 1890

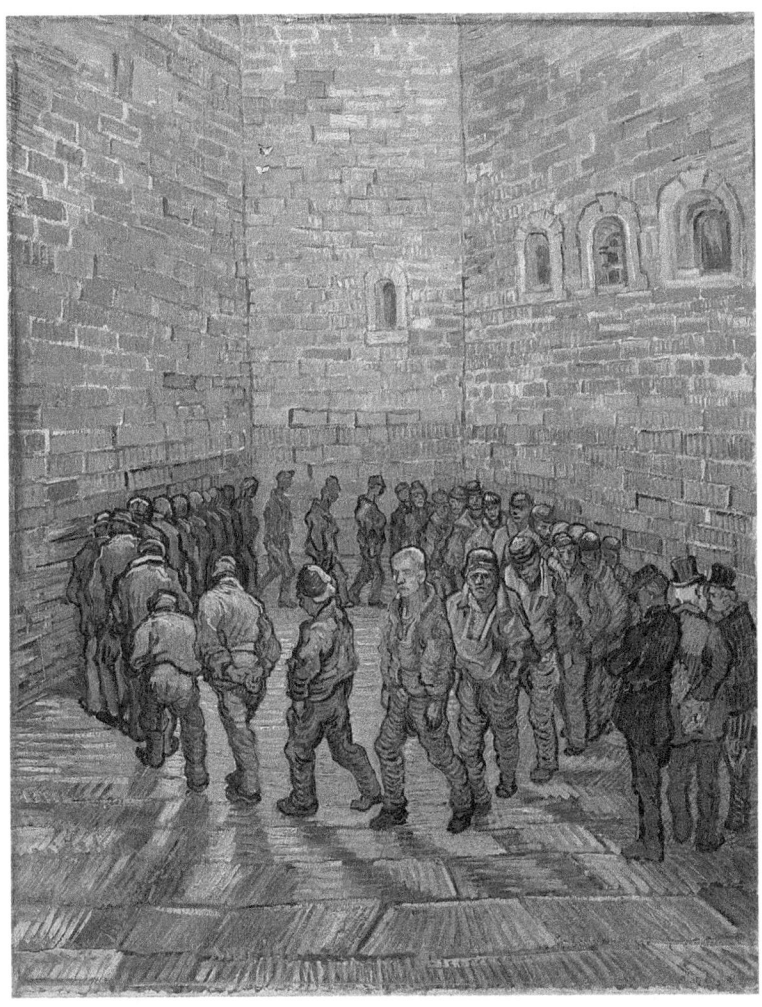

In 1888 Van Gogh suffered a complete psychiatric breakdown. By early 1889 he found himself admitted to the Saint-Paul Asylum in Saint-Rémy under the care of a one Dr. Peillon. There, he was encouraged by his brother, Theo, to paint as a sort of therapy. Without inspiration from the outside natural world he turned his attention to the existing works of other painters and was so moved to create **Prisoners' Round** inspired by an engraving by Gustave Doré of the exercise yard at Newgate Prison. One of van Gogh's most haunting paintings it currently resides on display at the Pushkin Museum in Moscow, Russia.

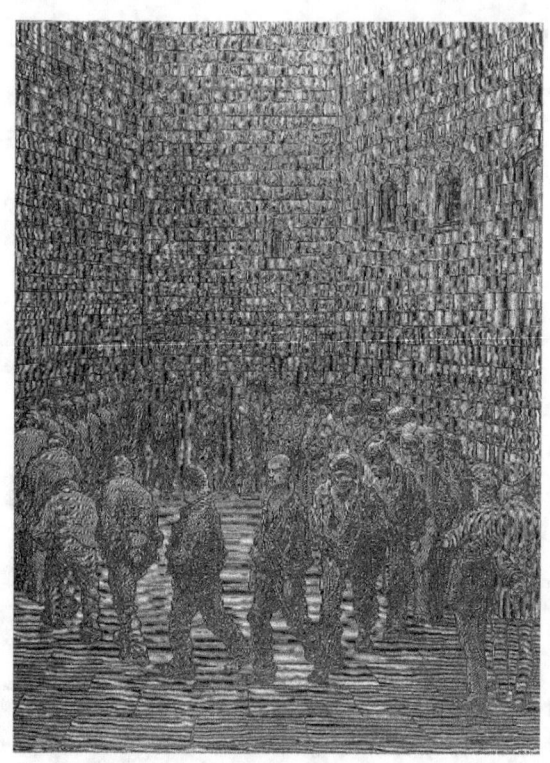

Gustave Doré - The Exercise Yard
(Newgate Prison), 1872

The Old Church Tower at Nuenen, Le Vieux Clocher, 1884

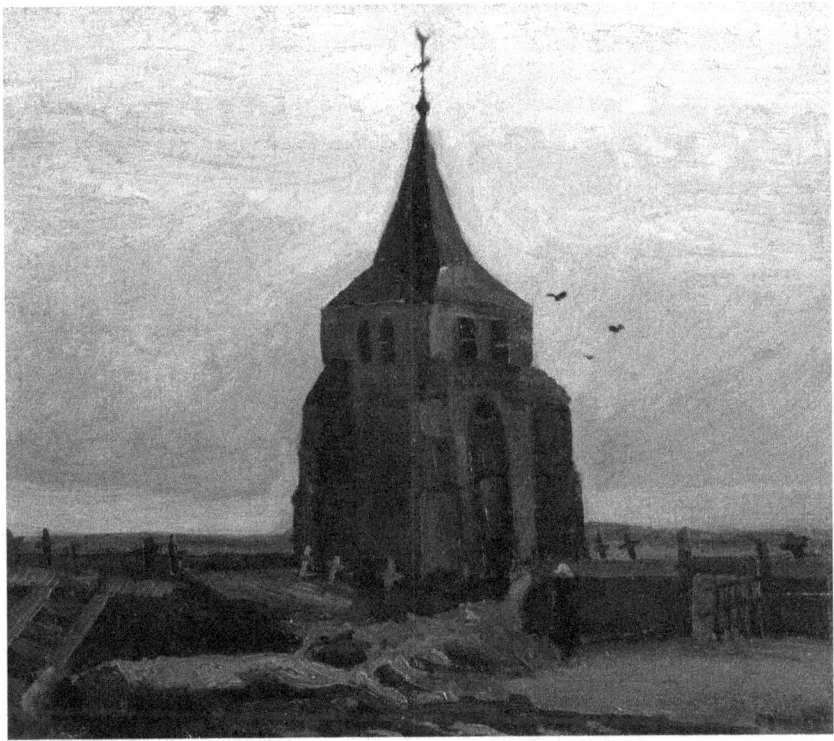

An early work, the 1884 *Le Vieux Clocher* shows no expression of van Gogh's broken brushstroke style that will later be so recognizable in such iconic works as *Starry Night* and *Olive Trees with the Alpilles in the Background.*

Here autumn grays, menacing ravens, and death rule across a gothic landscape with van Gogh's focal point being the condemned 12th Century Church at Nuenen as though H.P. Lovecraft or a pallid Nosferatu might creak open the lid of a wood coffin from a nearby open grave, where years later vibrant blue dreams, floral swirls and tufts of green, and swimming brushstrokes of gold explode across every canvas. The painting currently resides in the Foundation E. G. Bührle Collection Museum of Art in Zürich, Switzerland

The painter on the way to Tarascon, July 1888

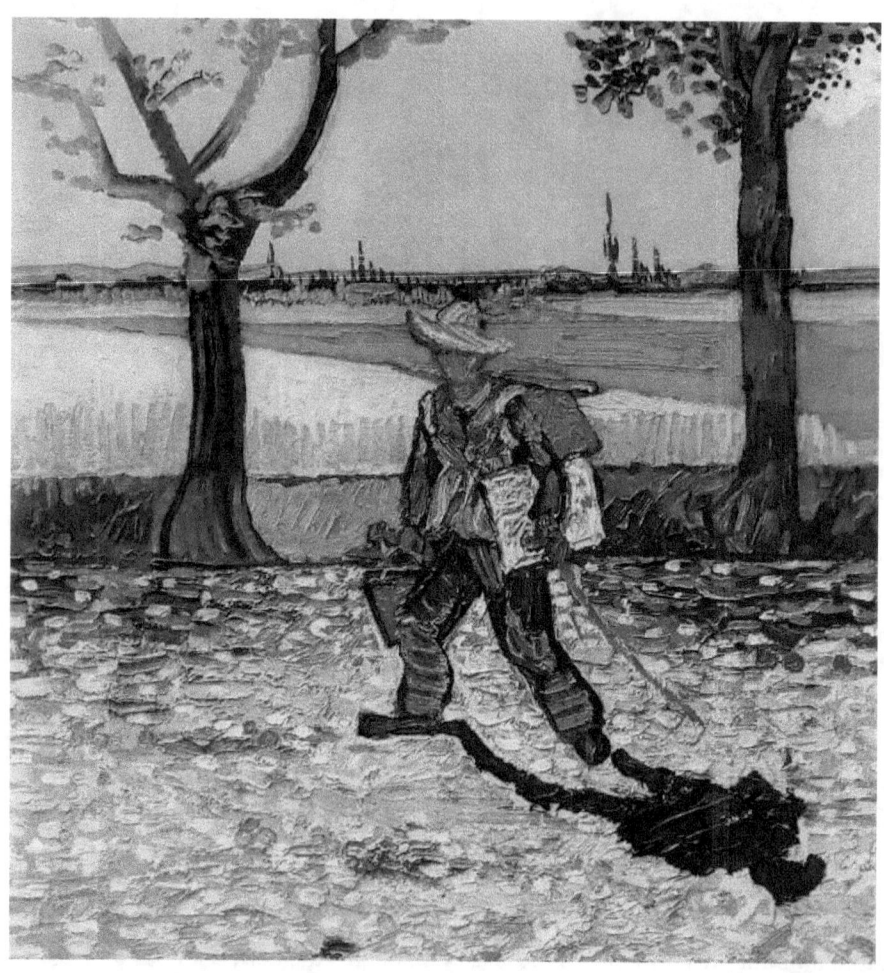

As mentioned earlier in the introduction this beautiful portrait of Vincent van Gogh on his way to Tarascon with easel, paint brushes, sketchbook, and canvas in hand, painted sometime during July 1888, was tragically destroyed by fire in Magdeburg, Germany April 12th, 1945 when Allied bombers attacked and bombarded the city from the skies.

Owned and placed on display at the Kaiser-Friedrich Museum long before the war began, the museum took all of its art out of its museum doors and transferred it all to the nearby Stassfurt salt mines for safe keeping. Alas, the flames of the bombardment licked their callous way down the interior mine walls and shaft and into the main nave of the salt mine, where all the artwork from the museum was boxed and stack up high, stored Indiana Jones movie style, where unfortunately the van Gogh met its demise. The Monuments Men brigade put together by the U.S. Army to retrieve and identify stolen Nazi art and artifacts made note in a ledger that *The painter on the way to Tarascon* by Vincent van Gogh was a "loss in the Stassfurt mines collection" dated spring, 1945. And so it is.

Portrait of Dr Felix Rey, 1889

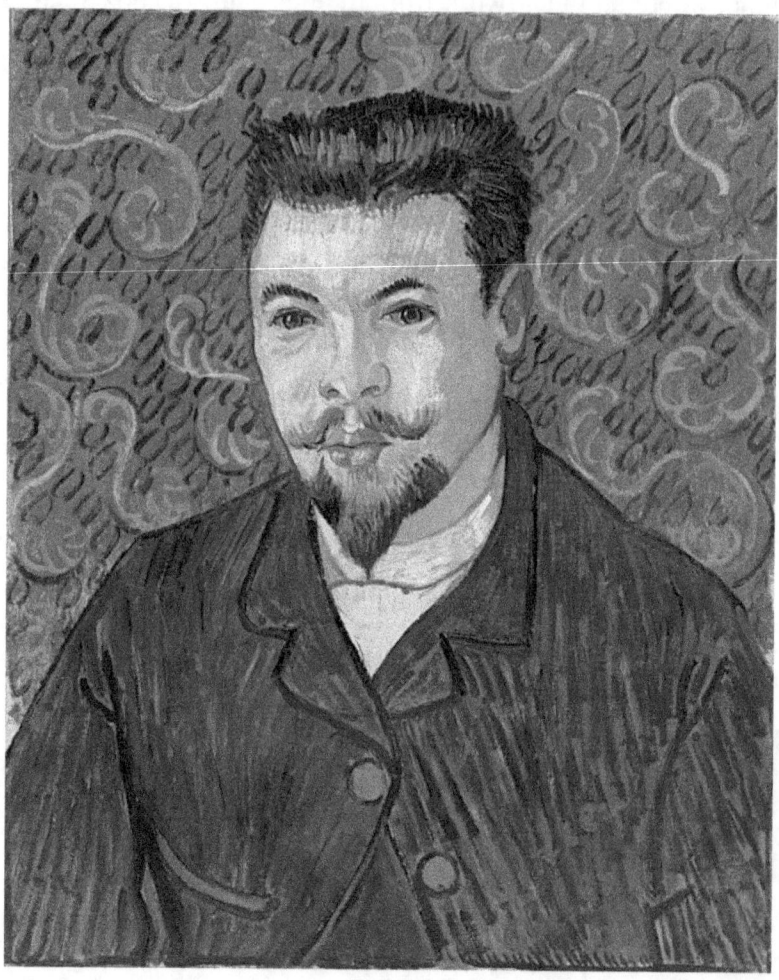

Doctor Félix Rey was a young intern at the hospital in Arles during the tumultuous winter of 1888 in which Vincent suffered from a psychotic break and famously cut part of his own ear off. While Vincent was recovering in the psychiatric ward he was given great comfort from the calm and generous Doctor Rey.

After his discharge some weeks later the two men stayed friendly, and in a fit of mania van Gogh decided to paint a portrait of his new friend as a gift to him for being so kind while he had gone off the rails.

Unfortunately, the young doctor still lived at home with his mother and she hated the portrait of her son that van Gogh so tiredly painted between the 7th of January, 1889 and the 17th of the same month that she reputedly stole the painting off the bedroom wall of her son, brought it out the house, and used it unceremoniously as a hole stopper over a hole in the henhouse of her chickens for the next ten years.

Years later when van Gogh's work began to become slowly recognized within the art world the painting was brought inside, cleaned up a bit to get all the chicken poop removed, and bought and sold several times until 1908 it found its ways into the sweaty hands of Russian collector and businessman Sergei Shchukin.

Of course, like the Nazi regime to come, this work was considered bourgeois after Czarist Russian fell to the Bolsheviks in 1917. So what do you do with bourgeois works of art when you are a Bolshevik? You seized all of it and the mansion it come, which belonged to Sergei Shchukin who timed his escape off to Paris perfectly, and you turn his extravagant estate into the People's State Museum of New Western Art (Государственный Музей нового западного искусства).

Over a century has passed since all the hullabaloo, and the Portrait of Doctor Félix Rey of Arles, France now sits rather cold and dim against the walls of the Pushkin Museum of Moscow, Russia. Rumor has it now that Vladimir Putin himself can often be found sitting cross-legged and alone atop the cold chessboard marble floors right in front of the portrait late into summer evenings doing God-knows-what to himself while the calm eyes and listening ear of Doctor Rey looks down at him as its head nods from side to side in shame. At least that is what friends of Russian opposition leader Alexei Navalny, and the those who run in the underground of Russia, have to say. Now that is when it is helpful to say you have a body-double on the payroll, huh, Vladimir?

Meules de blé (Wheat Stacks), 1888; stolen by the Nazi's

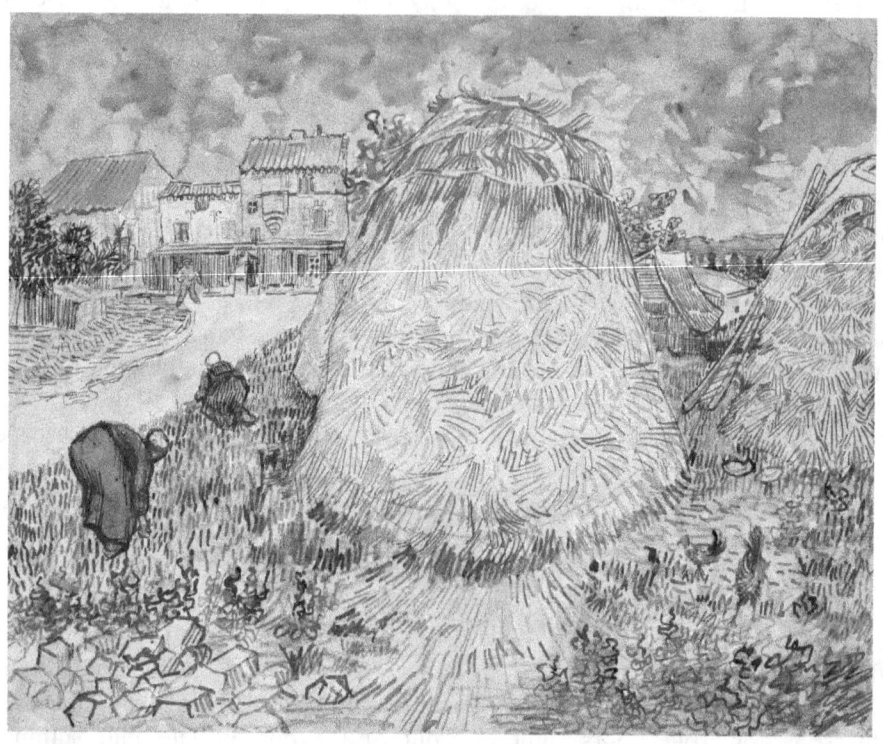

Unseen by the public for nearly a century, the pastoral *Meules de blé (Wheat Stacks)* dates back to 1888 Arles and once belonged to Vincent's brother Theo who eventually sold the work to Max Merensky, a wealthy German Jewish industrialist just before the outbreak of WWI.

Years later when the Nazi regime came into power the Jewish Meirowsky saw that it was too dangerous to stay in Berlin or Paris or even Barcelona and was forced to flee for his life to Amsterdam and then on to Geneva, but not before he discreetly handed over the painting to a German arts broker called Paul Graupe & Cie in Paris for "safe keeping," where, of course—it was a German arts broker in 1938 after all—it unwittingly yet surreptitiously found its way into the possession of Miriam Caroline Alexandrine de Rothschild, who herself wound up having to flee Paris and into neutral Switzerland following the outbreak of German led WWII.

During the German occupation of Paris, the Nazis jackbooted their way around De Rothschild's estate and salon like sugar-high Oompa-Loompas, looting her entire collection of priceless art, stealing the gilt, as it were, of luminous *Meules de blé* right off the silk damask wall of the salon along with many other pieces of priceless European art, of which included several landscapes by Paul Cézanne, Paul Gauguin, and hundreds of literary, musical, and first edition books and manuscripts that were all a part of the collection of Alexandrine De Rothschild.

After WWII the painting went from Nazi possession through the hands of many dealers and collectors throughout Europe all the while Alexandrine de Rothschild desperately tried in vain to get her van Gogh back, but all to no avail. It was not until Texas oil magnate Edward Lochridge Cox passed away that both the Merensky and De Rothchild heirs put in a dispute for ownership of the looted *Meules de blé* that it surfaced out into wide blue open again.

Somehow a settlement agreement was reached between the parties of the Cox family and the Merensky and De Rothchild heirs (a percentage of the proceeds that would be split by each family when Christie's the painting on November 11th, 2021 for $35.8 million dollars; and all's well that ends well?). And who does not like a good happy ending; or perhaps three?

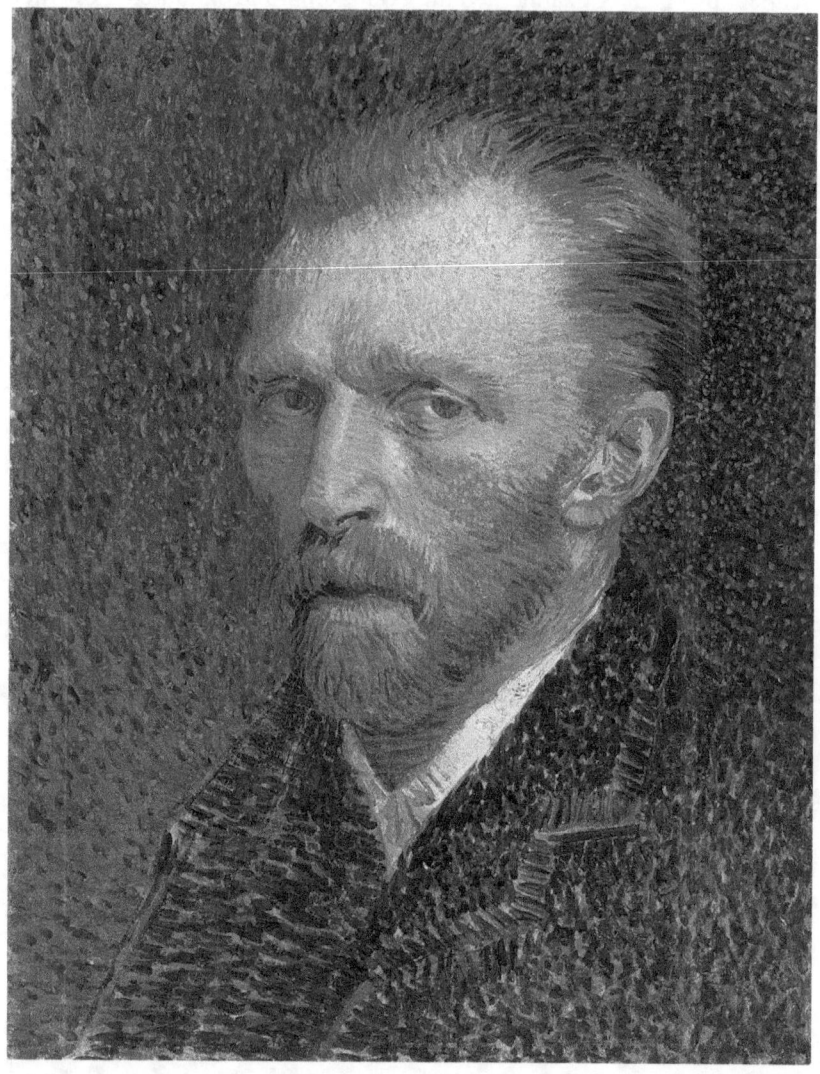

One of the dozens of self-portraits that he painted of himself, *Self-Portrait, 1887* was created as an oil on artist board, mounted on cradled panel, and exudes the fiery red bluster of Vincent van Gogh's orange-red beard. It also showcases his illustrious burnt sienna orange, blue, aqua, and oxblood red brushstrokes that swirl in eddies and tides around his bright red noggin and multi-colored double-vested wool coat. It currently resides on display at the Art Institute of Chicago in Chicago, Illinois.

A Pair of Lovers (Eglogue en Provence), 1888

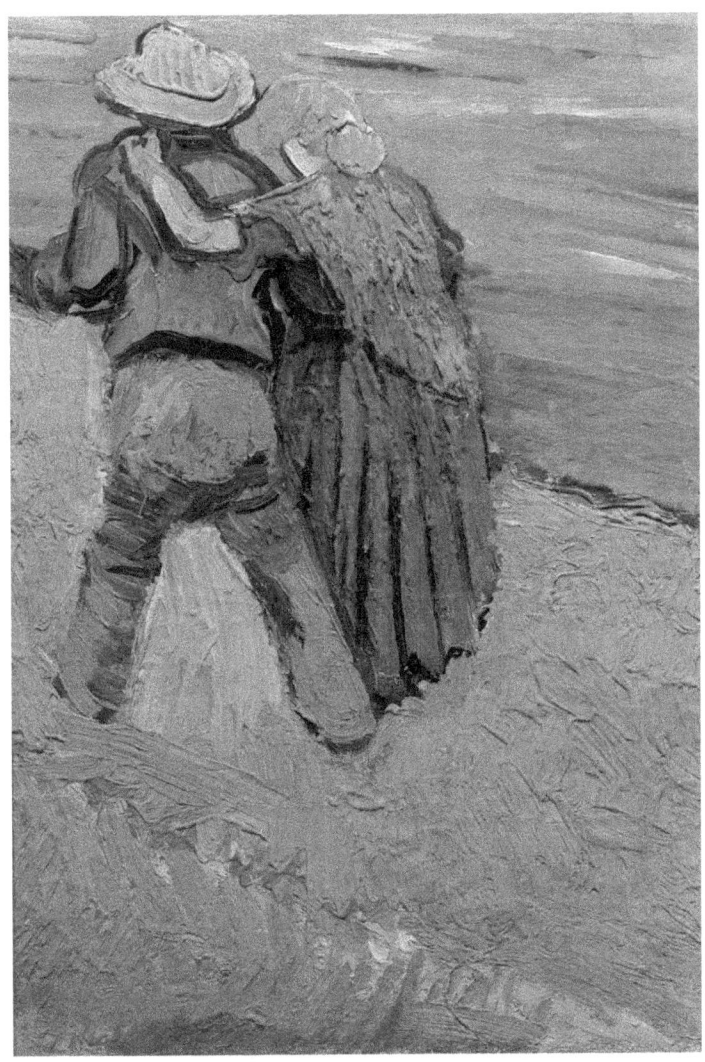

Originally a section of a much broader landscape that depicted a couple en route along the canal toward the Pont de Réginelle bridge, **A pair of Lovers** came into existence when van Gogh encountered bad weather throughout Arles, fought bouts of deep depression, and without the clear days and early evenings that he needed mentally to paint sky and a brilliant yellow sun plein air—painted outside—he literally cut out the above stretch of canvas and preserved it as its own work. In a letter to Emile Bernard dated March 18th,

1888 one can observe an outline of the original landscape that he eventually cut out and scrapped altogether.

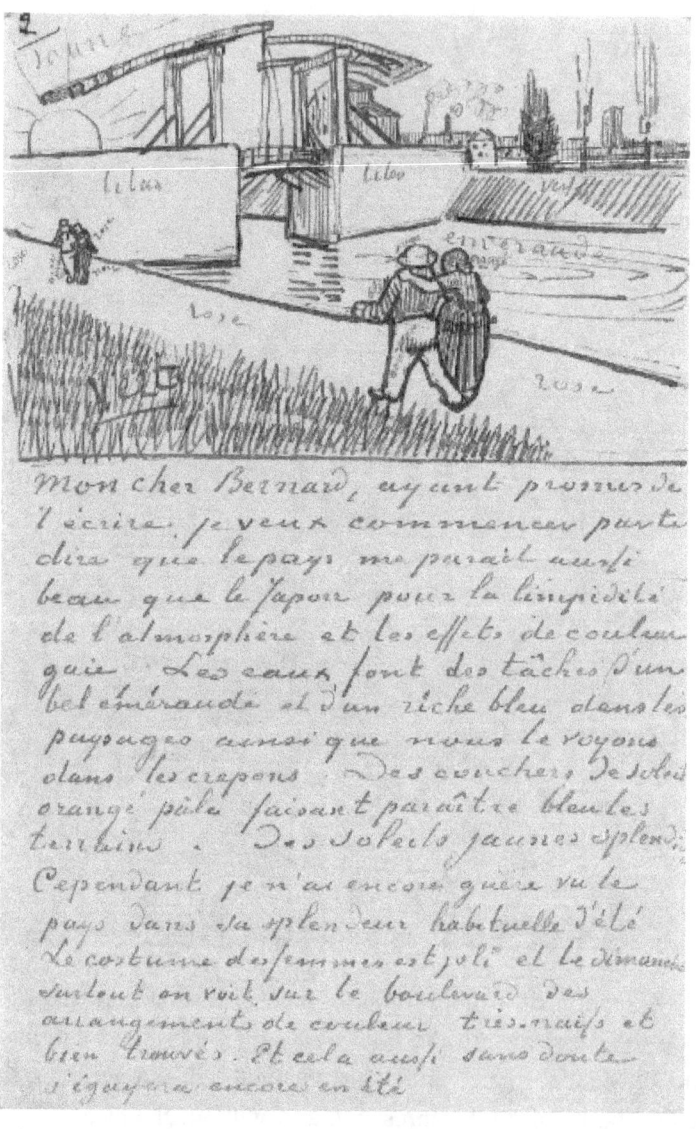

Flowerbeds in Holland, 1883

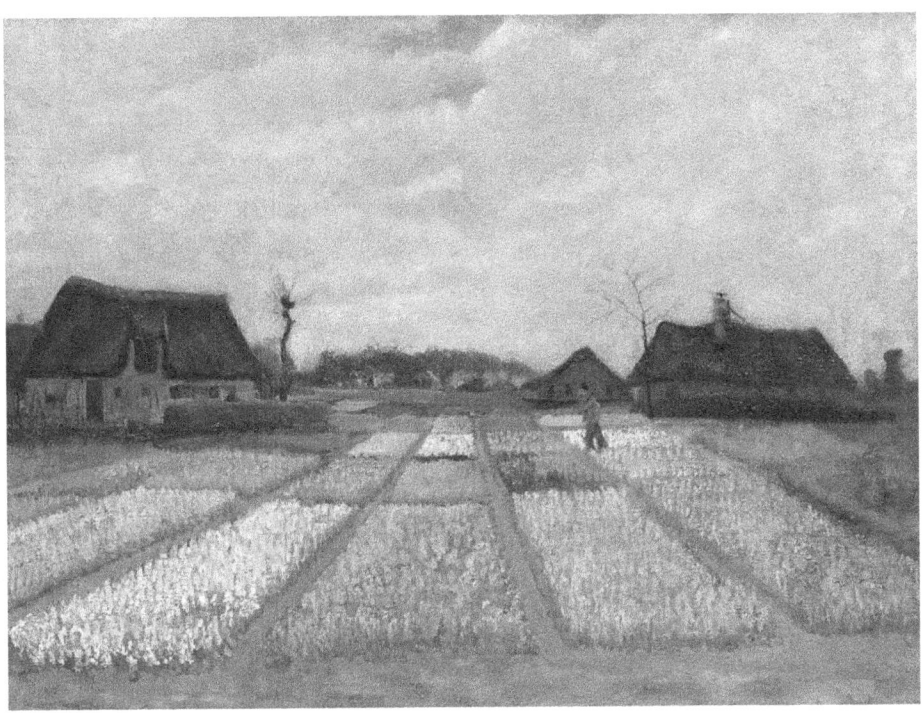

Painted near the city and municipality of The Hague in the Netherlands sometime during 1883, *Flowerbeds in Holland* depicts beautiful quadrants and tartans of flowers, most likely tulips, in rows of baby blue, silvery-white quartz, yellow, and rose-pink with hatched houses and bare spring trees that linger in the background. This is the very first van Gogh's garden painting he put to canvas. A typical early van Gogh it is one of his most beautiful works that does not feature his renown broken brushstroke style he would soon become known by. It has been on display at the National Gallery of Art in Washington, DC since 1983

Coin de jardin avec papillons (Garden corner with butterflies), 1887

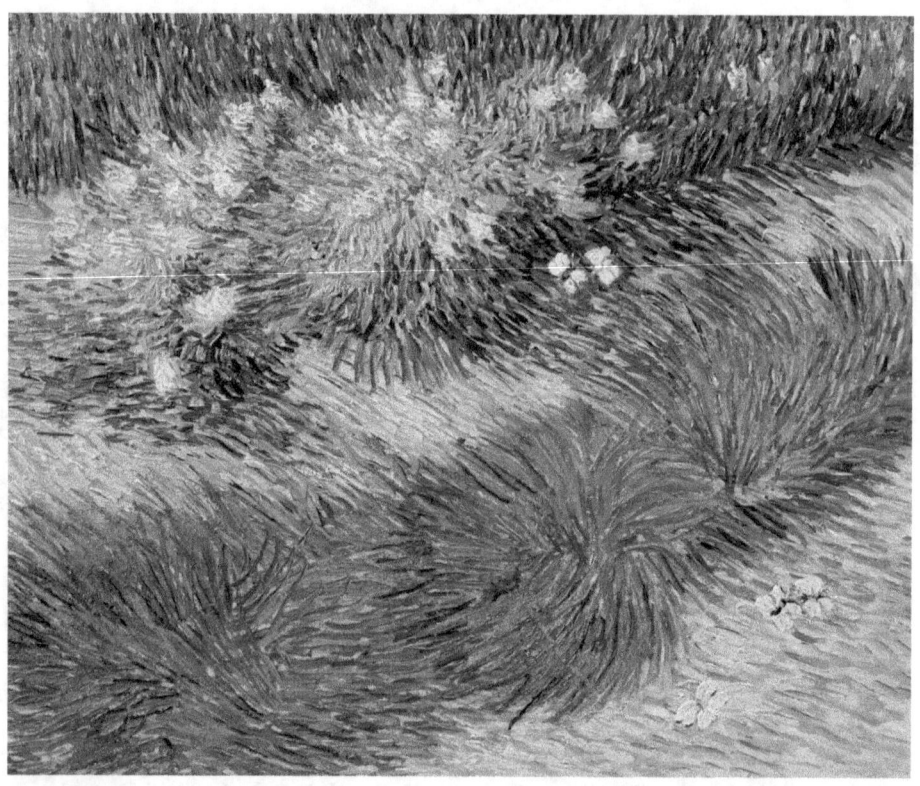

The magnificent 1887 *Coin de jardin avec papillons (Garden corner with butterflies)* is considered one of the true lodestars by van Gogh connoisseurs as it marks his progression from his earlier earthen tone and flat realism brushstroke style to his new radical expressive brushstroke bravura influenced by Pointillism, Japanese woodblock prints, and the color theories of more contemporary artists such as his friends Émile Bernard, Paul Gauguin, and Georges Seurat. Painted along the Parisian banks of the River Seine in the Asnières section of the city, *Coin de jardin avec papillons* was recently sold by Christies in November 2023 to a private collector whom rumor has it snuggles with the painting and a bright red Maine Coon cat named Catrick Swayze every night. But you did not hear this from me!

Lane of Poplars at Sunset, 1884

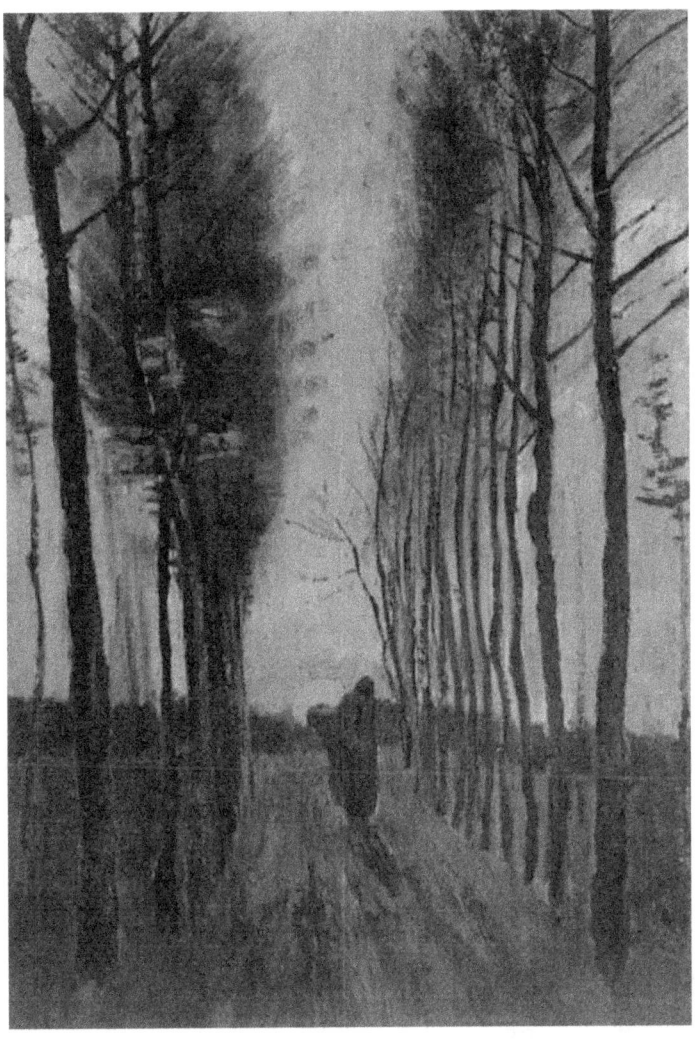

A lonely figure in between man-made planted poplars along the road as the person heads for a setting pink sun, *Lane of Poplars at Sunset* was completed in 1884 and is representative of van Gogh's early period and style. The painting now resides at the Kröller-Müller Museum in Otterlo in the Netherlands.

Peat Field, 1883

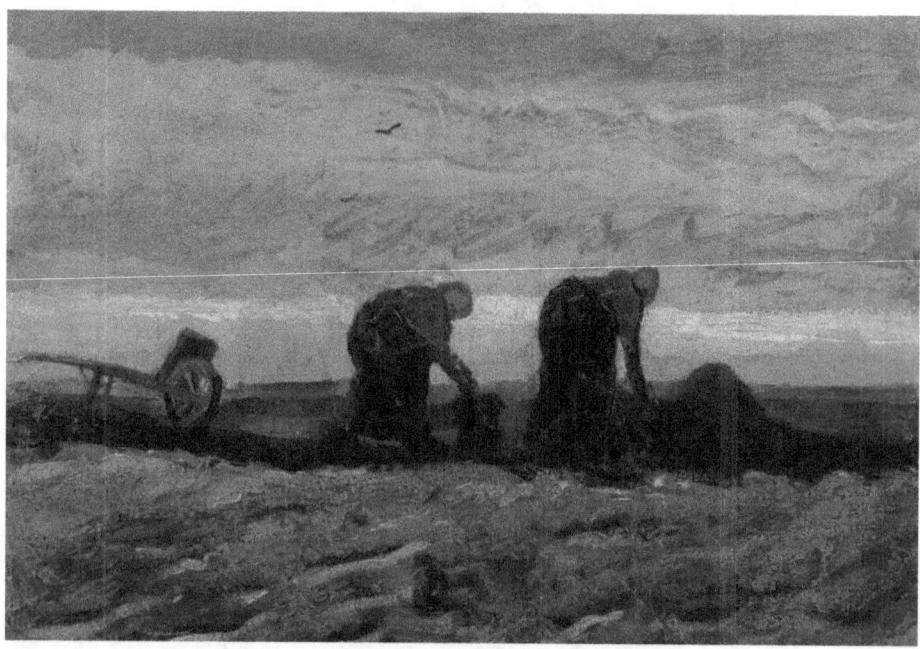

Painted soon after his move to rural Drenthe in the Netherlands, 1883's *Peat Fields* evokes van Gogh's passion for painting the native agricultural peasant going about their daily labor of planting and cultivating dried-out peat sods under stark striations of pink, dark green and winter gray. The painting now resides at the Van Gogh Museum in Amsterdam in the Netherlands.

Still Life with Bible, 1885

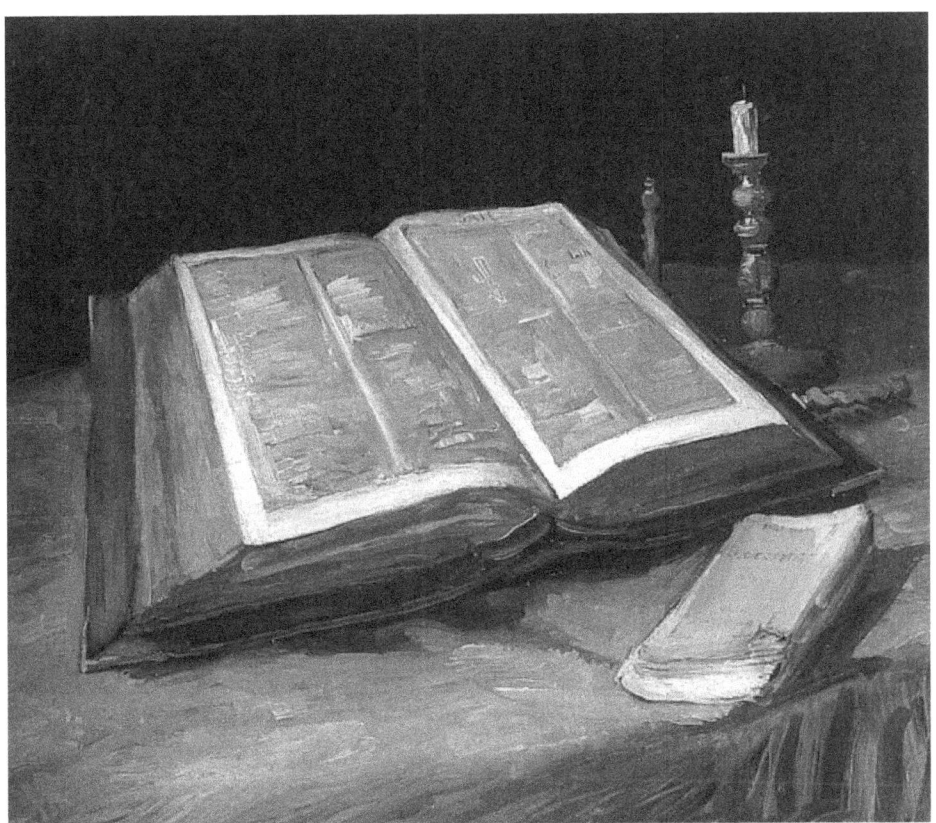

Little known is the fact that Vincent van Gogh studied theology at the age of 24 and then served as a lay preacher in the Borinage mining region, where he taught the gospel, visited the lame and sick, and occasionally gave sermons from the Bible. This spiritual part of van Gogh's persona remained with him for the rest of his life even when he thought life itself may have been in vain. *Still life with Bible*, 1985 is a beautiful portrait of his Protestant minister father's own hefty Bible that he painted only a few months after his dad's passing. Knowing this fact adds to the gravity of his portrait, which is quite haunting under any circumstance whether you know the footnote about it or not. The painting now resides at the Van Gogh Museum in Amsterdam in the Netherlands.

Sheaves of Wheat, July-August, 1885

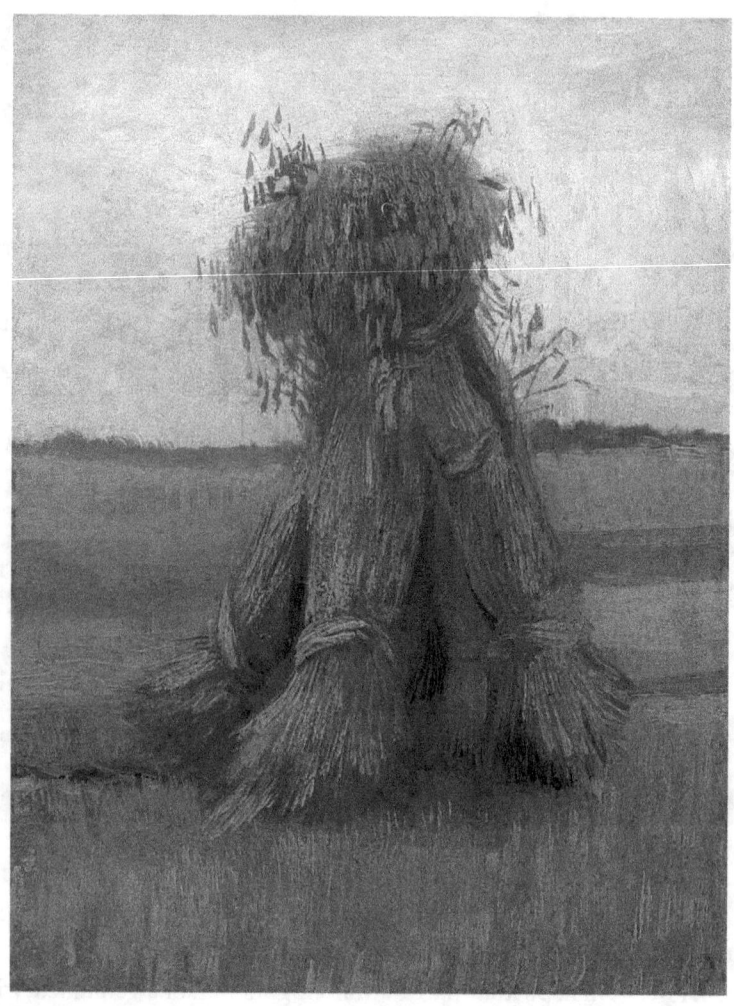

Sheaves of Wheat is an iconic symbol throughout van Gogh's artistic repertoire and can be seen in different interpretations throughout his lifetime catalog of outside landscapes done in various styles and forms. This early oil on canvas of *Shaves of Wheat* is not only beautiful in execution and form, but hints at the many vibrant wheat-themed landscapes to come. The 1885 version of *Sheaves of Wheat* resides at the Kröller-Müller Museum of Art in Otterlo in the Netherlands,

Sheaves of Wheat, 1890

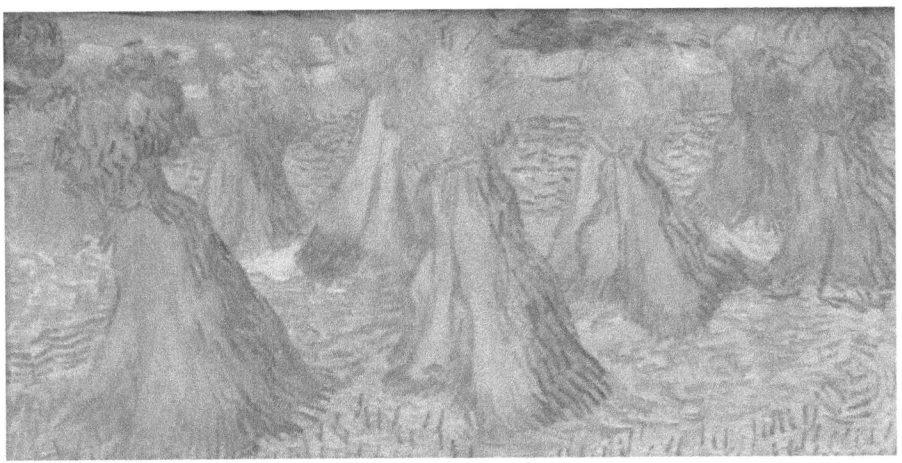

Just a few short years later and a new *Sheaves of Wheat, 1890* is transformed into vibrant oxbow blues, golds, yellows and greens full of broken brush strokes and childish exuberance. It begs the onlooker to take notice. Swirl in between the lines like ocean waves on a summer day. The artist is transformed, a metamorphose one cannot help but take note of; swim in, take a picture in one's mind they can never forget The artist has become an artist for the first time. This is a van Gogh. The fields of gold are alive and moving like water. *Hallelujah! Hallelujah!* The painting now resides at the Dallas Museum of Art in Dallas, Texas.

Wheatfield with Crows, 1890. Van Gogh Museum, Amsterdam

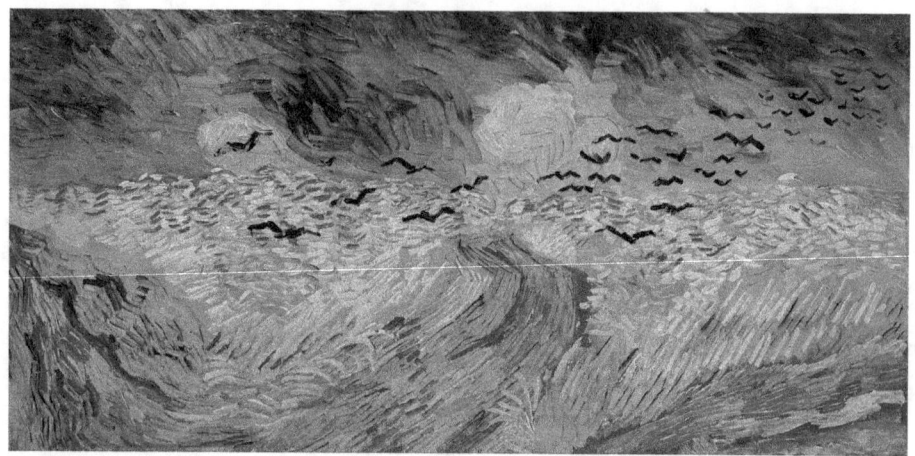

God, weather, nature, strife, life and death, the howling wind, H.P. Lovecraft, Edgar Allan Poe, and a winding carriage scarred road that leads to nowhere, to everywhere comes alive in 1890's *Wheatfield with Crows*. The shrugging blues of sky lick the tops of golden stalks of wheat as ominous crows fly aloft to remind mankind they are simply passengers on Planet Earth amid a universe filled with a myriad of two trillion galaxies. *Wheatfield with Crows* resides in the Van Gogh Museum in Amsterdam in the Netherlands.

Skull of a Skeleton with Burning Cigarette, 1885–86

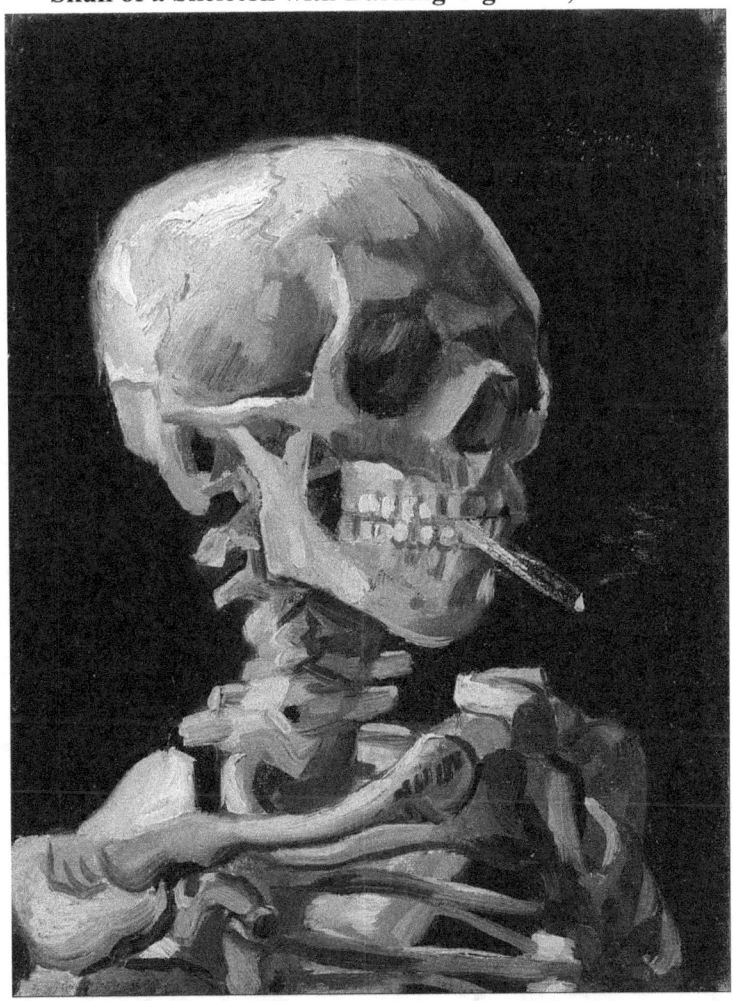

The evocative *Skull of a Skeleton with Burning Cigarette*, 1885–86 is equally dark, humorous, and existential. Van Gogh must have visited the underground catacombs of Paris and saw the myriad of piled up skulls, tawny candlelit walls lined with femurs and arm bones from the millions of Parisians who had been disinterred and stored underground like castoff seashells upon a coastal shore. Life is as short as one brief cigarette. It is both humorous and macabre. So say Vincent van Gogh. The painting now resides at the Van Gogh Museum in Amsterdam in the Netherlands.

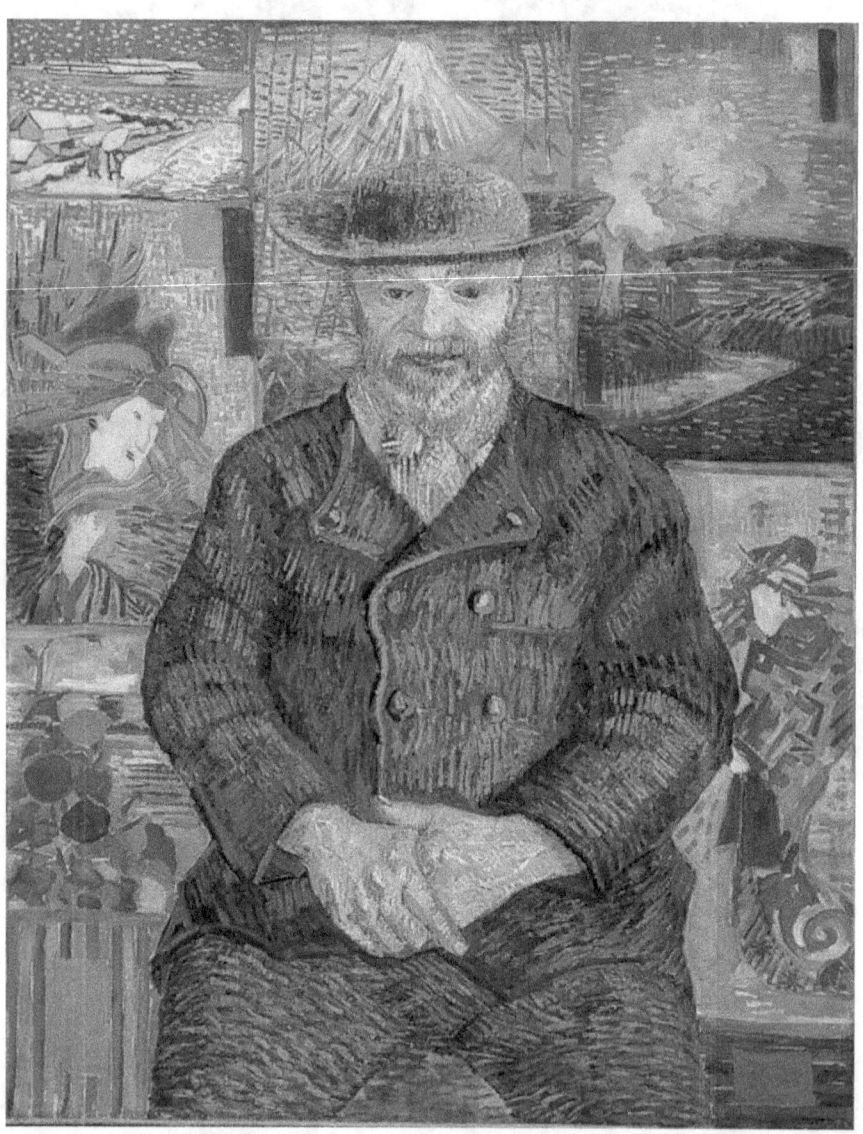

Pointillism, Japanese woodblock art, and contemporary colors and style highlight 1887's *Portrait of Père Tanguy*. The painting is a collage of all the fractal thoughts Vincent has on his mind throughout 1887 that he wants to incorporate in his work now—only this painting literally has them written down as glimpses of pictures using the elements and words van Gogh wishes to incorporate from his mind's eye. One may not find a more literally

31

translation of what van Gogh wanted to do in his art going forward than found right out in the open amid this wonderful portrait. We literally know what van Gogh is thinking from his work. Artists can be snarky and a bit cheeky when having a confident day. Perhaps van Gogh is having a little fun with us here. We can only hope so as this would be quite grand!

The Sower with Setting Sun, 1888

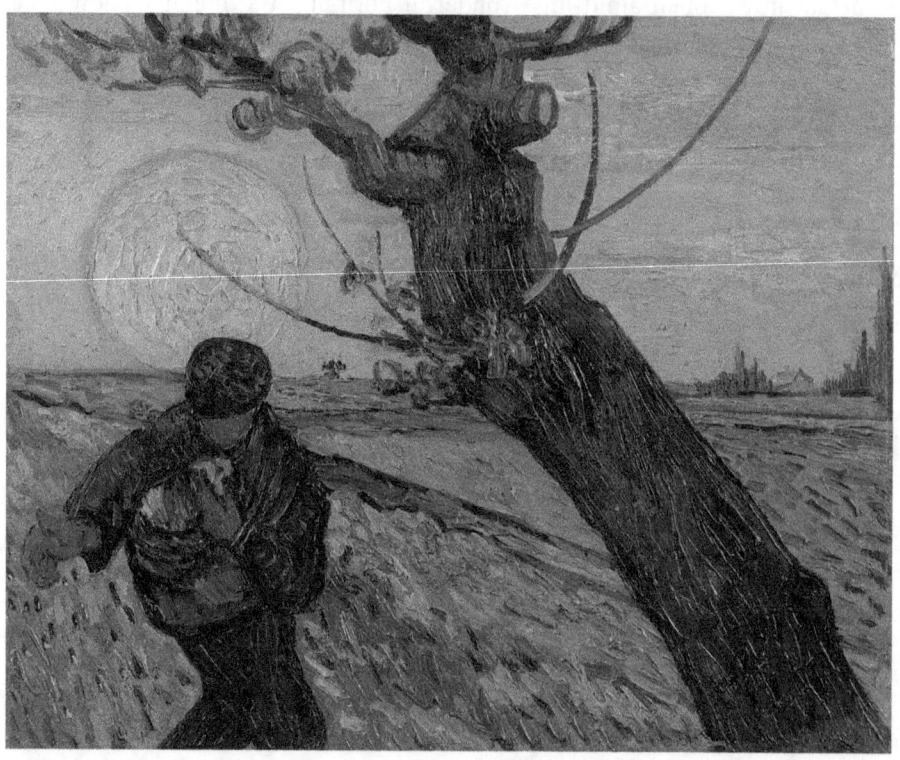

What better time to paint plein air—paint outside—than in the springtime in the countryside of France. The furrowed fields are lush, the olive and peach trees are coming alive, and a bright yellow sun sets into the horizon turning the shadowy fields cool in a luscious purple hue. The weather must have been fine during this fine spring week when van Gogh painted *The Sower with Setting Sun* during the spring of 1888. It is a happy portrait of a man full of hope and optimism.

Self-Portrait with Straw Hat, Paris, Winter 1887–88

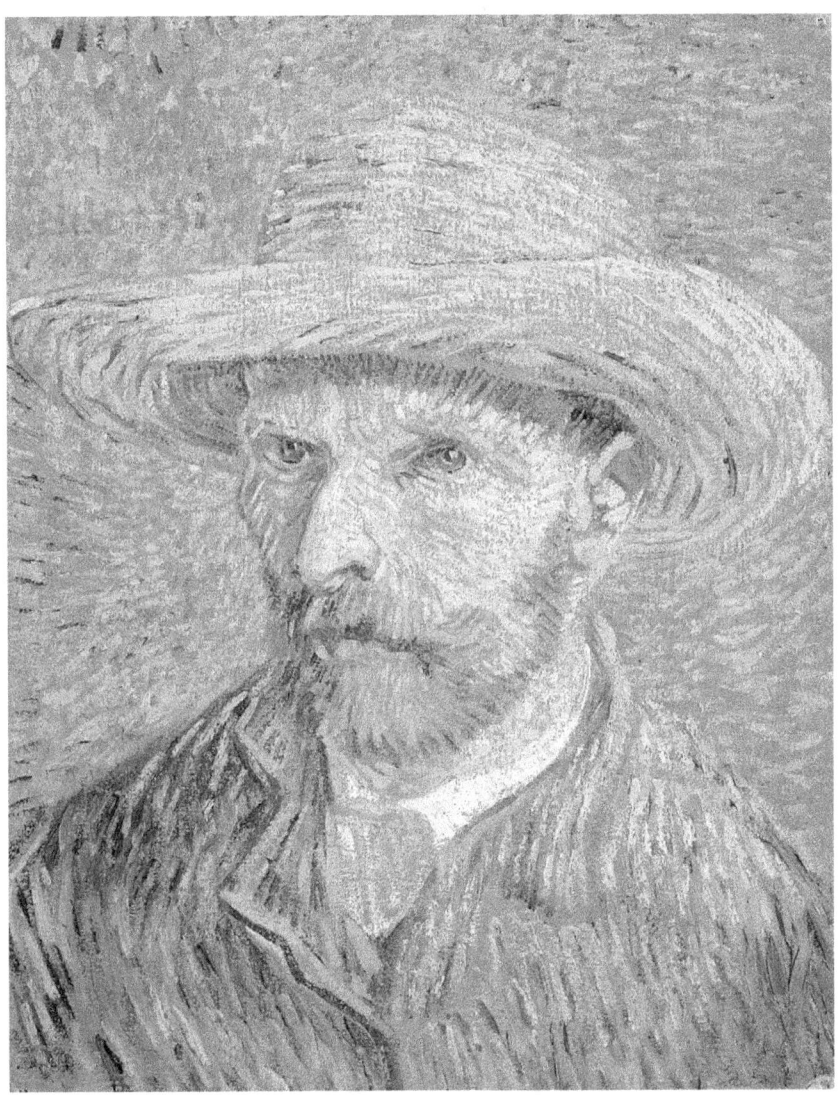

Academy award winner actor Dustin Hoffman once asked his legendary co-star of the movie *The Marathon Man*, Sir Laurence Olivier, "why is it that we do what we do?"

The Shakespearean trained legend Sir Olivier responded right away: "The reason we do what we do, dear boy? *Look at me! Look at me! Look at me!*" What great artist isn't a great showoff as well? Even when nobody knows your name. *Self-Portrait with Straw Hat*, done in Paris during the Winter of

1887–88, dares one to look away from the artist. The rapid brushstrokes. Its pink tides and eddies. The golden straw hat. Those penetrating green eyes. A work of art that makes even the Mona Lisa blush. If there is a such thing as perfection in art *Self-Portrait with Straw Hat*, 1887-1888 may be the ultimate winner. Resides in the Metropolitan Museum of Art, Manhattan, New York City.

Woman Walking In A Garden, (Femme dans un jardin), 1887

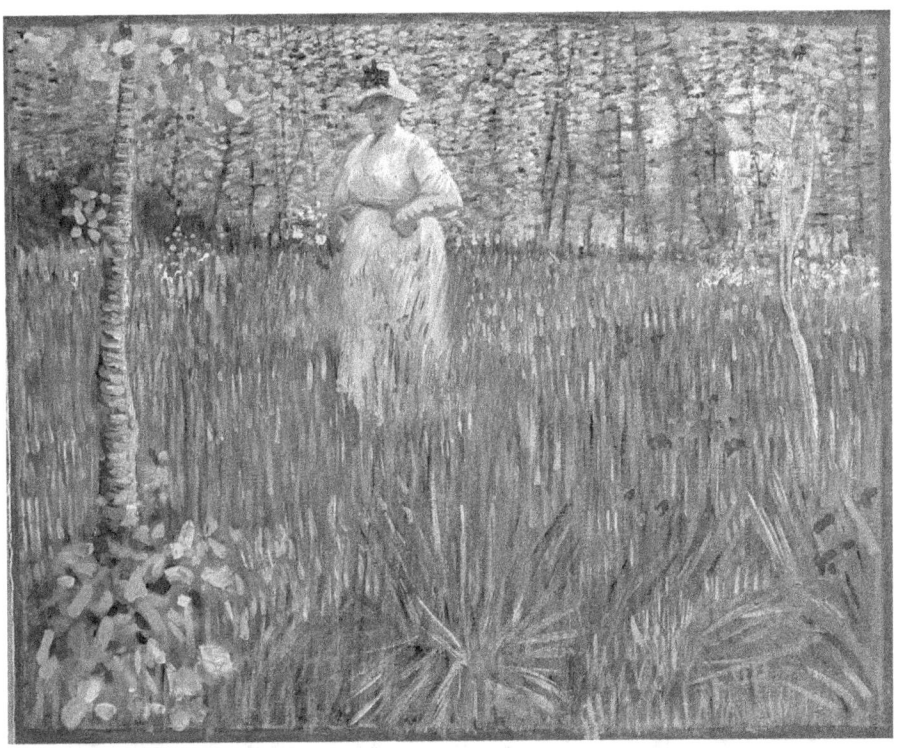

Painted during van Gogh's Paris years, this one in particular done in June and July of 1887, *Woman Walking In A Garden* shows all the new influences that Vincent has been picking up being around and studying the Impressionist artists of the day around the Latin Quarter and Montmartre in Paris, such as the likes of Claude Monet, as seen in the above work, as well as Edgar Degas, Auguste Renoir, and Georges Seurat. The hand and brushstrokes may be of van Gogh, but works like the above show a lot of Monet and Seurat influence in its subject matter and setting. The reds and yellows are vivid and bright and traces of Pointillism can be seen all about the edges of the nearby forest of Asnières in the background behind the focal point of the woman in the painting. How no one bought this fantastic beaty in the 19th Century seems mindboggling to us now. *Woman Walking In A Garden* resides completely neutral to all countries around it within the Kunstmuseum Basel Museum of Basel, Switzerland.

Road with Cypress and Star, May 1890

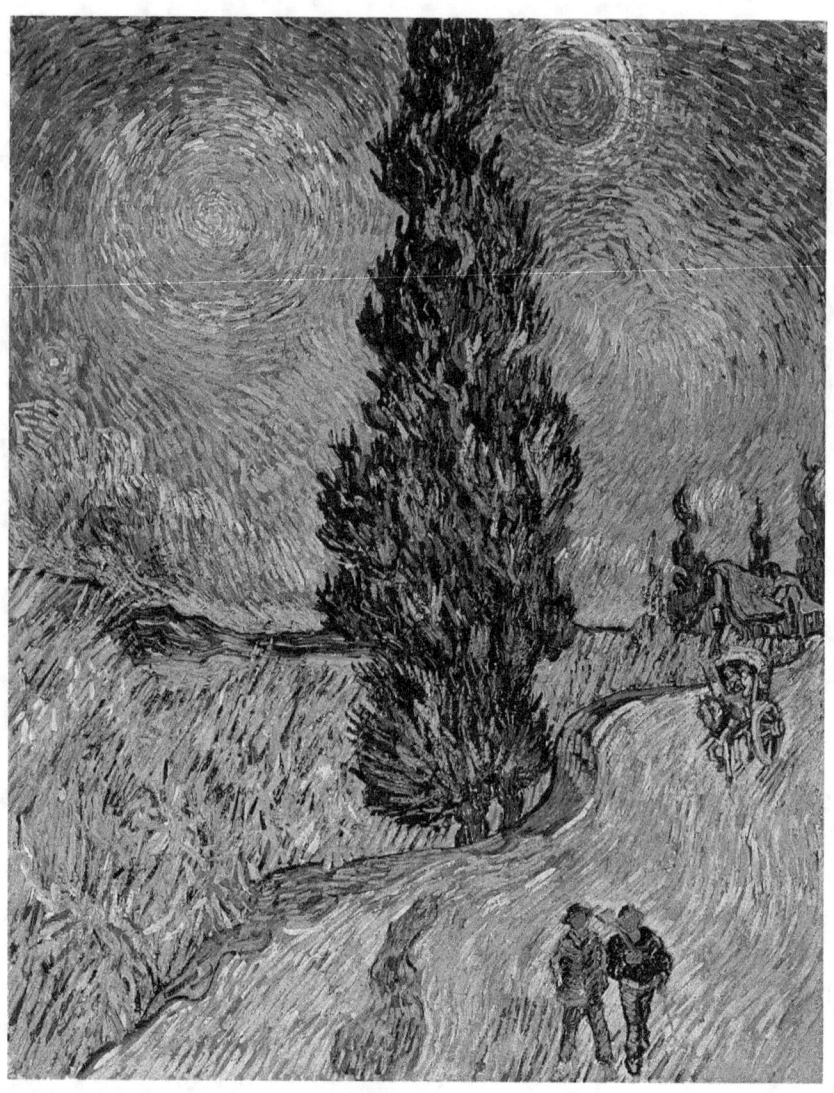

Road with Cypress and Star, also known as *Country Road in Provence by Night*, is a stunning late work from 1890. It is renowned for being one of van Gogh's most beautiful landscapes and also as the last painting he painted in Saint-Rémy-de-Provence, France before he died of a self-inflected wound (literally and figuratively). It is now on display at the Kröller-Müller Museum in Otterlo in the Netherlands.

Wheat Field with Cypresses (National Gallery version)

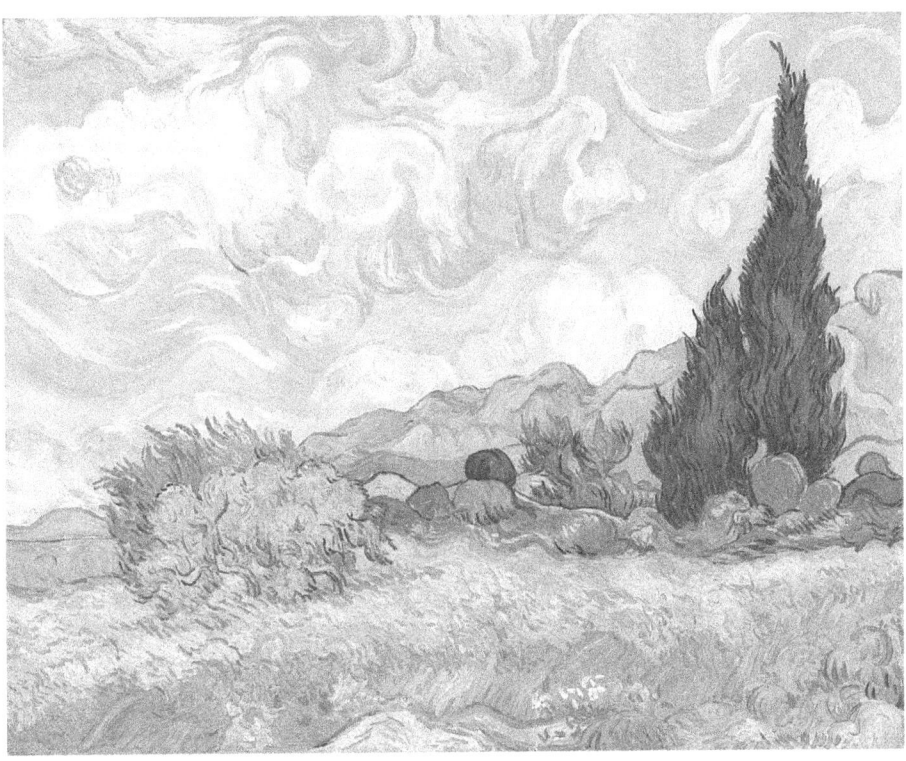

Three versions of *A Wheatfield with Cypresses* were painted by van Gogh in 1889. Each is a slight variation of the other in regard to tone and lightening. One could look at them as being the same landscape during a different time of day: dusk, noon, and twilight. They were painted and exhibited at the Saint-Paul-de-Mausole mental asylum at Saint-Rémy near Arles, where van Gogh was a patient in 1889 and 1890. The wheatfield and cypresses were inspired by the view from his bedroom window at the asylum that framed the valley and nearby Alpilles mountains as though begging to be painted.

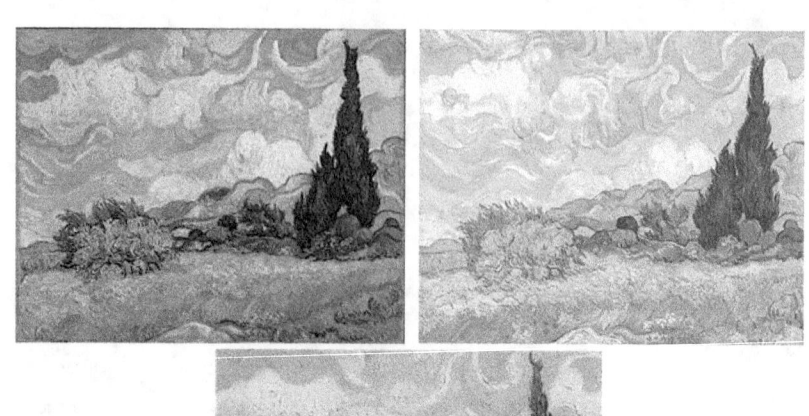

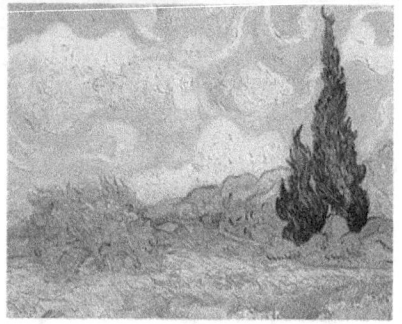

Farmhouse in Provence, 1888

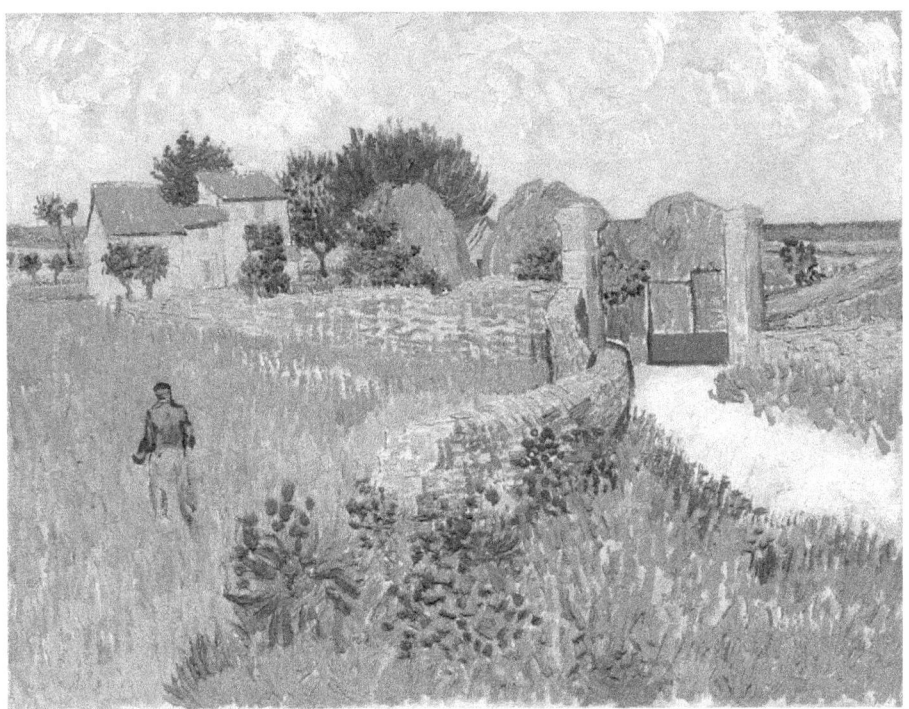

Farmhouse in Provence, also known as *Entrance Gate to a Farm with Haystacks*, is an oil-on-canvas painted during 1888 in Arles, Provence, Southern France. It was known to be a bright and sunny area in and around Arles all through the summer and the light of Southern France became ensconced on van Gogh's canvas, where the colors and sky and flowers and fields popped and came alive in light Mediterranean blues and teals and silken golds.

Avenue near Arles with houses, 1890

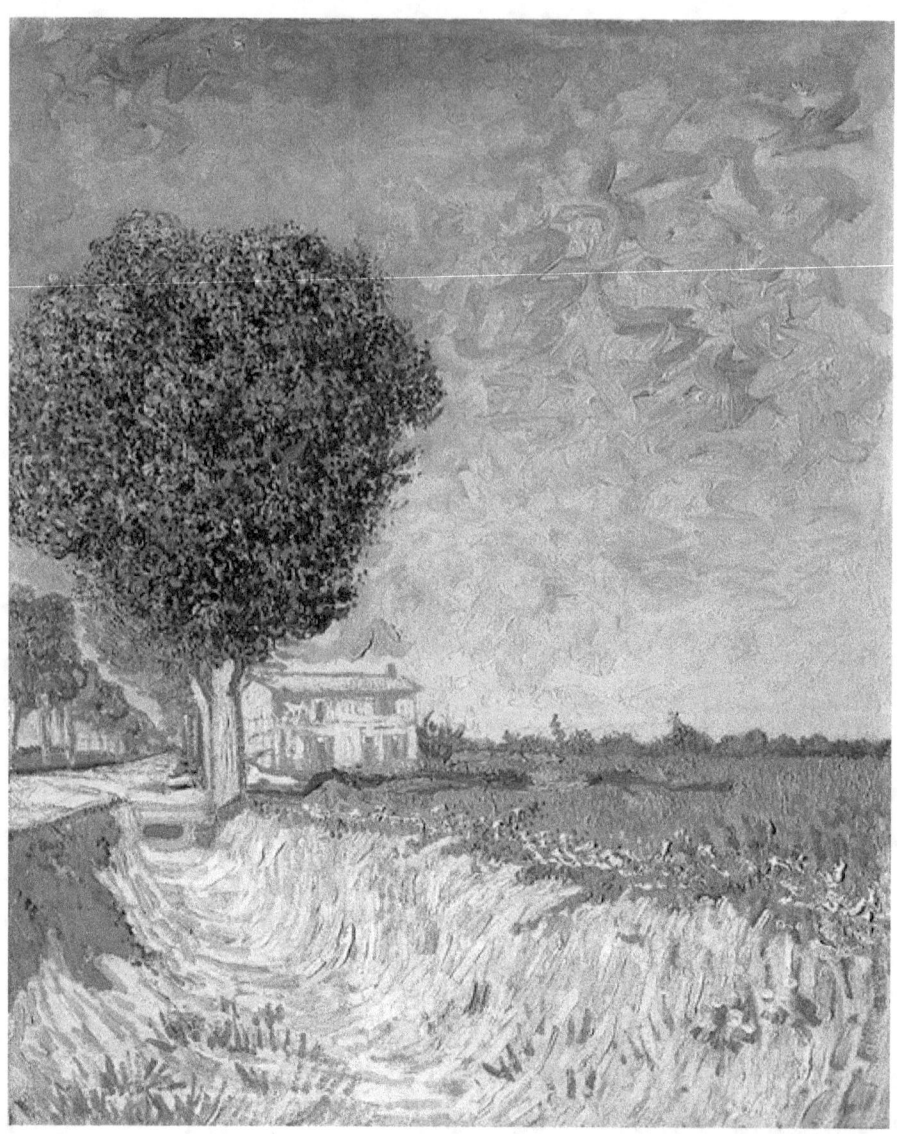

The gorgeous blue skies, colorful wildflowers, and lush poplars of *Avenue near Arles with houses*, 1890 make the heart skip a beat. Van Gogh's own heart must have rejoiced after completing such a magnificent landscape the way every struggling artist thinks their latest work is the one that will put him or her over the top. Alas, he was wrong, and it probably broke his heart a little piece at a time from the lack of recognition that came and passed like the thought of a ghostly kiss on the cheek that never came. The painting now lives in the Pomeranian State Museum in Greifswald, Germany.

Interior of a restaurant, 1887

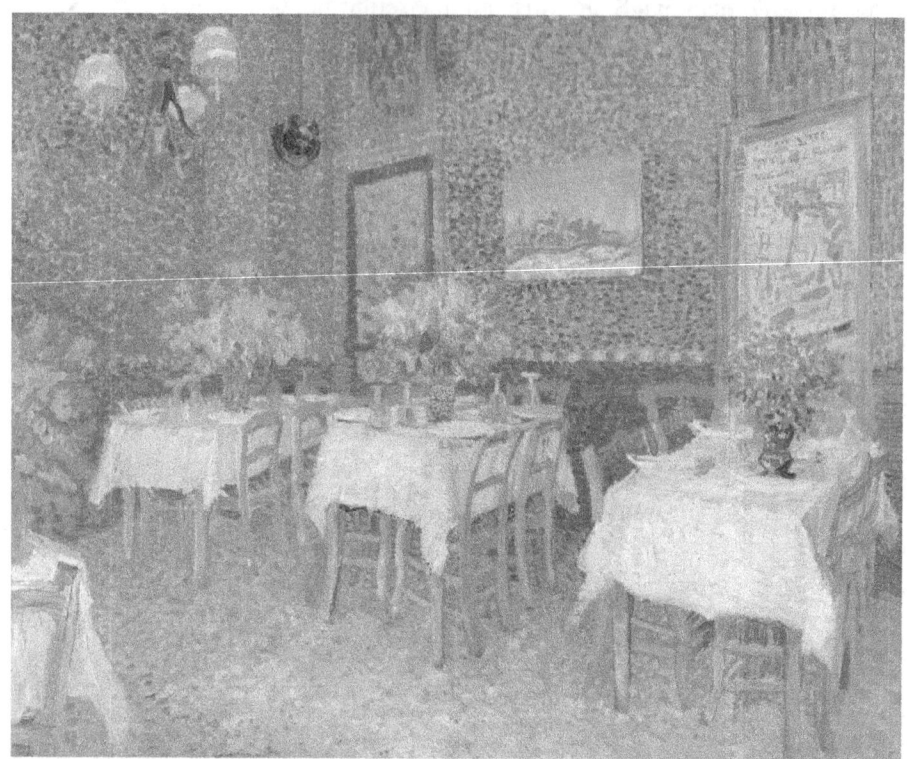

By the middle of the 19th Century along the *Quai de la Tournelle* and the *Rue du Pont Neuf* there were over 3,000 restaurants, cafés, and brasseries throughout Paris. Decorated walls with second empire hand-painted wallpaper, fine blue Italian table skirts, an elegant perfume from vases that overflowed with cut peonies, giltwood Louis the XIV mirrors behind the zinc bar, and a hook for every gentleman's hat, food went hand in hand with every artist and writer. If you wanted to run into your friends or wanted to be jolly where everyone knew your name you simply headed down from Montmartre and went to one of the many open-windowed restaurants for dinner and a few glasses of absinthe.

Van Gogh was no stranger to the restaurants and cafés of 19th Century Paris. He and his brother Theo along with fellow denizens and brothers-in-arms, Émile Bernard and Paul Gauguin (his real first name is Eugène), used their entrepreneurial skills to try and massage liaisons with the wealthy patrons and gallery owners who were there who they hoped to hawk their landscapes and portraits so they could continue to paint. In the above work from 1887, *Interior of a Restaurant*, we see one of van Gogh's experimental pointillist works he must have simply been trying on for size. It is a beautiful work and a foregleam at what might have been. The painting is not just an exercise of artist melding colorful dots and brisk brushstrokes across canvas, but its teases the long exuberant brushstrokes that Vincent will be known for soon and subtle gradations of color to suggest shadow instead of islands of dark dots to paint it in. These are tools of the trade that come from his early realism works and not true pointillism like one finds in a Paul Signac or a Georges Seurat. *Interior of a Restaurant* resides at the Kröller-Müller Museum in Otterlo in the Netherlands where it probably still dreams of those old perfumes of braised lamb, salmon with spring onions, black cherry clafoutis, and the scent of empty Champagne bottles from all around.

Edge of Wheat Field with Poppies, 1887

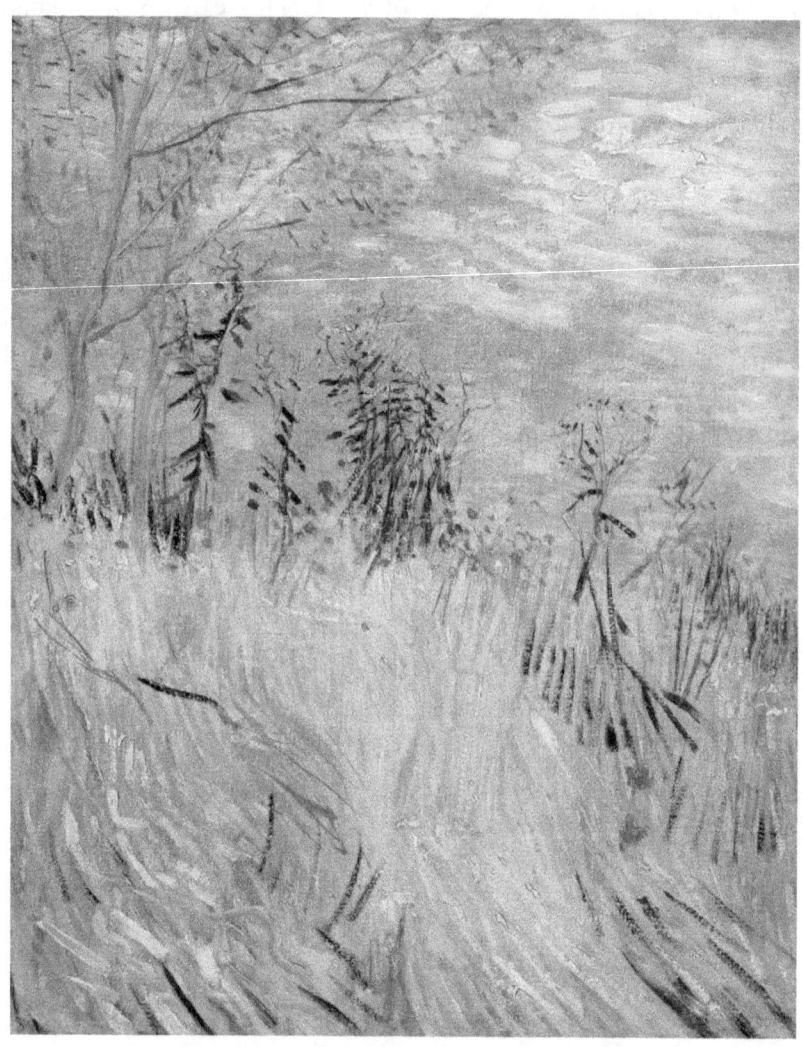

Patches of flowing gold grass, the burst of fading vermillion poppy, and green shoots of alfalfa could still be found here and there scattered throughout 19th Century Paris, where Theo and Vincent holed up at their apartment that overlooked the diamond jubilee of the city from atop Montmartre. Even using Google Earth you will be hard pressed to find even a spec of grassy field or red poppy anywhere within Paris city limits, never mind Montmartre nowadays, but Vincent saw fit to preserve this slice of outdoor life with oil on canvas on pasteboard for all of prosperity. It now lives at the Denver Art Museum in Denver, Colorado where there still exists today plenty of grassland prairie, and in some secret places even some strawberry marks from the air of red poppy.

Green Ears of Wheat, 1888

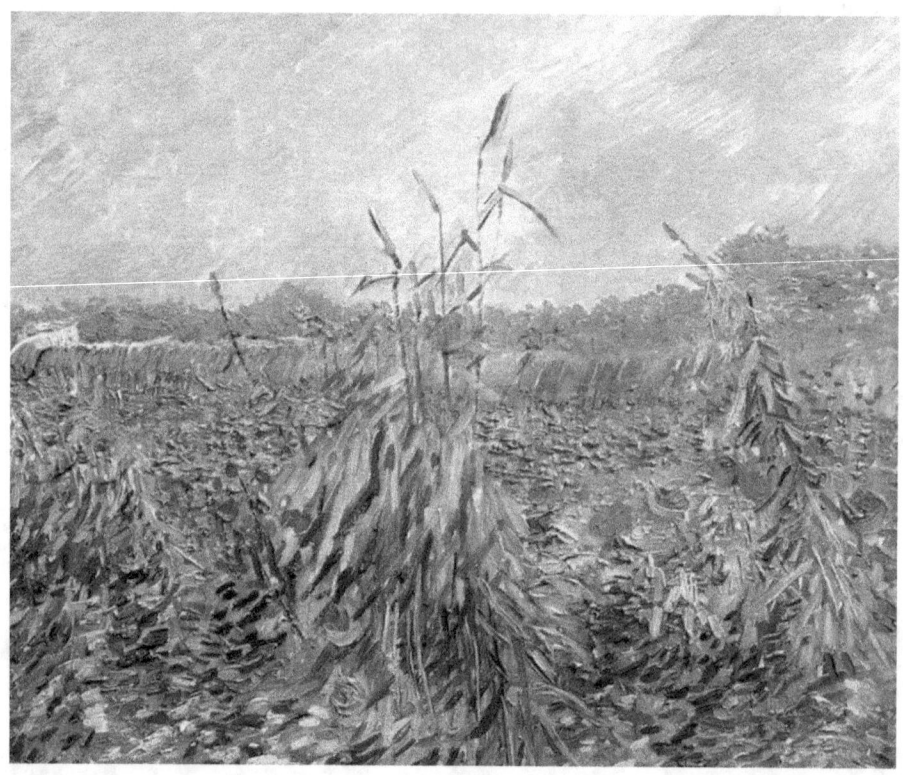

Green Ears of Wheat, circa 1888, from the period he spent painting outside in Arles, France should honestly be re titled *Green Ears of Wheat with Red Poppy*. It is the circuitous red brushstrokes of blossoms along with the movement of the surrounding variations of green that give this landscape such breathtaking gravitas. With a blue sky not as detailed as usual for a van Gogh of this time period our focus is forced on the field, the blood-red flowers, and the wheat whose energy will soon be harnessed for the cows and horses that Vincent wants us to look at. And when you do this what you see is almost the flow and rivulets of emerald and red rapids like a fast moving river perhaps like the Great or the Little Rhône. *Green Ears of Wheat (with Red Poppy)* resides now at the Israel Museum of Art in Jerusalem, Israel.

Ears of Wheat, June 1890

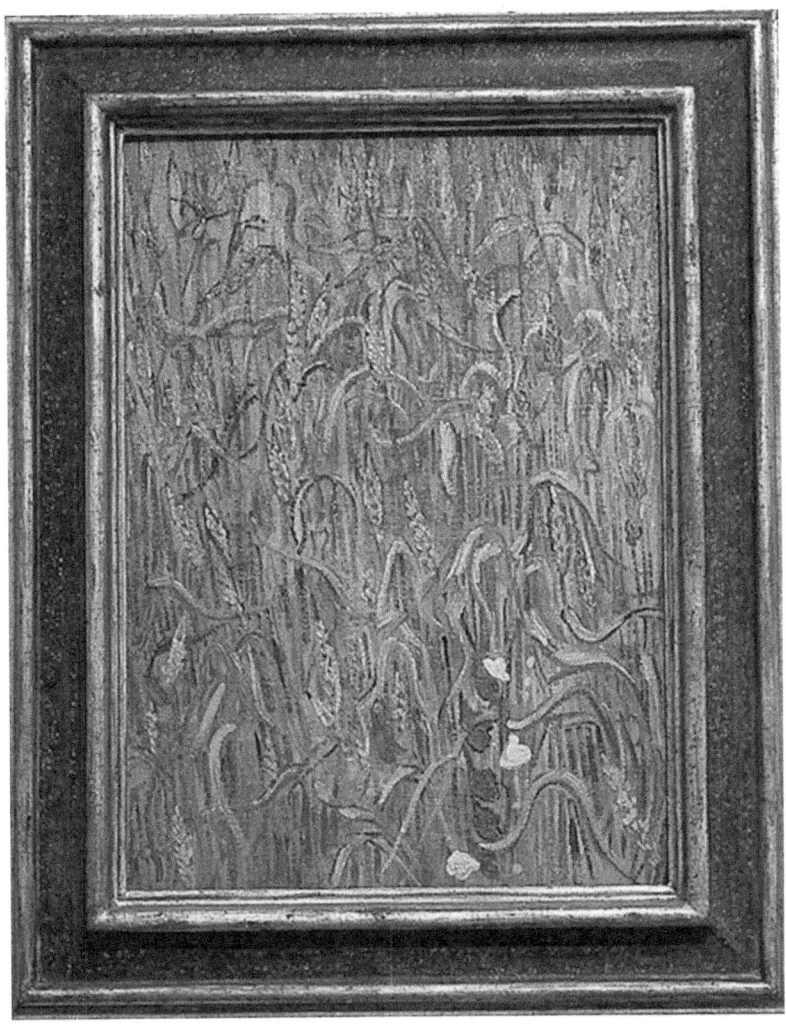

There is nothing for me to describe that can be any better than how Vincent described *Ears of Wheat* himself in a letter to his friend Paul Gauguin:

"Nothing more than ears of wheat, green-blue stalks, long, ribbon-like leaves, under a sheen of green and pink; ears of wheat, yellowing slightly, with an edge made pale pink by the dusty manner of flowering."

It was as though van Gogh could use the AI in his own head to simply type out the words in the cerebellum and his hand could mechanically dashed out whatever it was that he could envision. Computers are only as intelligent as the people who program them. And art is only as good as the artist's mind and its ability to interpret what the eyes see. You can almost imagine an exuberant Vincent snow-shoeing in large steps through the grass out there with easel and paint brushes in hand with wheat high up to his waist as he stood in the middle of the field there in Auvers-sur-Oise and painted the above. All it does is leave us with a smile from ear to ear. Only the best of friends can do that. Or perhaps the mind's eye of Vincent van Gogh!

Resides now at the Van Gogh Museum in Amsterdam in the Netherlands.

Street in Saintes-Maries, 1888

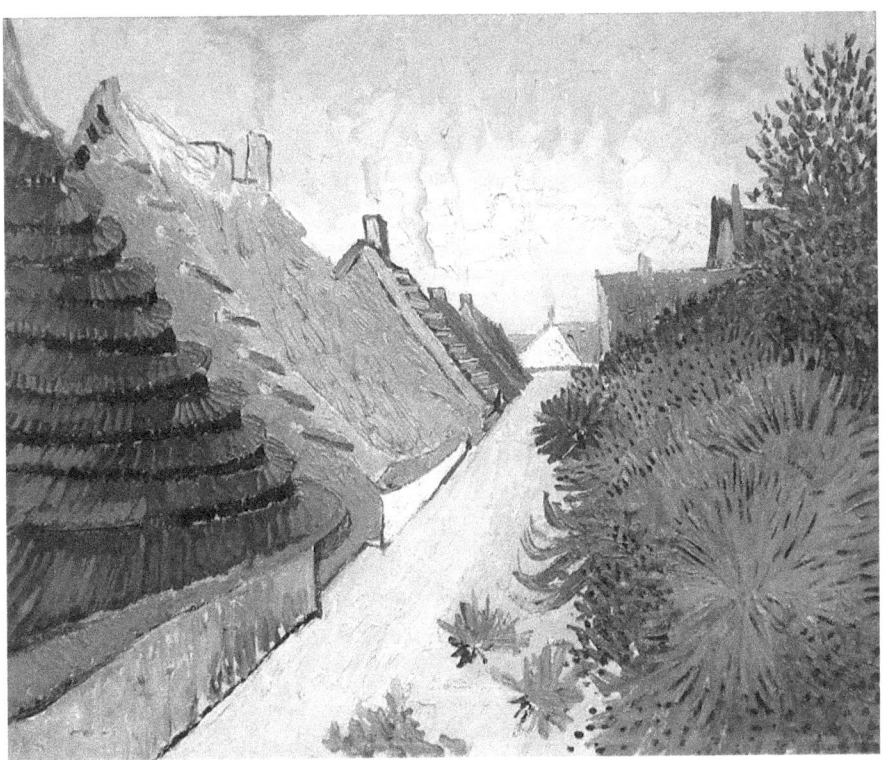

In May of 1888 it is a well-known fact that Vincent made a trip to the sun-drenched fishing village of Saintes-Maries-de-la-Mer along the Mediterranean coast of France. There he executed many drawings that he used after he returned as a blueprint for two seascapes and one small portrait that was of the snug cottages of the fishing village of Saintes-Maries-de-la-Mer itself.

The above represents the latter with its snaking woodsmoke twisting up and out from cottage chimneys along with tropical Mediterranean greenery of fragrant eucalyptus, agave, and strawberry trees that frame a landscape already sculpted and laid out in natural pathways and islands of green by centuries of sea-spray that watered the coast before any human ever set foot there. The painting is built on muted thatch browns, blues, and grays set against gold sky and the water-thirsty plant life that occupies the entire right frame of the painting. It is a feast for the eyes and a work that if hung on your writing room wall or library would leave you delighted and content wanting only for maybe a good tumbler of brandy late at night. Well, maybe, if you still got any lifeblood left in you at all, a little bit more than that. But not always.

View of Saintes-Maries, 1888,

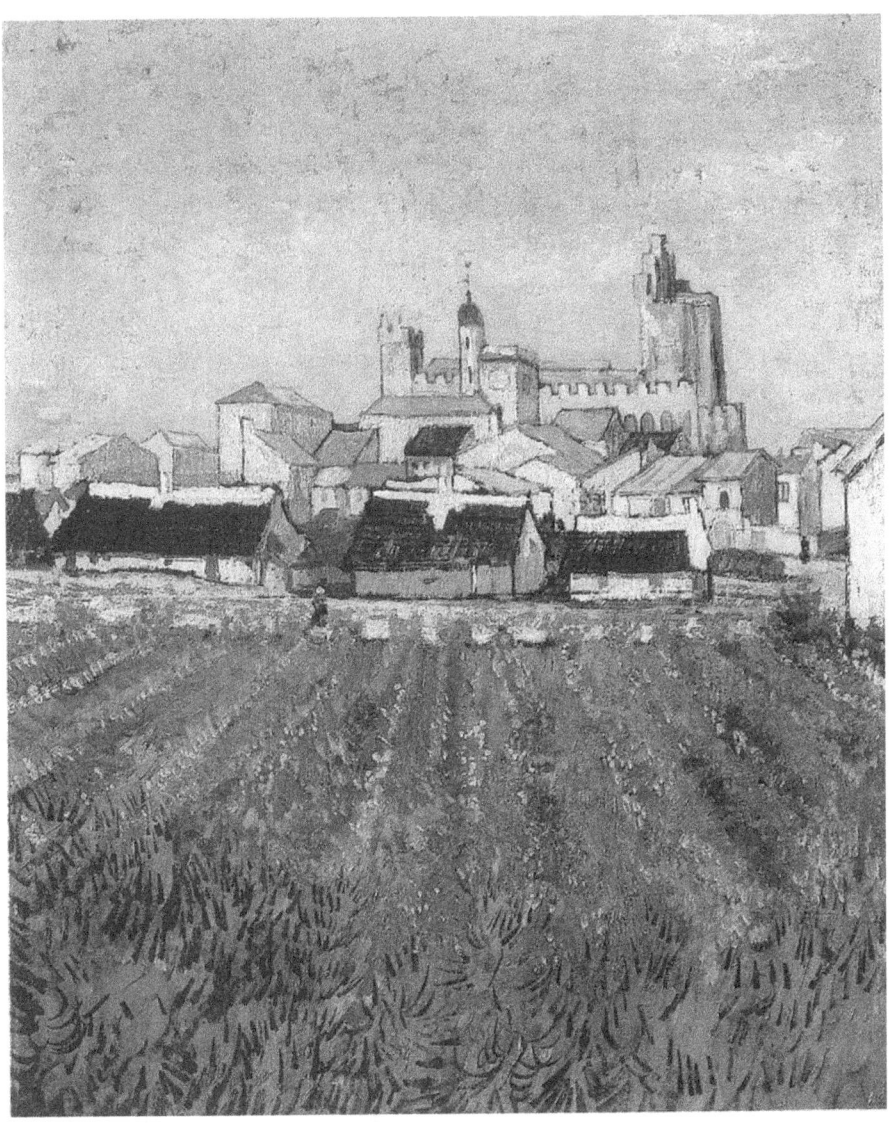

I first saw a photograph of this painting in a book as a child sometime during the early 1970's. It was a sunny summer day outside in Rhode Island and Glen Campbell's *Gentle on My Mind* was playing on JB105 on the radio. Right away, not even knowing who van Gogh was yet, it struck me how special and unique this landscape was.

There are plenty of landscapes from his era that use Florence or other European provincial cities across Tuscany and Provence that show flowering fields of manmade rows of flowers, but most are painted with a view of capturing the city as the focal point. But here you can tell that the artist actually loves the field of lavender and simply wants to use the dark rooftops, stucco cottages, and the monastic walls of Saintes-Maries to frame in the natural wonder that nature has painted herself even when man's hand has tried to intervene and tame it into submission. *View of Saintes-Maries* resides at the Kröller-Müller Museum in Otterlo in the Netherlands. Be sure to play some Glen Campbell for it whenever you stand before its frame. It will pay you forward with reams of dopamine and also some good karma (if you happen to be lucky).

Evening - The End of the Day (after Millet), 1889

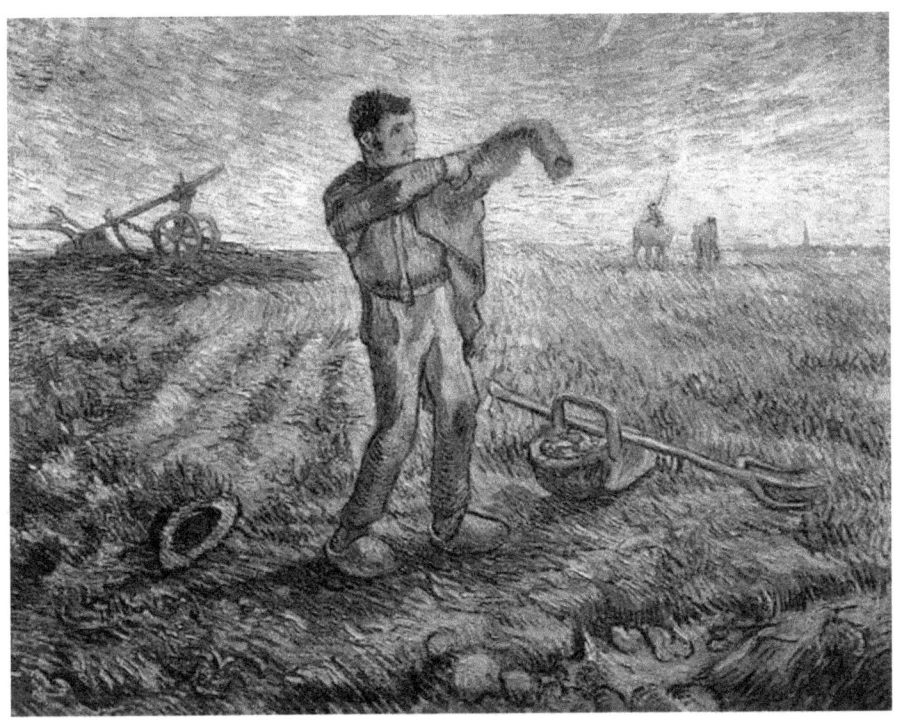

Is this painting a Thomas Hart Benton or a Vincent van Gogh? It would be hard to tell if it were not for the giveaway of van Gogh's hand that is hidden in the brushstrokes of waves of grass and the draining portal of sunset seemingly being pulled down toward the horizon like a shade.

There are only three colors used here, but *Evening – The End of the Day* is like a big piece of placer nugget one wants to slip into their pocket like a talisman instead of taking it to the claims office and exchanging it for weight's worth in gold. There are little Easter eggs hidden all over the vast gold landscape. And it would be a shame to point them all out to you instead of simply letting you spot them all on your own to interpret each one personally the way we each like to do with a great song or a novel. To visit in person *Put the message in the box, Put the box into the car, Drive the car around the world, Until you get* to the Menard Art Museum in Komaki, Japan.

The Little Stream, October 1889

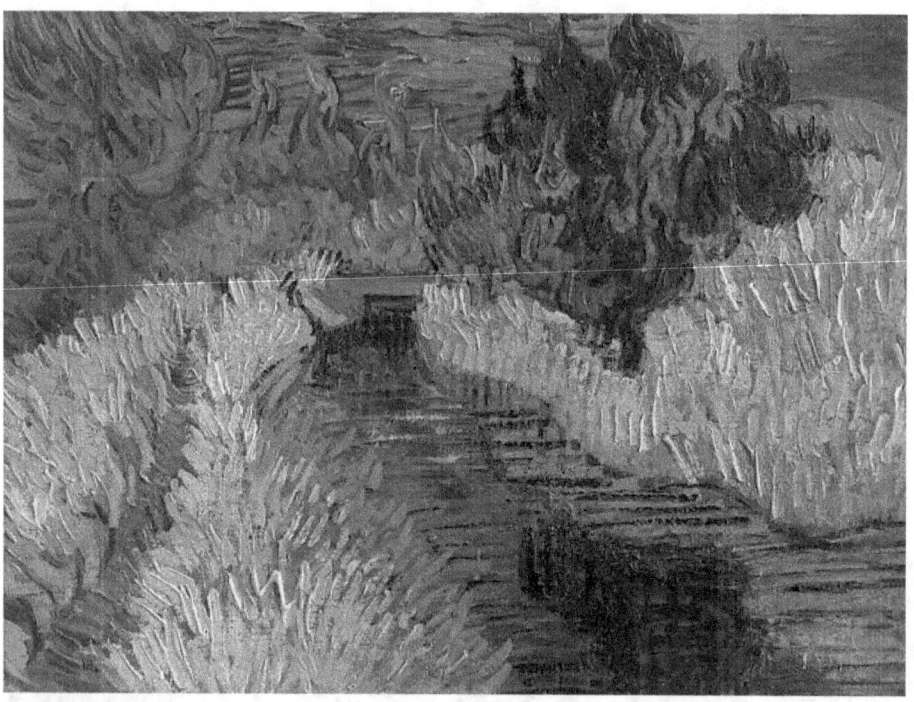

A symphony of frogs and crickets ignite a cool late autumn air near an unnamed blue ribbon of stream that meanders through a field of Auvers-sur-Oise. Vincent seems to almost light the autumn foliage on fire across and behind the bridge. Gold, orange, and muted red set them themselves afoot meticulously, but barely, down atop the mirrored stream. This is not a light-soaked landscape like *Evening - The End of the Day (after Millet)*, but every bit as haunting. Framed in a room mahogany lined room it has no choice but to finger you over to it over by the wall. Someone is trying to talk to you about Sri Lanka or Taylor Swift or Sam Bankman-Fried while you stare intensely at it, but you cannot hear their voice (the way men cannot hear two conversations at once), because *The Little Stream* whispers, gently, like the wind that traverses its flowers, pistils, and lines of ripple atop the stream.

If you are alone and in need of a quick visit to twilight in Auvers-sur-Oise you can find *The Little Stream* currently on loan at the Metropolitan Museum of Art, Manhattan in New York City. Afterwards treat yourself at the little kosher Jewish deli over in the East 70s and get the fatty pastrami on rye and a Coke. The pastrami is better than anything they have in San Sebastian, Irún,

Hendaye, Biarritz, and Bayonne. If you tell them Frank O'Hara sent you there—they may even give it to you for free. Au revoir. Shalom.

Landscape with Bridge across the Oise, 1890

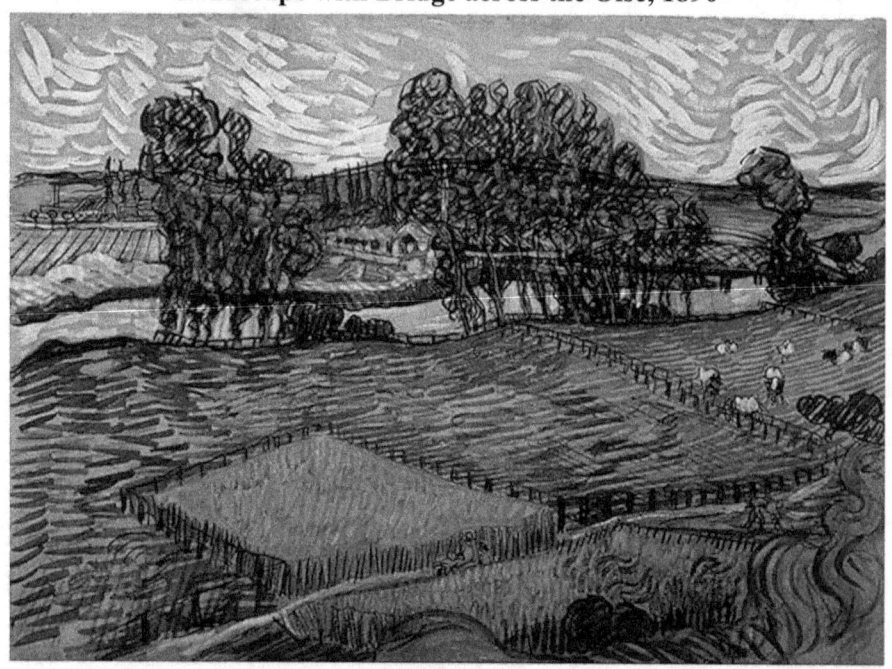

If you travel to the fair countryside of Auvers-sur-Oise today you can still find this vista right there along the riverbank near the masonry arch bridge half hidden behind the poplars and willows seen in the mid-righthand side of this landscape. The sky is usually blue around those parts, but there sits a house in place of the once furrowed field and the fenced in vegetable garden. There are also no more cows or sheep at this particular place and it has all grown in a bit unwieldy and wild. Also, the blue arched bridge has been supplanted by a more stunted and mundane spat of a bridge, because obviously the captain of the French department of transportation who planned the newer construction had no idea about a painting Vincent van Gogh had painted in 1890 called *Landscape with Bridge across the Oise* (and its importance to those who love the artist.) Plus there were French cigarettes to be smoked, fresh warm baguettes to be bought for the noon meal, and blonde French models with light hazel eyes and beautiful white bikini tan lines tattooed against their otherwise taut bronze-brown skin.

The trees in the above are still there though, which gives us a bit of comfort, but maybe just a far too little. Our handsome bronze-brown landscape is much faded now from an intense sun that it must have been exposed to throughout the years near a window, but much like our blonde French young models that ruined the new bridge from ever having the chance to own a nice arch's line of thrust it is mostly all still there. Nonetheless one can observe, albeit a bit faded, the once great arched bridge of Auvers-sur-Oise half hidden by van Gogh behind some poplar trees at the Tate Gallery in London, England.

Three White Cottages in Saintes-Maries, 1888,

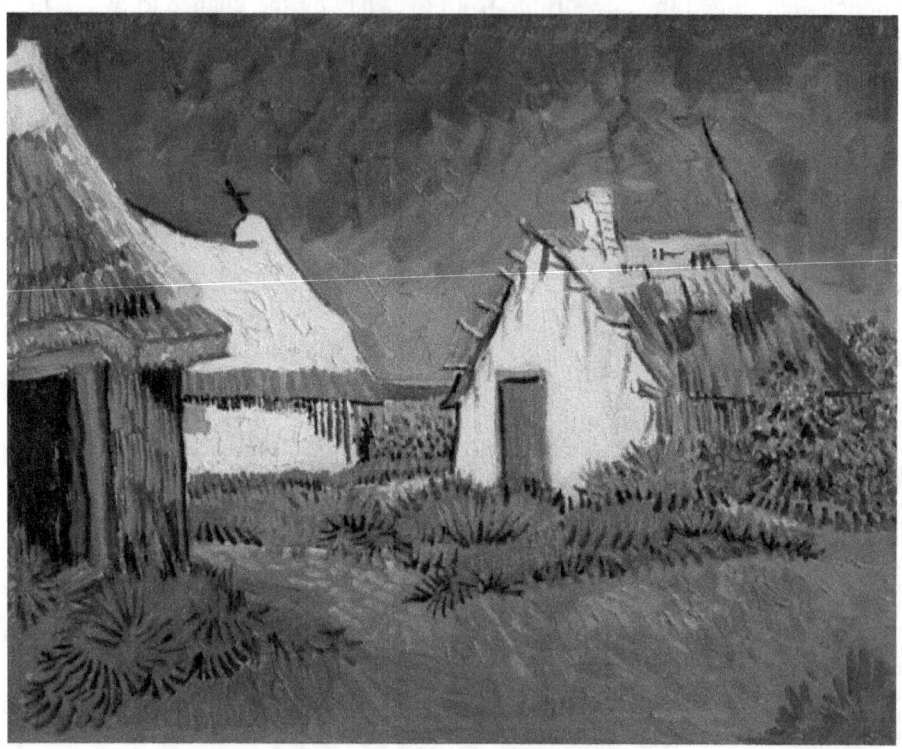

Painted in Auvers-sur-Oise, France, circa 1888, the smallish 12.5 inch by 17 inch *Three White Cottages in Saintes-Maries (Cabanes blanches aux Saintes-Maries)*, was one of the first of the new wave of van Gogh landscapes and portraits. It truly marks an important turning point in his artistic style with his new use of contrasts and colors in a deliberate exaggeration that clearly screams out to everyone now: I am a Vincent van Gogh! It is currently on display at the Kunsthaus Zürich Art Museum in Zürich, Switzerland.

Les Ponts d'Asnières, 1887

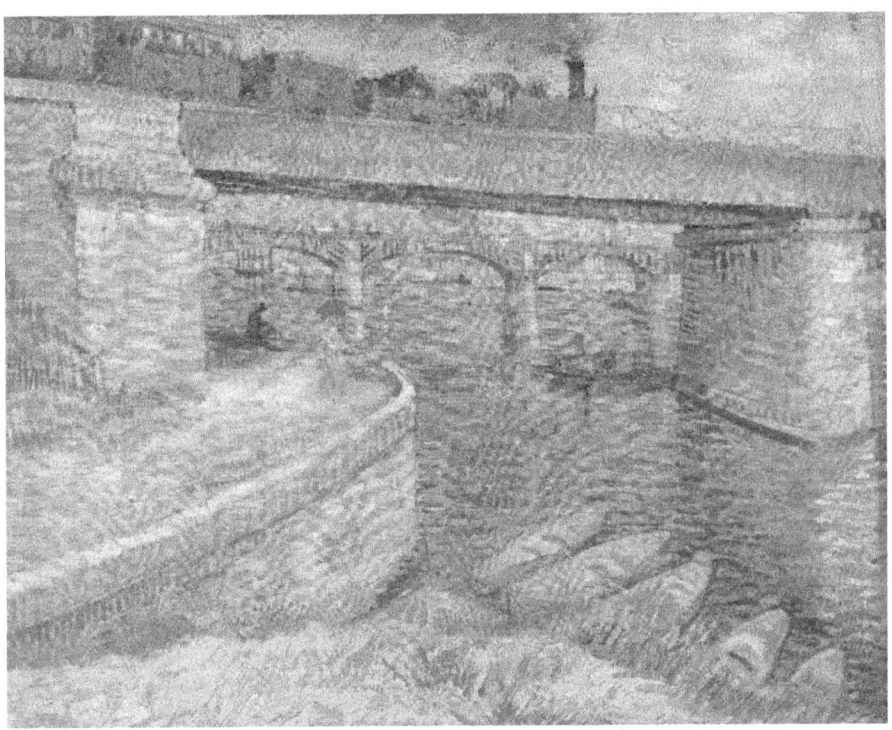

Painted in Paris during 1887, *Les Ponts d'Asnières*, is part of what we now call the Asnières-sur-Seine series of paintings that van Gogh painted made up of Parisian bridges, river landscapes, French city parks, café settings and was influenced by his introduction to Pointillism, Impressionism, Symbolism, and Japanese woodblock prints from Japan. The painting now resides in the Foundation E. G. Bührle Collection Art Museum of Art in Zürich, Switzerland.

Roses trémières, 1886

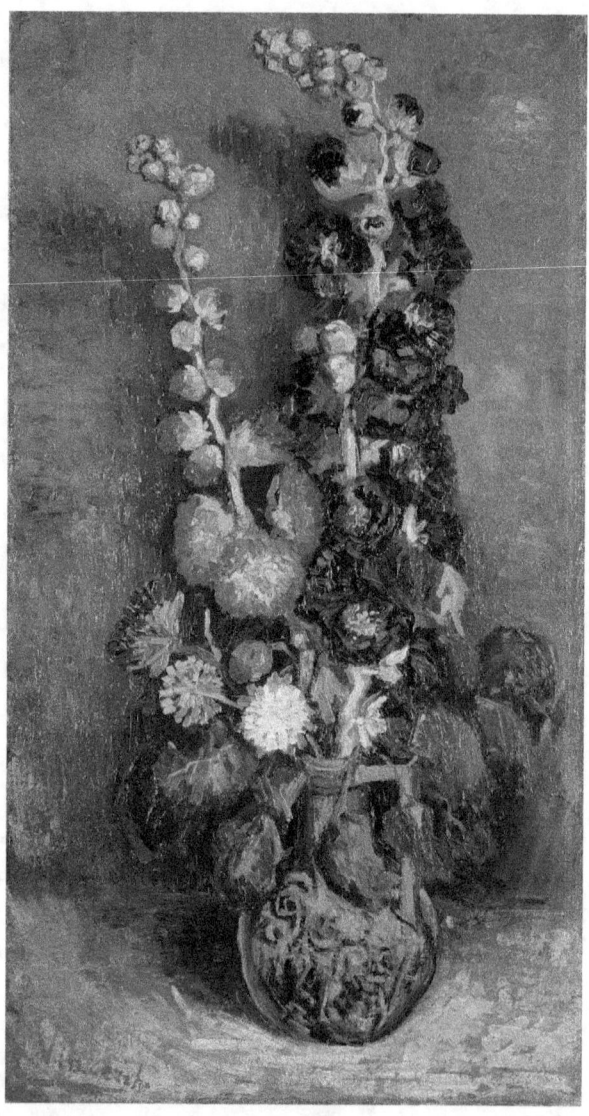

An early still life from 1886, *Roses trémières* looks as though it could have been painted by any number of artist of the era save for the distinct "Vincent" trademark signature in the lower lefthand corner. Although, beautiful, there are only hints of van Gogh brushstrokes throughout and atop the table the vase sits upon. It is currently on display at the Kunsthaus Zürich Art Museum in Zürich, Switzerland.

Branches de marronnier en fleur, 1890

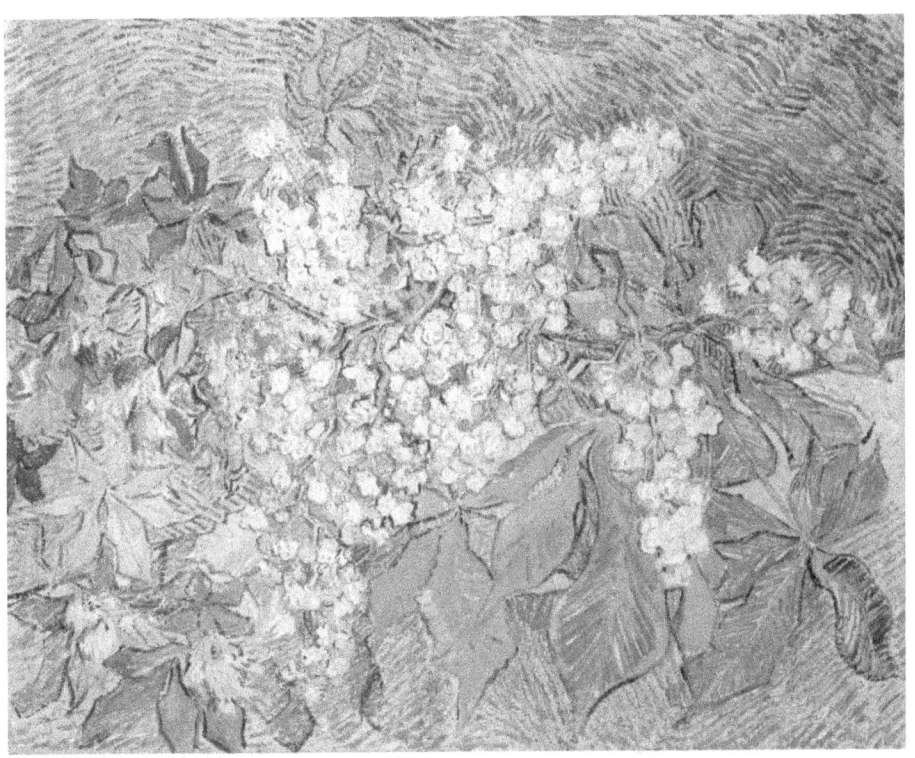

Four years after 1886, *Roses trémières* the 1890 *Branches de marronnier en fleur* is more of a rhapsody in blue and white blossoms with flowing lines like ripples swimming outward atop an otherwise still blue pond. It is currently on display at the Kunsthaus Zürich Art Museum in Zürich, Switzerland.

Self-Portrait with Dark Felt Hat, 1886

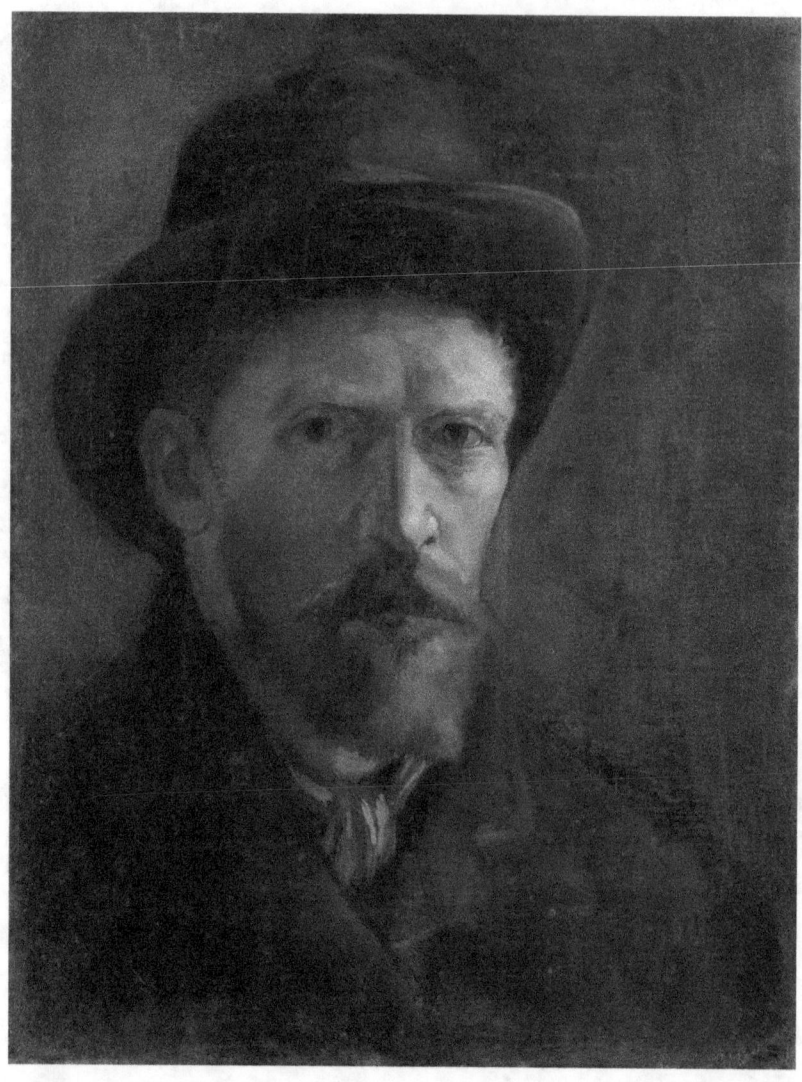

Self-Portrait with Dark Felt Hat from 1886 seems to almost depict an artist who does not know who he is or where he is going. There is no bravado or luster as in later works and self-portraits even during that manic time when van Gogh began to fall apart. Madness and genius work well for the artist. Lack of vision and self-awareness do not as seen by this portrait. The painting hangs on display at the Van Gogh Museum in Amsterdam in the Netherlands.

The De Ruijterkade in Amsterdam, 1885

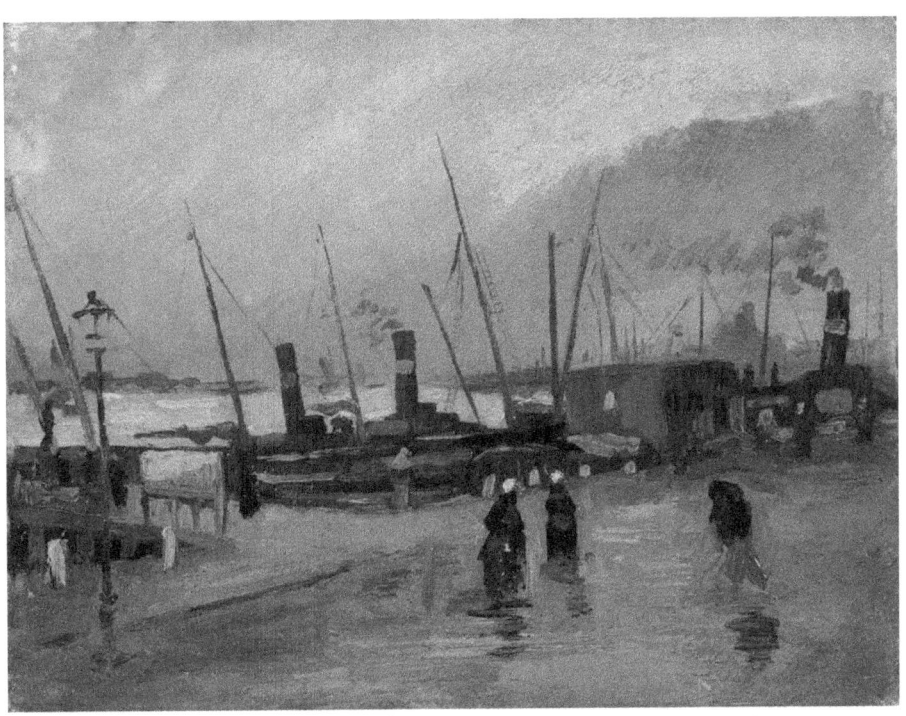

Vincent van Gogh painted *The De Ruijterkade in Amsterdam* in 1885 upon his arrival at Antwerp, Belgium, in November of the same year. With his easel set upon the wet cobblestone in front of the nearby docks van Gogh painted the harbor, boats, docks, and bonnet clad subjects day after day, but found no buyers for his work within the local Antwerp art world.

The Parsonage Garden in the Snow, 1885

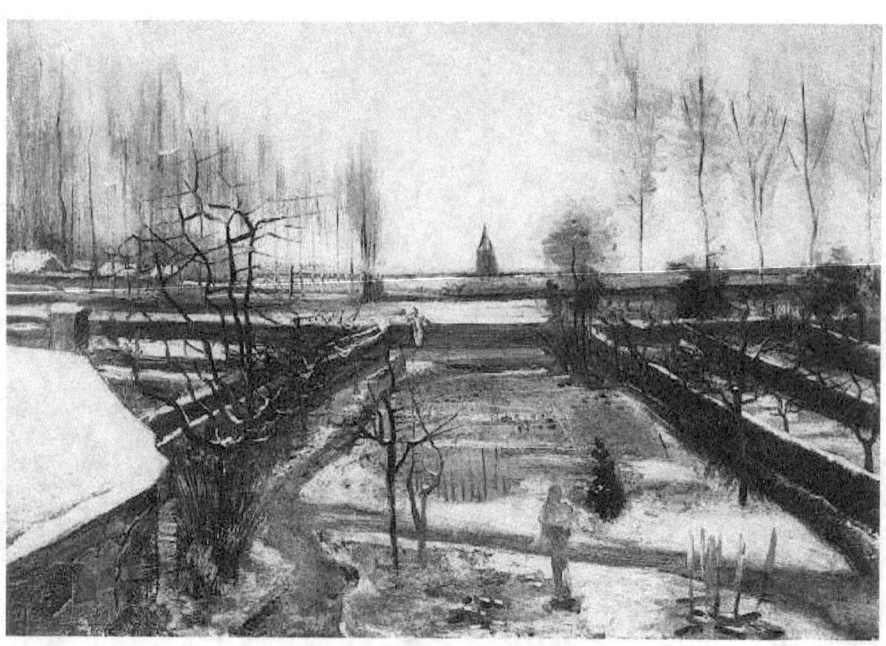

In 1885 *The Parsonage Garden in the Snow* shows a bleak landscape barren of leaves, harvest growth, color, and but off on the horizon light! A glow of hope for what lies ahead. The landscape now resides in sunny California at the Hammer Museum (University of California), Los Angeles.

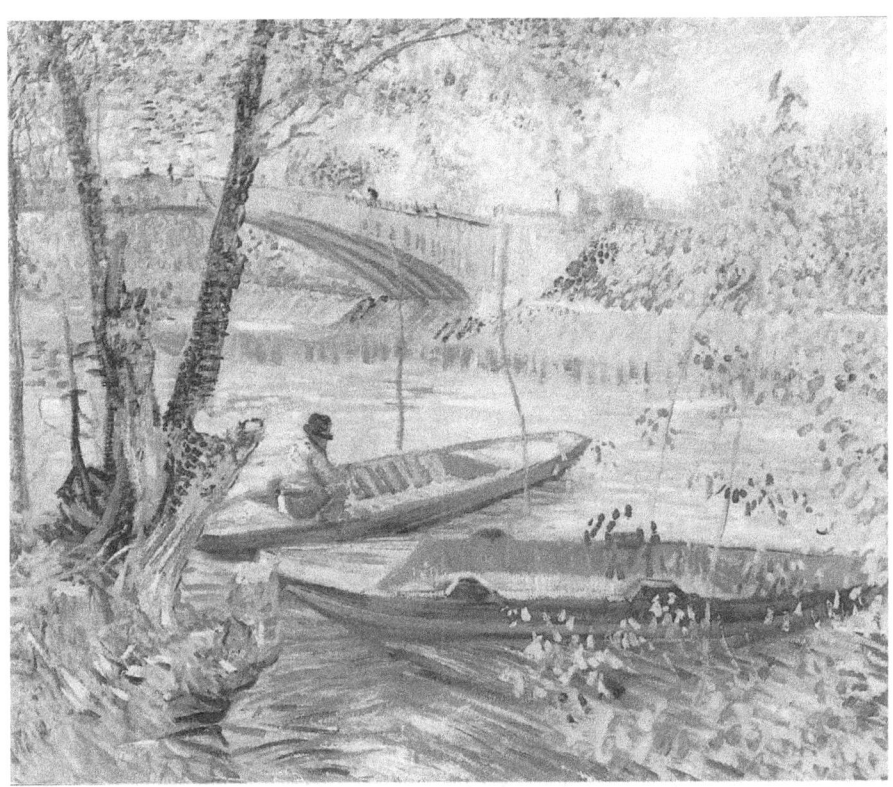

Fishing in Spring, the Pont de Clichy (Asnières), 1887 is another in the Asnières-sur-Seine series of paintings that van Gogh painted whose focus was made of Parisian bridges, river landscapes, French city parks, and café settings that he soaked in during his years in Paris. Home now for the painting is at the Art Institute of Chicago in Chicago, Illinois.

View of Paris from Vincent's Room in the Rue Lepic, 1887

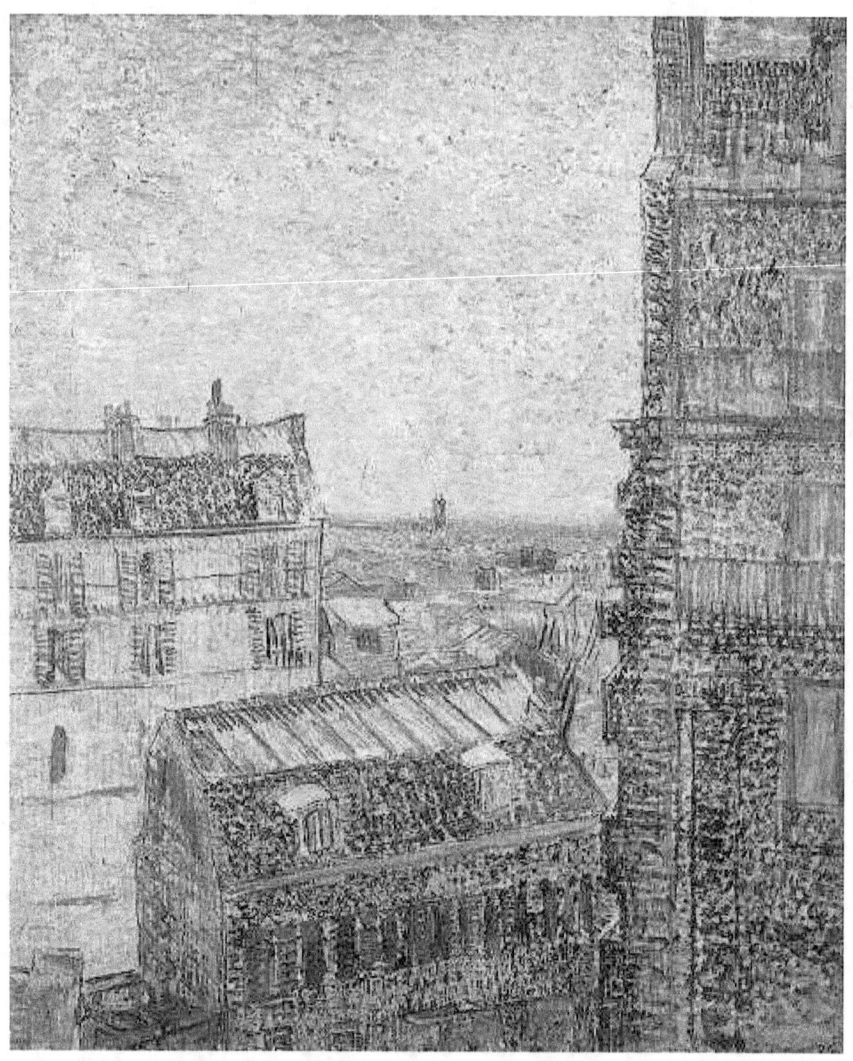

Another in the Asnières-sur-Seine series of paintings that van Gogh created in 1887, *View of Paris from Vincent's Room in the Rue Lepic* shows off a skyline view of the nearby buildings and rooftops of a panoramic Paris with Notre Dame cathedral off in the distance. This intimate painting currently resides in the Van Gogh Museum in Amsterdam.

Couples in the Voyer d'Argenson Park at Asnières, 1887

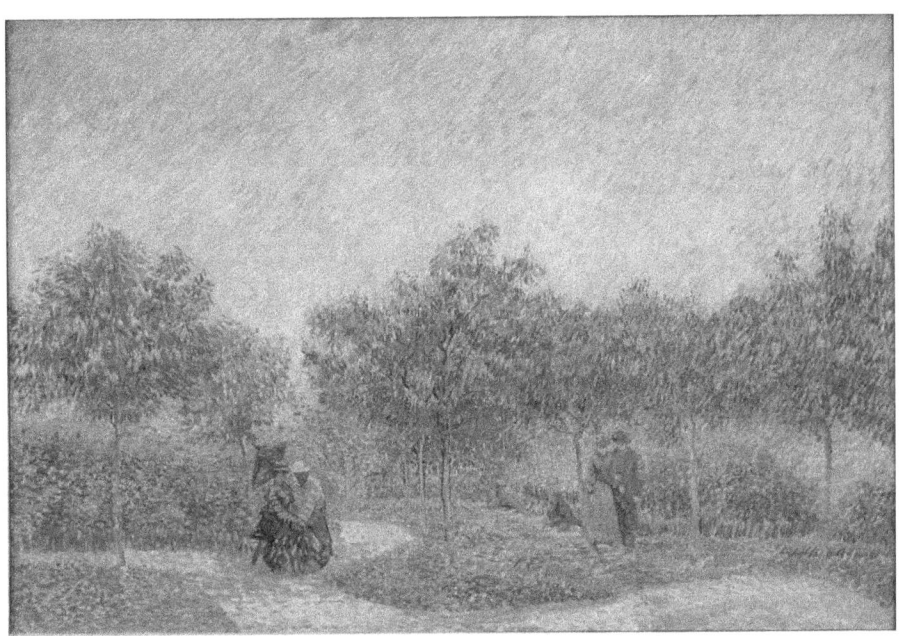

Another in the Asnières-sur-Seine series of paintings that van Gogh created in 1887 the sublime *Couples in the Voyer d'Argenson Park at Asnières* is a beautiful depiction of "sweethearts" strolling and sitting in the park full of blossoming flowers and fruit trees.

Square Saint-Pierre at Sunset, 1887

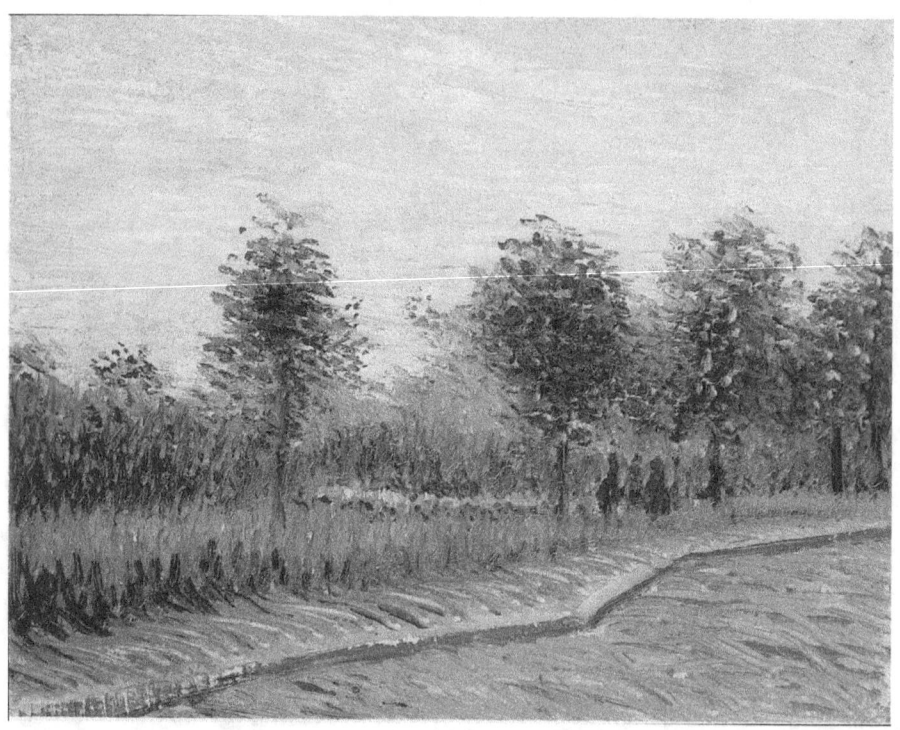

Another in the Asnières-sur-Seine series of paintings van Gogh created in 1887, Vincent began to paint what he termed "the glory of summer and the rich colors of the vegetation." Notice the result in the hues of yellow sun around the leafy vestiges of linden tree leaves and the afterglow of light arrayed in the bottle blue-green of the shadowy parts of the leaves and branches. *Square Saint-Pierre at Sunset* is a transformative work, an artist wreaking havoc with its wings as they try to break through their crystal stasis. The painting currently resides at the Kunsthaus Zürich Museum in Zürich, Switzerland where it still wreaks havoc to this very day.

Starry Night Over the Rhône, 1888

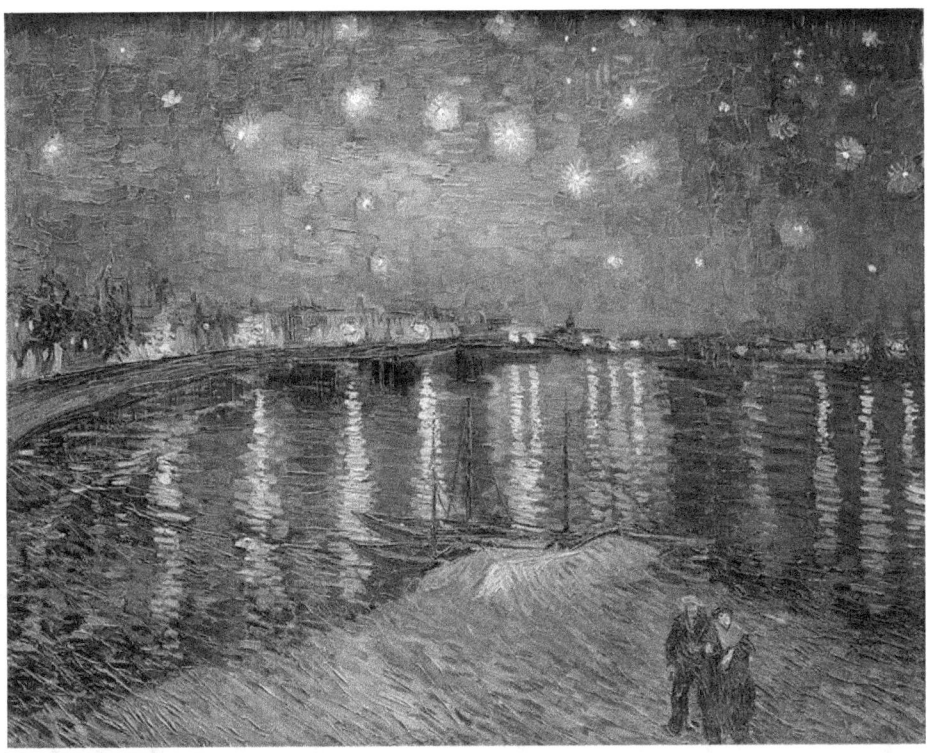

Starry Night Over the Rhône, circa 1888 is considered one of the most iconic and beautiful paintings of all-time. Romantic, otherworldly, reflective of the world around it both in the heavens and on the ground, *Starry Night Over the Rhône* captures the very essence of what it means to create great and memorable works of art. Is there another painting in the canon of art like it? No. Any other comparison to another painting? None. One more beautiful? Debatable. Van Gogh would be bowled over by his fame that now exists in traveling exhibitions from city to city, at art shows, and his influence on not only other artists but entire generations of writers, painters, musicians, and poets. *Starry Night Over the Rhône* is now currently on display at the Musée d'Orsay in Paris, France.

Das Restaurant de la Siréne in Asniéres, 1887

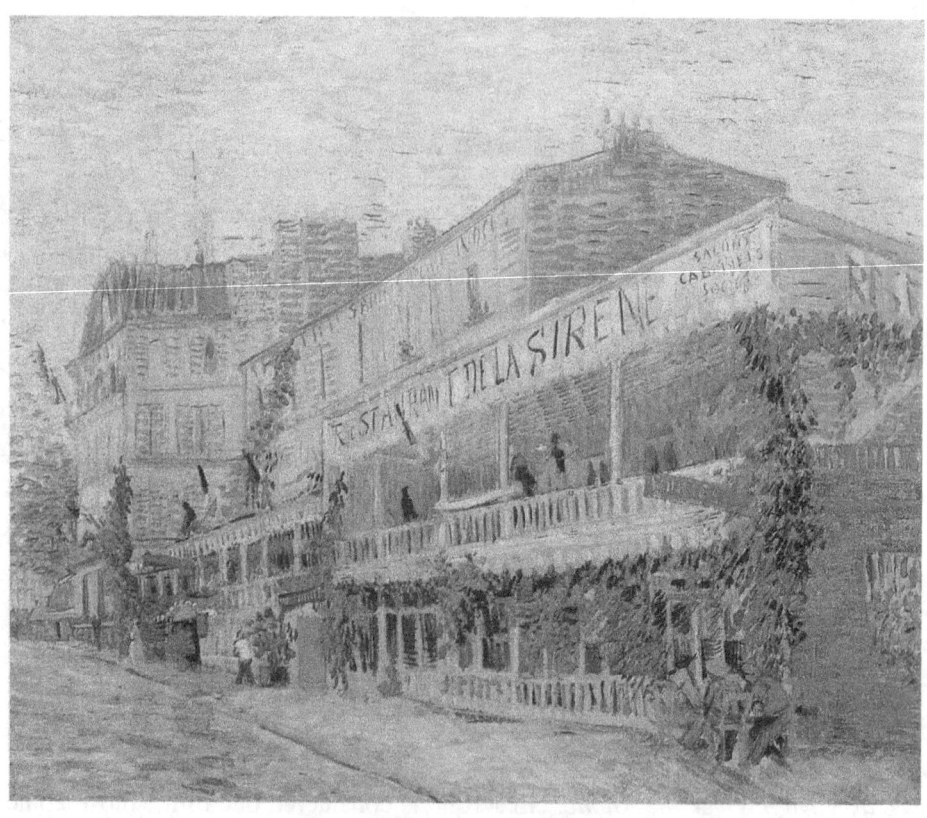

Das Restaurant de la Siréne in Asniéres, 1887 is a Paris street scene and a part of the Asnières-sur-Seine series. There is a little bit of a honky-tonk or perhaps a Créole-Po Boy vibe that wobble and lures the viewer from the party-like atmosphere that comes from the subjects so alive amid the porches and vine covered verandas. It is currently housed at the Musée d'Orsay in Paris, France.

The Rispal Restaurant at Asnières Summer, 1887

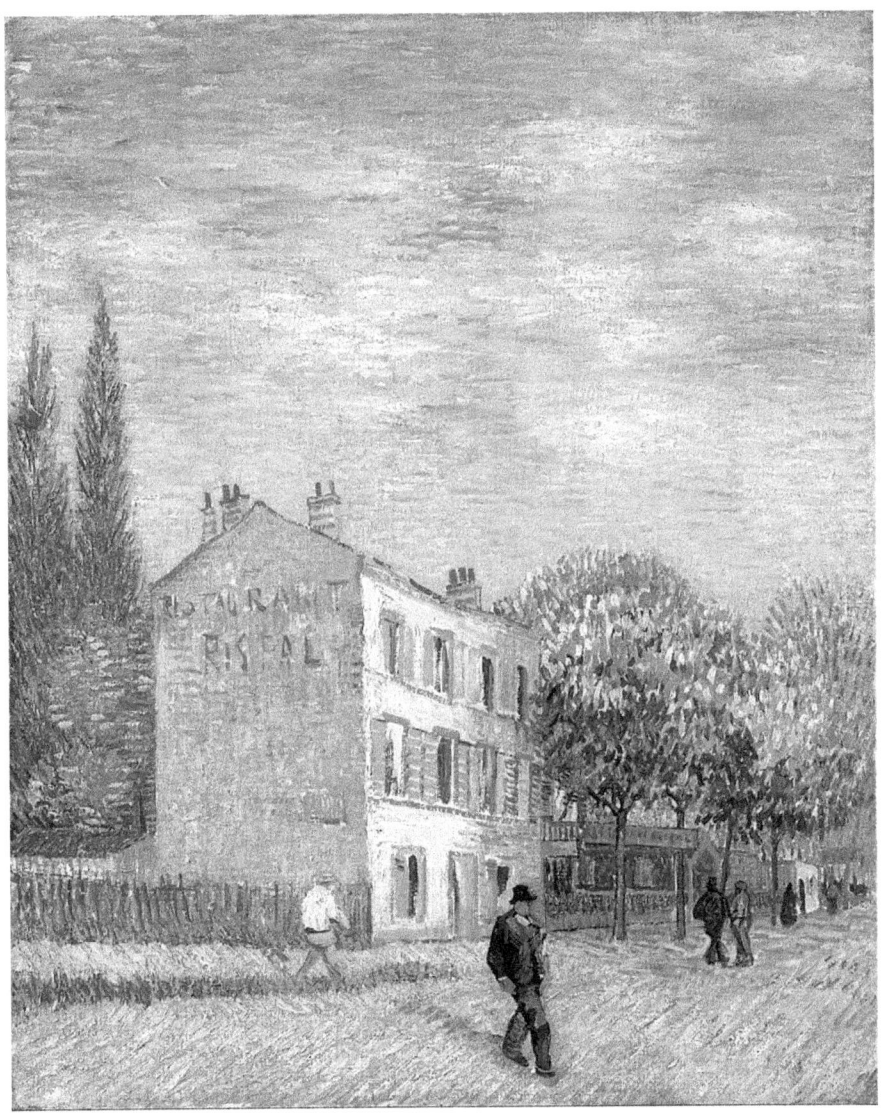

The Rispal Restaurant at Asnières is a breathtaking summertime Parisian street scene from 1887 with lively leafy trees and broken lined blue sky. It is currently housed at the Nelson-Atkins Museum of Art in Kansas City, Missouri.

Exterior of a Restaurant at Asnières, 1887

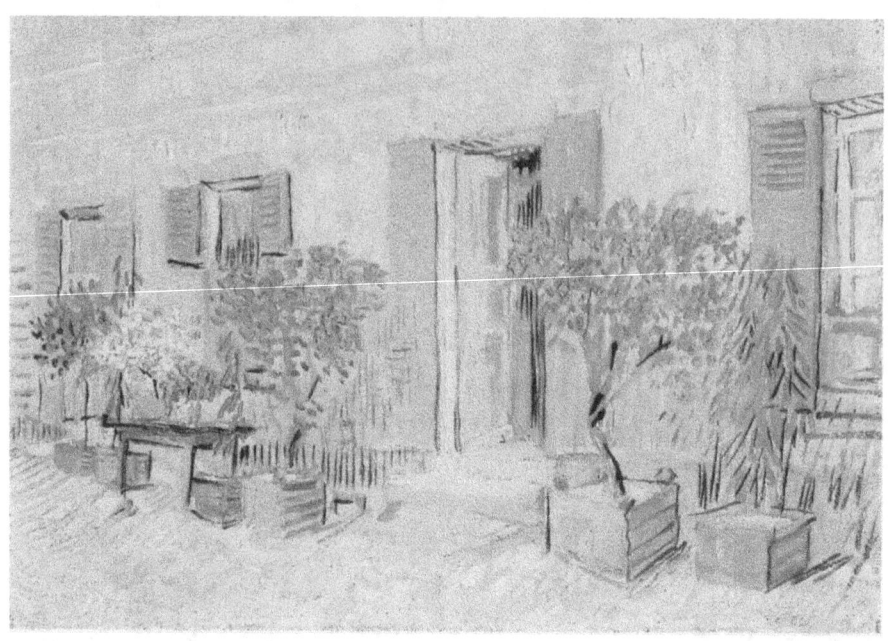

Bathed in gold-yellow, *Exterior of a Restaurant at Asnières*, circa 1887, is an excellent example of a van Gogh Parisian street scene lush with floral and leafy presentation.

Rain or Enclosed Wheat Field in the Rain, November 1889

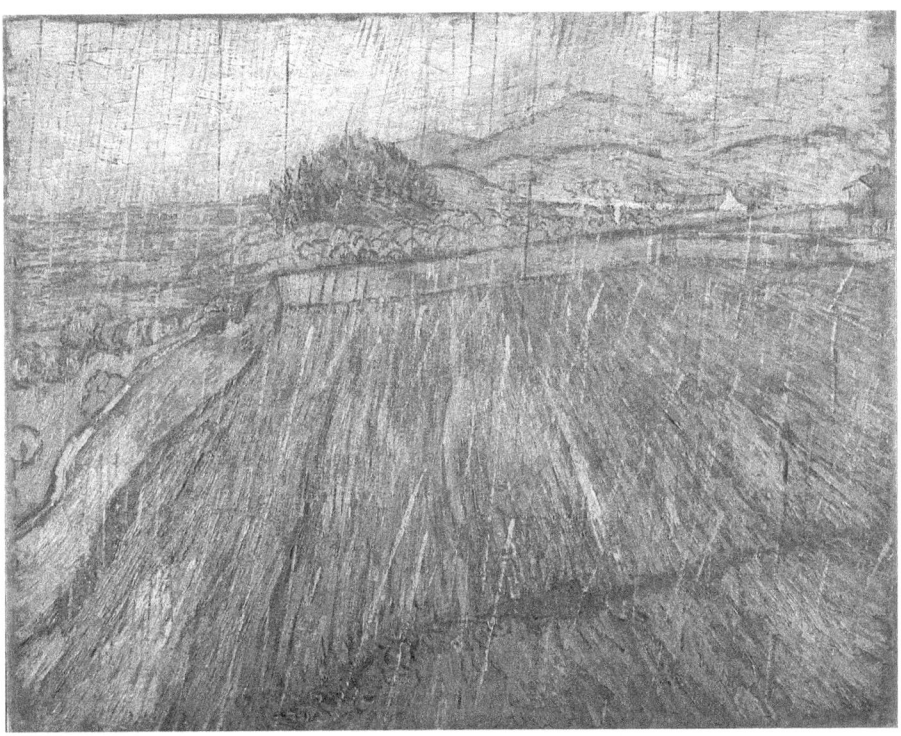

When one thinks of Vincent van Gogh they often think of round glowing balls of yellow sun, brightening wheat fields, lush red poppy, the streets of Paris, or Sowers sowing seed, but there can be no crop or harvest without the November rains, which van Gogh brings to life in his ominous and beautiful *Rain or Enclosed Wheat Field in the Rain* painted in the autumn of 1889. It is currently housed at Philadelphia Museum of Art, Philadelphia.

Wheatfield Under Thunderclouds, 1890

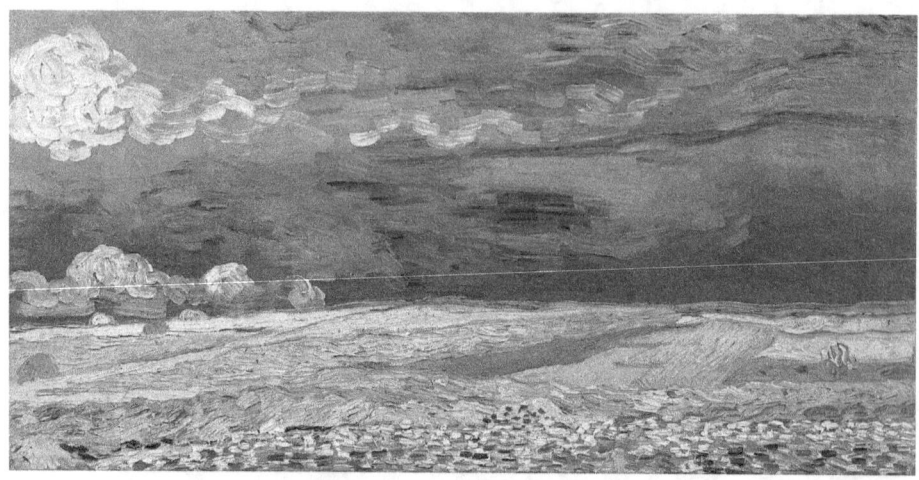

Wheatfield Under Thunderclouds, 1890, gives the viewer a beautiful exhalation of thunderstorm clouds being windblown across the French countryside sky with wheatfields and a smattering of red poppy in the foreground. It is currently on display at the Van Gogh Museum, Amsterdam in the Netherlands.

Wheat Fields, early June 1889

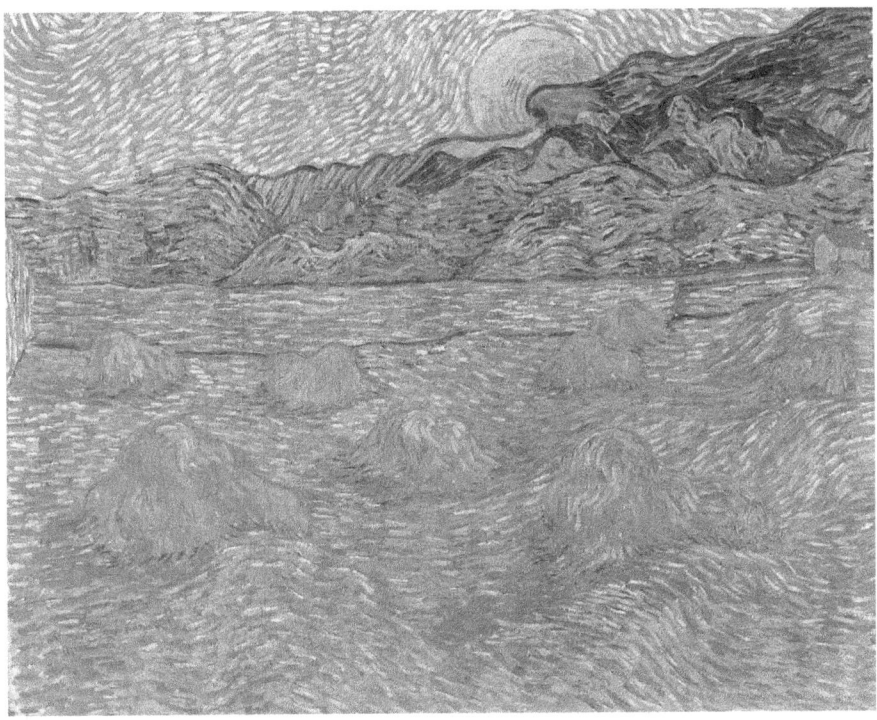

Before and after the rain comes the sun from behind the shoulders of alpine mountains. *Wheat Fields* from early June 1889 is full of flowing rhythms and movements like the very ground and sky is alive with all its quantum mechanics in plain view to the human eye. *Wheat Fields* is currently on view at the Kröller-Müller Museum, Otterlo in the Netherlands.

Irises, May 1889

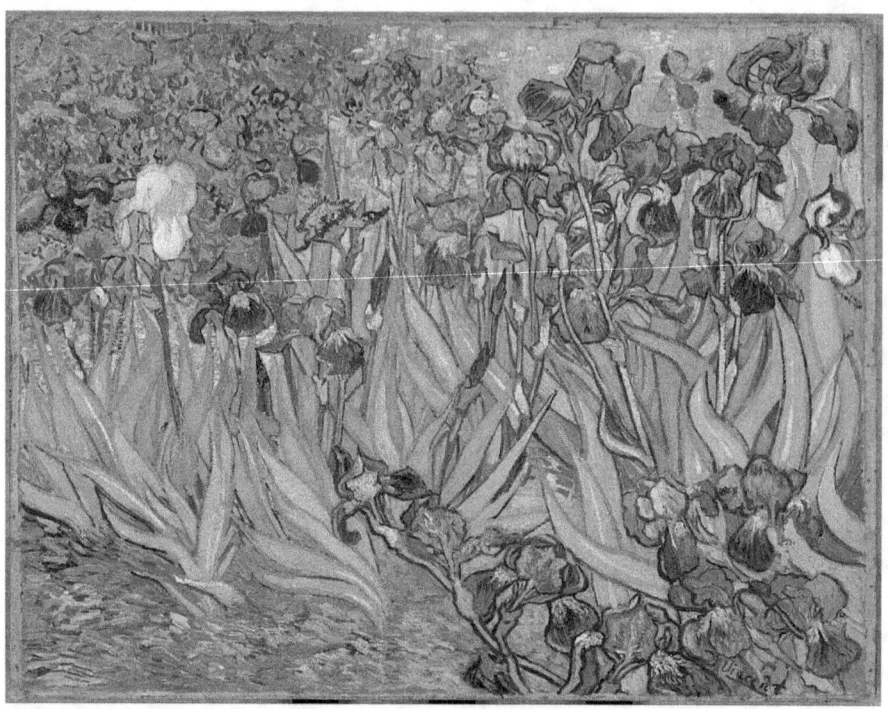

Irises was painted at the Saint Paul-de-Mausole asylum in Saint-Rémy-de-Provence, France, in the last year before van Gogh's untimely demise at age 37. It blurs the lines between old and new, life and death, flat and airy, springtime and autumn. The irises are set in a beautiful more-blue-than-purple hue and seem to come alive to counter balance the beauty and subtle orange-gold of the French Marigolds that grow in the background. One of the paintings van Gogh used to help himself keep busy while institutionalized otherwise he might continue down the road of insanity it is now considered one of his most iconic works and resides on display at the Jéan Paul Getty Museum in Los Angeles, California.

Self-Portrait, September 1889

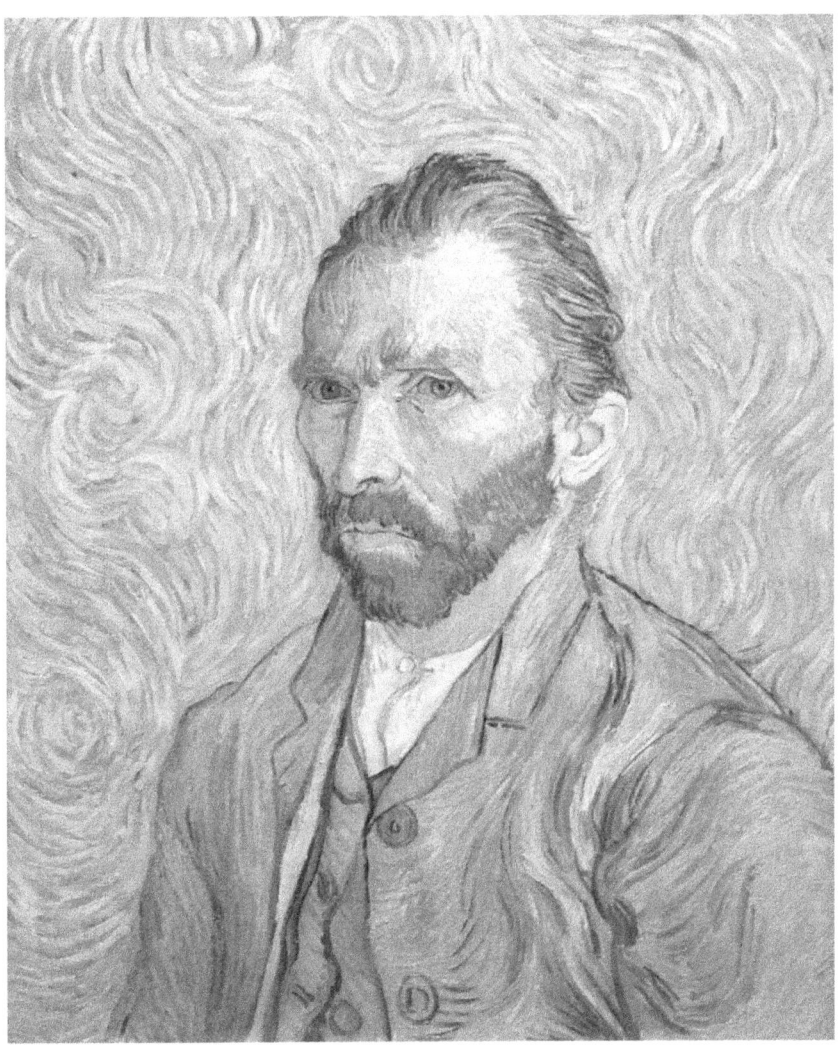

Self-Portrait, September 1889 was painted mere months before the tragic suicide of Vincent van Gogh. The world around him is in a whirlwind of chaos, exactly as he feels inside his mind and body. The weight upon his chest. The lead he feels filling up his legs. The pounding at the back of his head. All the world is blue with just a hint of light left cast upon the face of van Gogh himself, but little anywhere else. One can often see the soul in the eyes of someone at times. What does pain look like? Van Gogh shows us here in his tormented self-portrait from 1889. The painting is now on display at Musée d'Orsay in Paris, France.

Two cutted sunflowers, August 1887

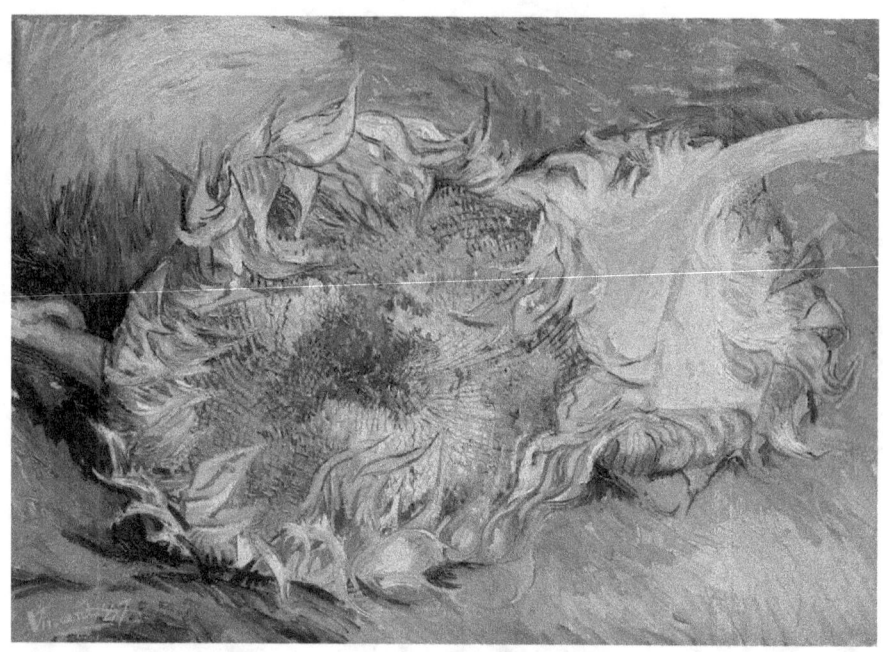

Painted during the late summer of 1887 somewhere in and around Paris, probably high upon the white hill of Montmartre, *Two cutted sunflowers* is a symbolic whirlwind of the cycle of life—even the most beautiful, vibrant things in the physical world must die. This sober portrait exemplifies this mantra. Or they are just two dried out sunflower heads with most of the black seeds plucked out by the thrush, goldfinch, and yellow canaries. Both options can be true at the very same time. And they are.

F. Scott Fitzgerald was once famously quoted as saying:

"The test of a first-rate intelligence is the ability to hold two opposing ideas in mind at the same time and still retain the ability to function."

That is the very epitome of the portrait *Two cutted sunflowers*. It currently resides in the Metropolitan Museum of Art in Manhattan, New York City.

Les Vessenots à Auvers, 1890

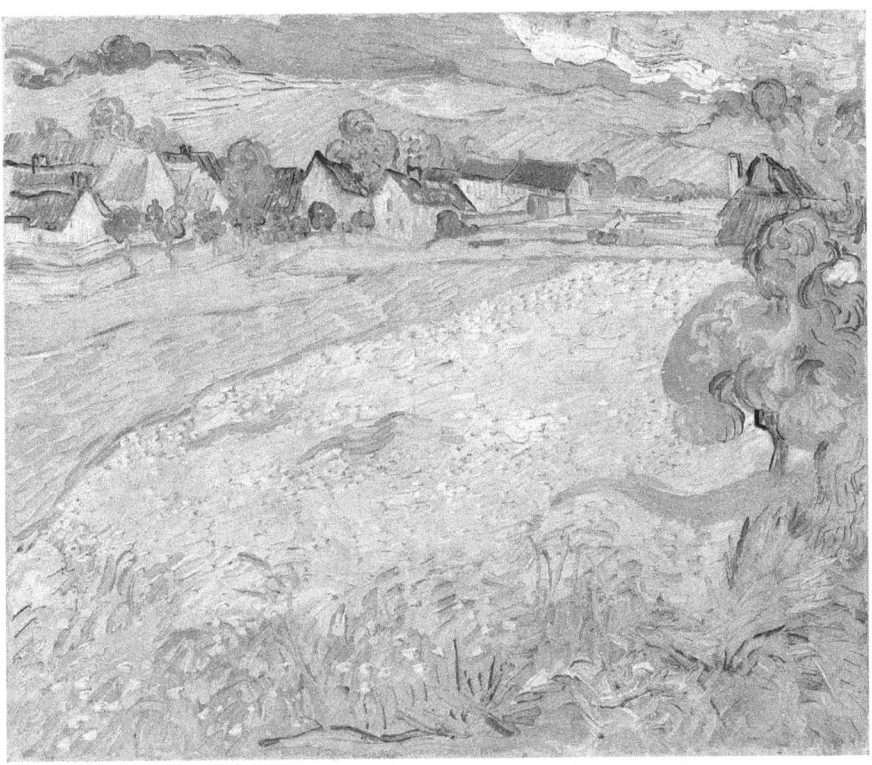

Few van Gogh paintings are so vivid and alive as *Les Vessenots à Auvers*, 1890 that he painted at Auvers-sur-Oise on the outskirts of Paris less than six weeks before the his death. In the last days of his life van Gogh painted over 70 landscapes and paintings, many that harked back to his days in the north of France, many he painted from memory. He was frantic, a man on a mission, desperate to be recognized as an artist thus the frantic pace of the dozens of paintings he created over the waning days of his life. This painting is currently on display at the Thyssen-Bornemisza Museum in Madrid, Spain.

The Church at Auvers, 1890

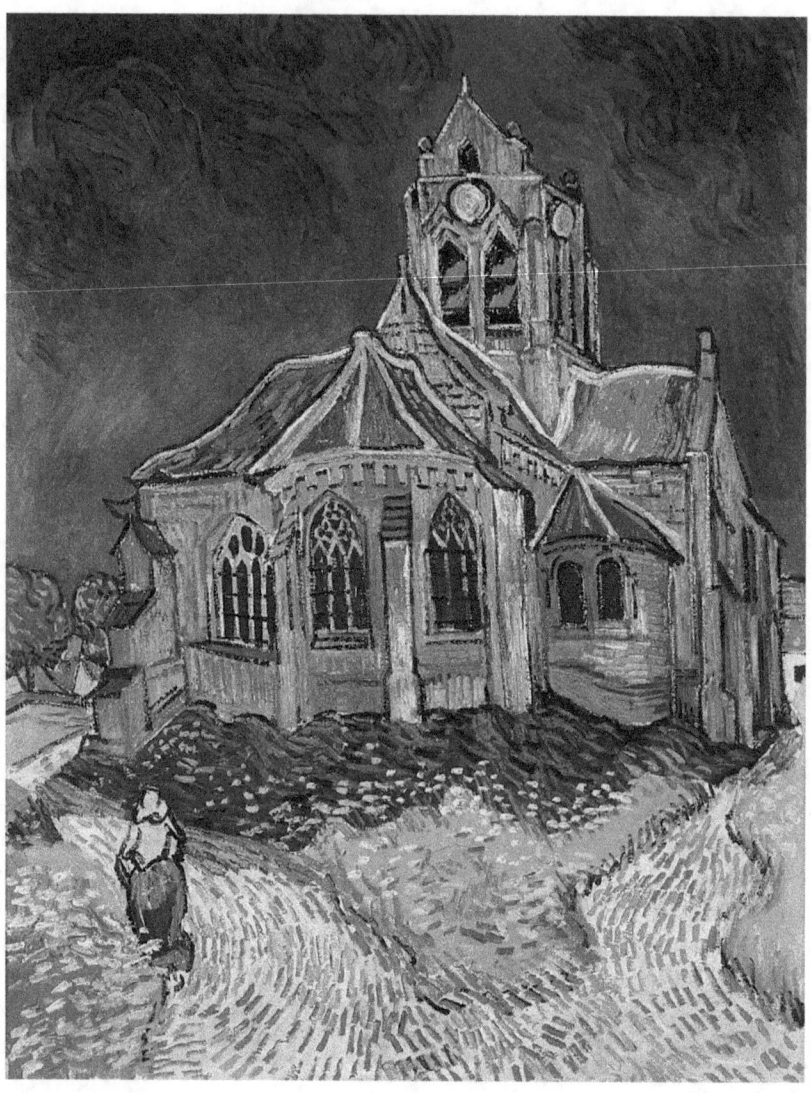

In 1890 van Gogh painted one of his many masterpieces, *The Church at Auvers*. It is a landscape of an actual cathedral, the Place de l'Eglise, that resides in Auvers-sur-Oise on the outskirts of Paris. The background is full of nothing but blue sky amid a spiritual setting with two roads, the wide and narrow, to chose from. In a letter that he wrote to his sister, Wilhelmina, June 5th, 1890 a couple of weeks before his death, he offered the following about his particular landscape: "*An effect in which the building appears to be violet-hued against a sky of simple deep blue color, pure cobalt; the stained-glass windows appear as ultramarine blotches, the roof is violet and partly orange.*

In the foreground some green plants in bloom, and sand with the pink flow of sunshine in it. And once again it is nearly the same thing as the studies I did in Nuenen of the old tower and the cemetery, only it is probably that now the color is more expressive, more sumptuous." The Church at Auvers is on display at the Musée d'Orsay in Paris, France

The Starry Night, June 1889

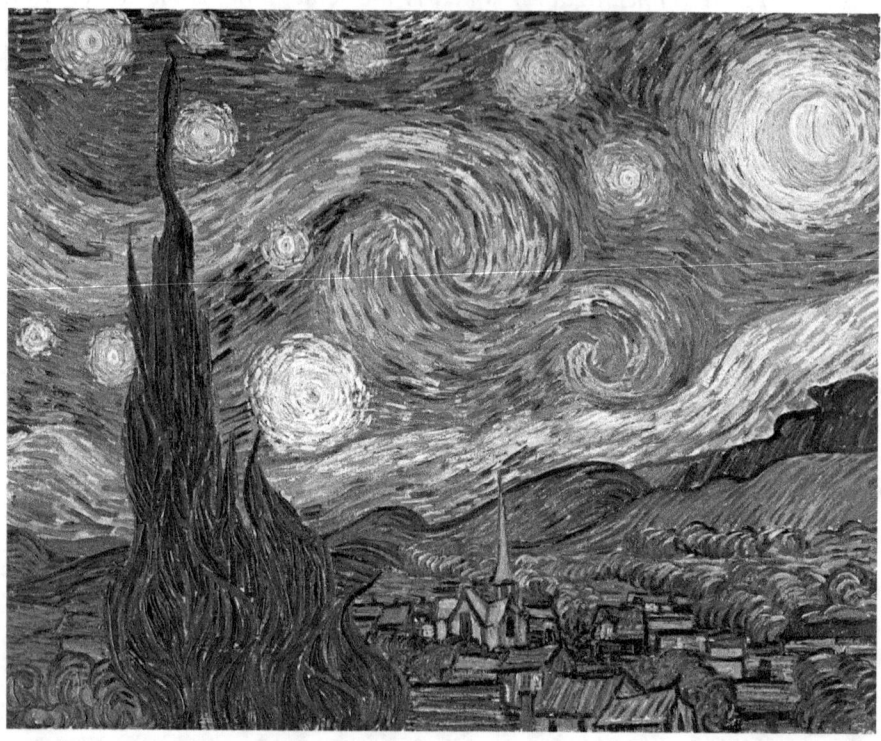

The Starry Night painted June 1889 again depicts the view from the east-facing window of his bedroom in the asylum where van Gogh was living institutionalize at Saint-Rémy in Provence, France.

It is the blue of dusk that exists immediately before sunrise, the westerlies blowing across the early morning French sky, swirling the air and clouds, a big yellow crescent moon glows as it slowly sinks toward the mountains below yet just like a fantastic future he dreamed of creating the addition of the idyllic village, church with steeple, and candlelit thatch cottages are completely imaginary. There exists no idyllic village outside the window where van Gogh kept so many hours while his demons visited him both day and night at will. Isn't it ironic that maybe one of the most famous paintings of all times depicts something completely made up in the man of someone slowly going mad. *The Starry Night* now sleeps at peace amid the glossy white hallways and walls at the Museum of Modern Art, New York, New York.

Ward in the Hospital in Arles, 1889

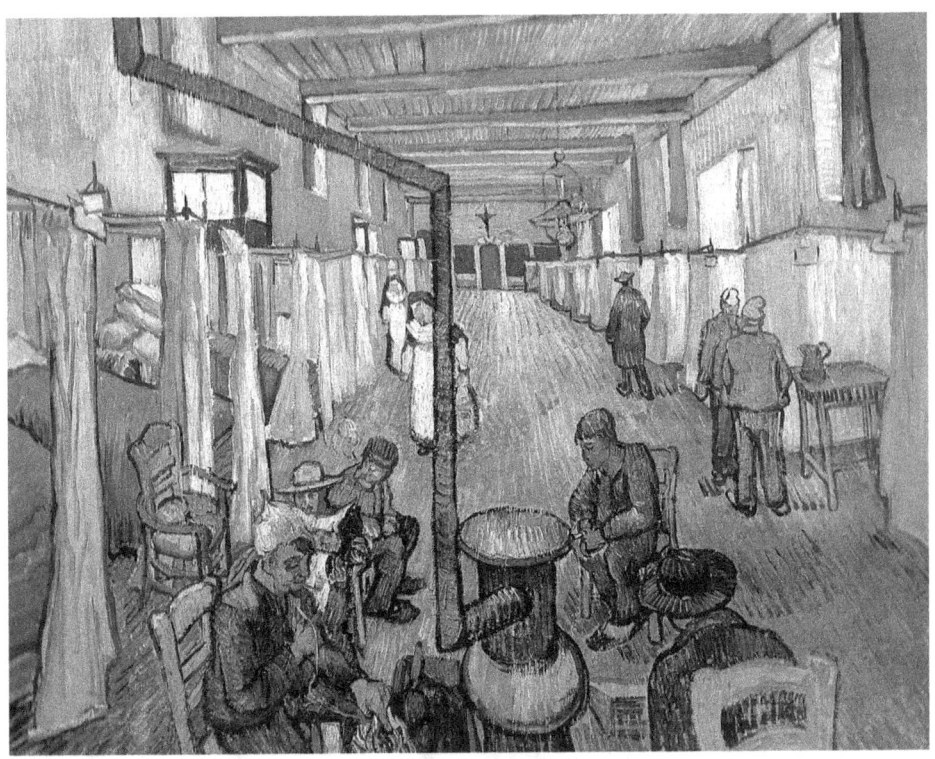

Ward in the Hospital in Arles, 1889, is a delicate depiction of life inside the asylum with other patients with what looks like van Gogh reading a newspaper with his trademark straw hat at the left of the woodstove with the gold chair pulled out from the nearby hospital ward bed. *Ward in the Hospital in Arles* resides in the Oskar Reinhart Collection "Am Römerholz," in Winterthur, Switzerland.

Self-portrait with Bandaged Ear and Pipe, 1889

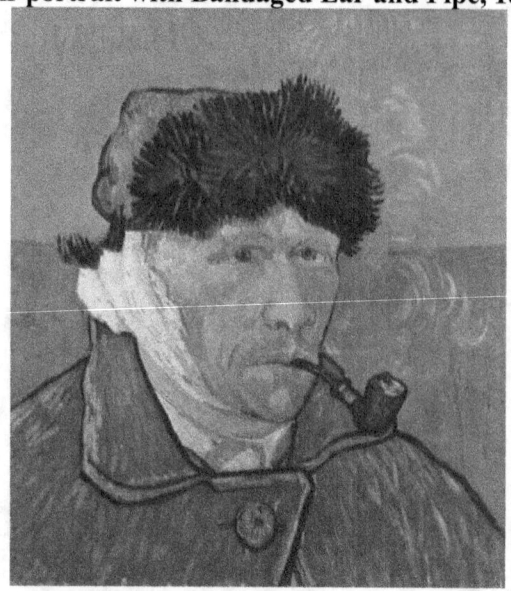

Self-portrait with Bandaged Ear, 1889

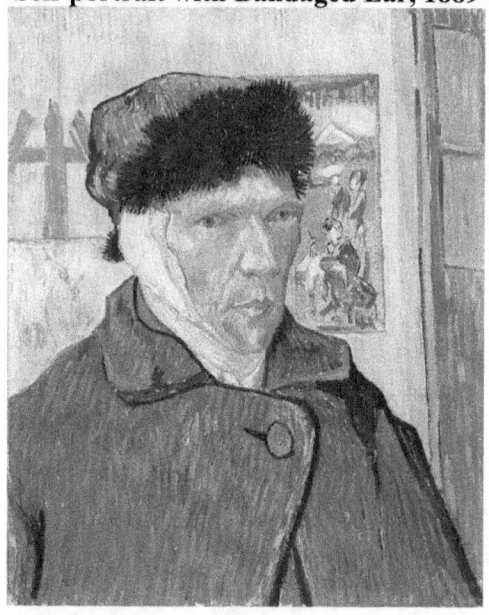

What do most artists, writers, and poets do when they create a piece and when finished they are completely revolted with what they have created? They create another as van Gogh obviously did with the two self-portraits he painted after his ear was cut off.

The Courtyard of the Hospital at Arles, 1889

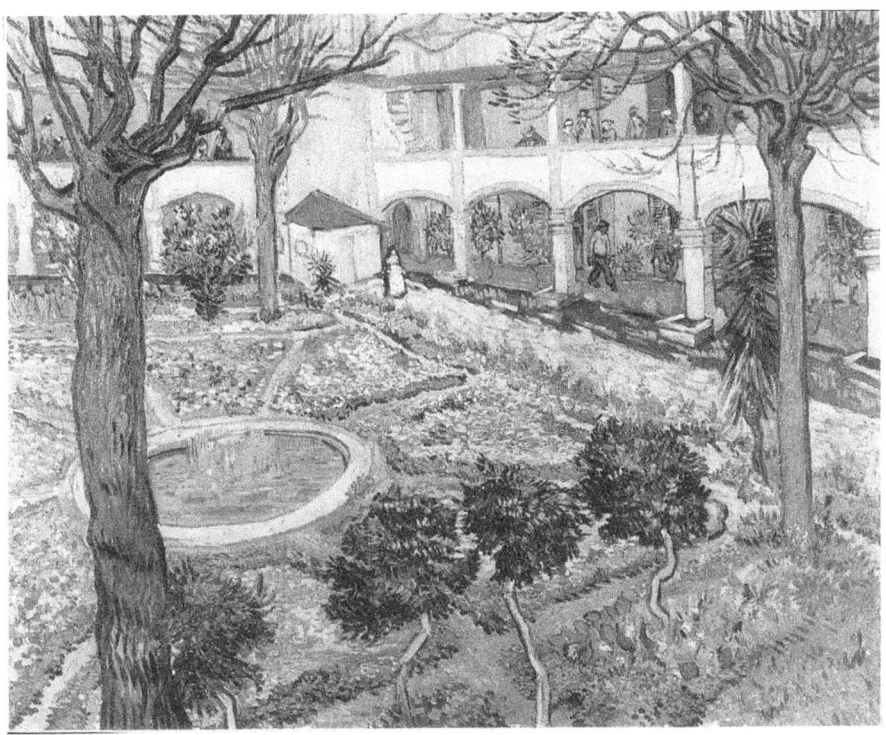

The Courtyard of the Hospital at Arles, 1889 where Vincent sat and thought and gazed for days and weeks on end. He was very self-aware of his unstable faculties and often blamed himself for much of it being self-inflected, which breaks the heart. The courtyard painting now resides at the Oskar Reinhart Collection "Am Römerholz," in Winterthur, Switzerland.

Almond Blossom, 1890

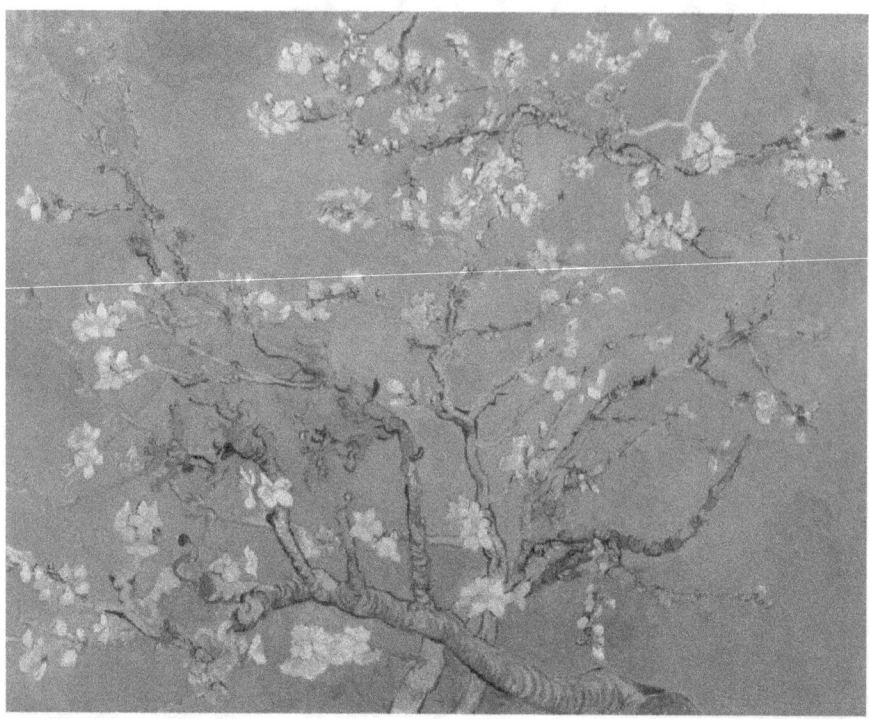

Almond Blossoms with its almond tree branches and whitish-pink hued blossoms set against a pale blue sky background harks back to the fabulous Japanese woodblock prints that became one of the many building blocks and components of van Gogh's later works.

Like every great master such as a Bob Dylan, Elaine Sturtevant, F. Scott Fitzgerald, Andy Warhol, Banksy, the Beatles, or Grand Master Flash and the Furious Five, Vincent van Gogh took a little nugget of memory from here, a little nugget of brushstroke and light from there to create something altogether new and different. No Japanese woodblock influenced work of art could be so heavily predisposed to the Japanese form and yet so Vincent van Gogh as ones that came into being off the deft hand of van Gogh. Great art is like different ingredients inside the cupboard of the chef's kitchen. Alone they are simply components in glass bottles, but mixed together they become something to light the neurons and the synapsis of the brain on fire! *Almond Blossoms* currently is on display at the Van Gogh Museum in Amsterdam, the Netherlands.

Deux Paysannes, 1890

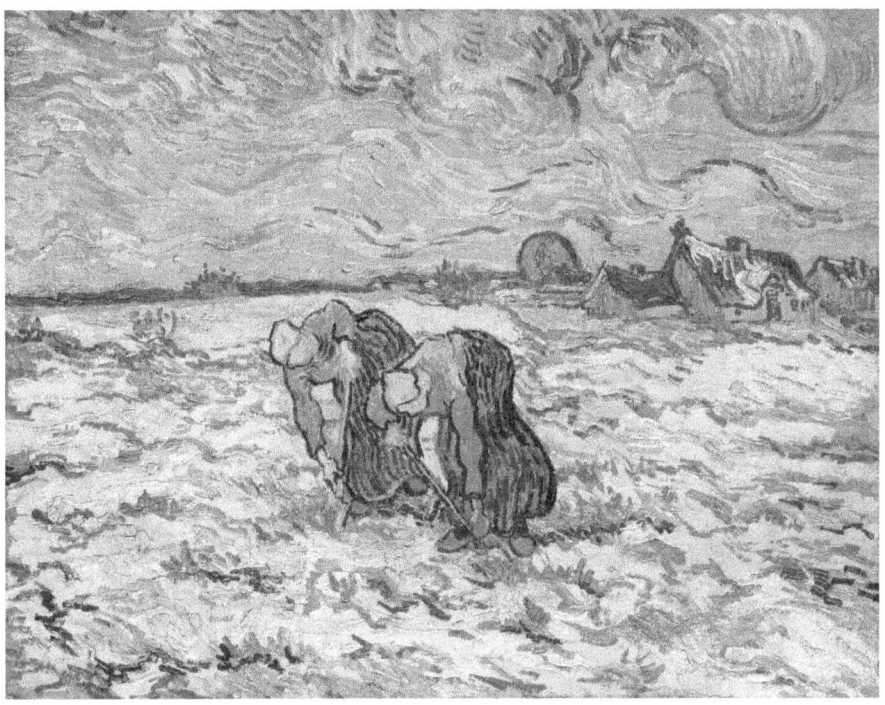

Two Peasant Women in the field blends the old subject matter of 1880 and 1881 with the peasant models of van Gogh's earlier work with the rich movement and tones of his later paintings. The landscape is from the Emil Bührle Collection, and is on long term loan to the Kunsthaus Museum in Zürich, Switzerland.

Landscape from Saint-Rémy, 1889

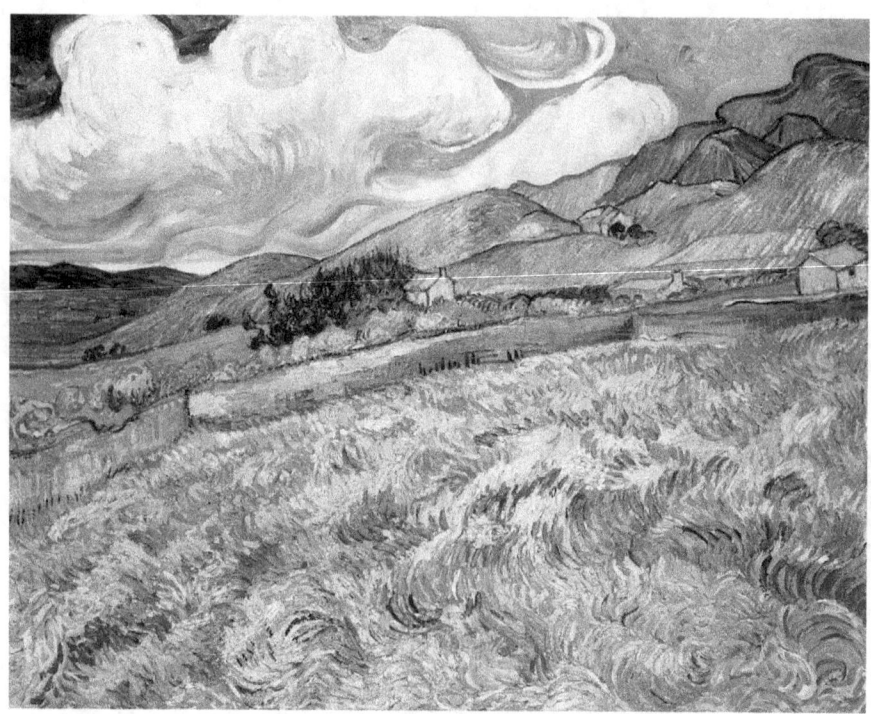

Landscape from Saint-Rémy was painted in the early summer of 1889, when Van Gogh remained in the mental hospital of Saint-Paul-de-Mausole in the south of France. The painting depicts the serpentine clouds, wavering nearby fields of wheat and timothy and alfalfa plus the rocky steep incline of Chaîne des Alpilles mountain range of Provence that sits approximately twelve miles south of Avignon. On display in the Ny Carlsberg Glyptotek Art Museum located in Copenhagen, Denmark.

The Red Vineyard, 1888

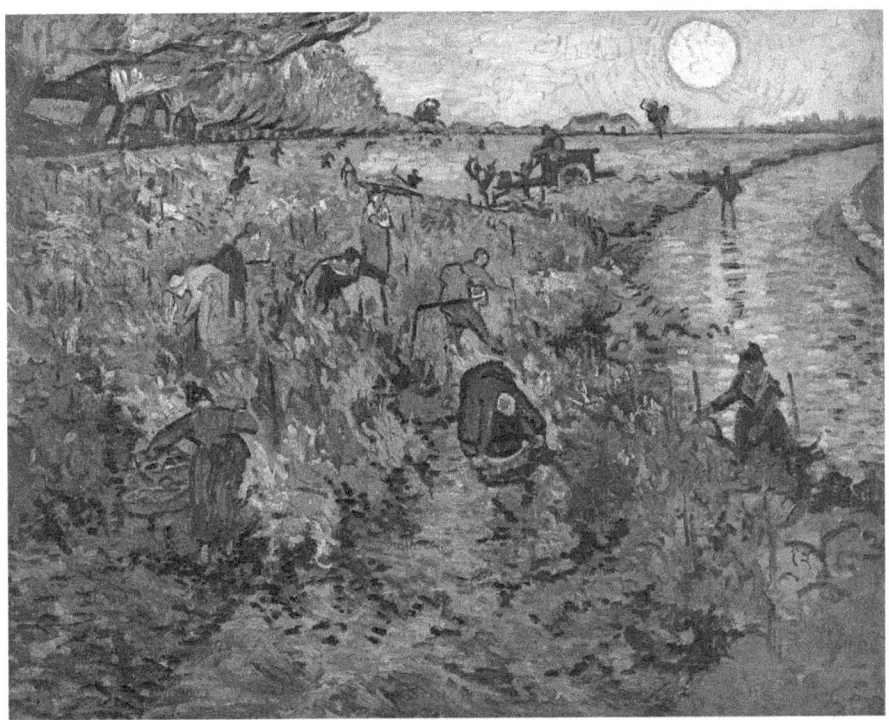

The Red Vineyard at Arles full of its tireless vineyard workers and autumnal reds and yellows is renowned for being the only work of Vincent van Gogh that sold during his lifetime. It was purchased for a mere 400 francs by Anna Boch, the only female member of *Les XX*, the group of twenty painters, designers and sculptors from Belgium, that was formed in 1883 by the Brussels lawyer, publisher, and entrepreneur Octave Maus. Anna was also the older sister of Eugène Boch, the famous Belgian artist and painter.

The Red Vineyard is also quite renowned for being painted by memory the day after van Gogh had visited the vineyard. The work lives and breathes the French autumn harvest. It makes the spine tingle like the bell tones of piano keys when you are alone in the dark listening to a haunting piano concerto with someone you have just fallen in love with. Yeah. A little bit like that!

The Bedroom, No. 1, 1889

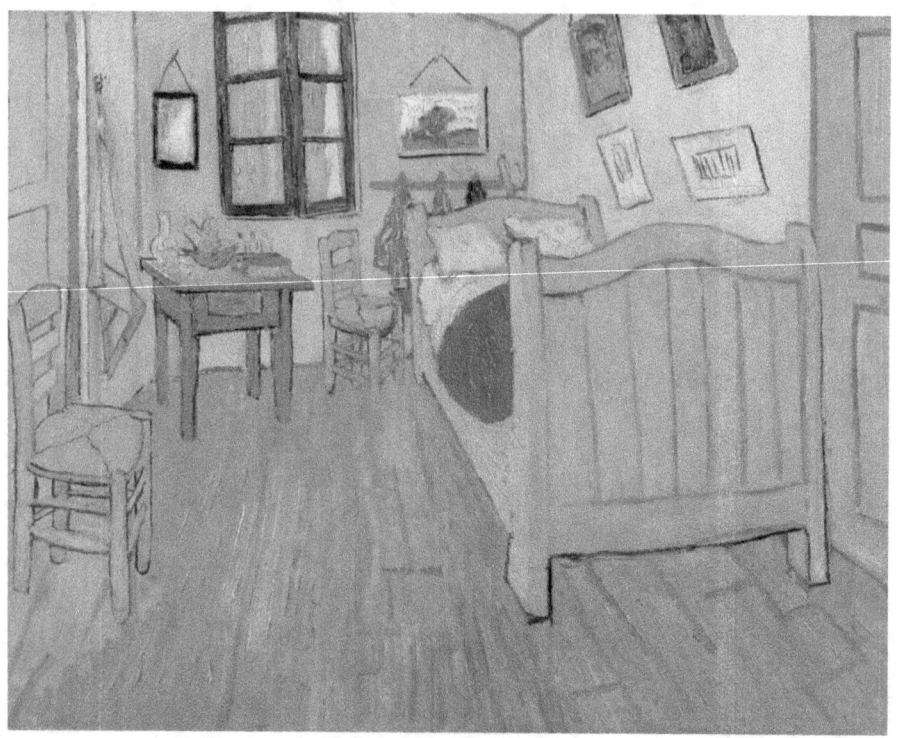

In October 1888, Vincent van Gogh moved into his beloved "Yellow House" at Arles, France, where soon his friend and fellow painter Paul Gauguin moved a week later. Van Gogh prepared his bedroom in a spartan manner with simple wood furniture of the time, two chairs, a small writing desk, a bed, a place to hang the straw hat that he wore while taking walks and painting his landscapes outside in Arles. He also filled the blue interior walls of his bedroom with his own landscapes and portrait paintings. Soon after he actually painted a literal still life of his lovely bedroom at the Yellow House as seen above.

So pleased was van Gogh by this bedroom portrait that he painted two more almost identical versions of the same painting. While at first glance they look identical, if one looks closely enough they will find that the subject matter of the portraits that hung on the walls of each version are completely different. So are the hues of some bedroom items such as the mirror, ephemera on the desk, and the cushion on the chair

In his original version of The Bedroom there are portraits of two men that hang above the righthand side of his bed. A portrait painting of Eugène Boch and The Lover (Portrait of Lieutenant Milliet), which he painted only one month earlier as a stand-alone portrait. In the second and third versions of The Bedroom those same two portraits of the two men are replaced with a self-portrait of van Gogh and the portrait of an unknown woman.

The Yellow House, (The Street) 1888

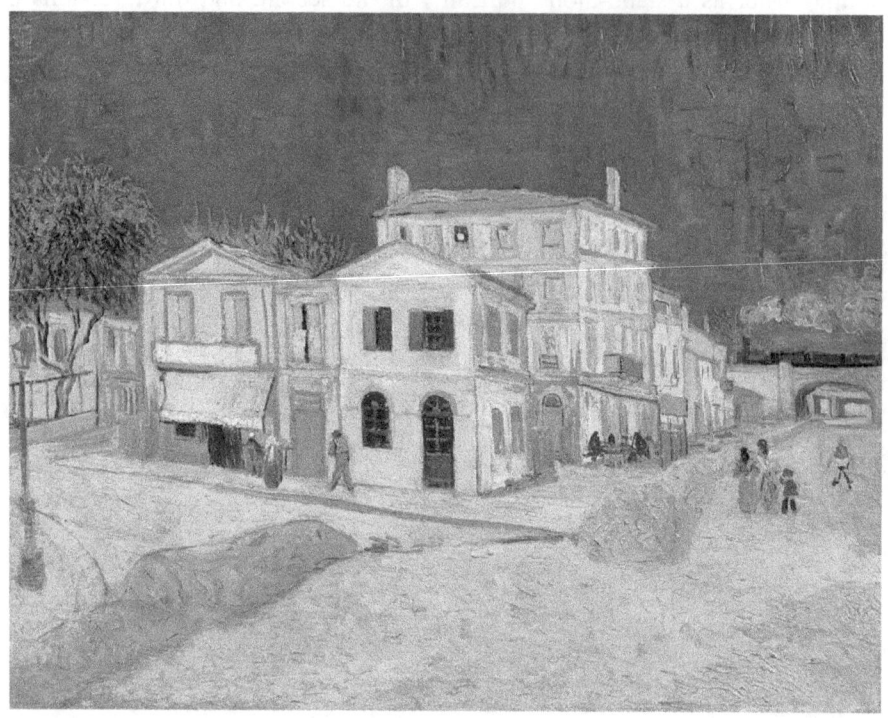

Did you not always picture *The Yellow House* set amid the countryside with flowering magnolia and olive trees and a cobblestone garden path that lead up to where the cottage sat half in sunlight, half in shadow? I know I did. But somewhere in Mrs. Thompson's art class, circa 1985, at Scituate High School in the northwest hill of Rhode Island I must have fallen asleep or was too busy writing notes to girls or day-dreaming about being the next Earnest Hemingway, because I slept right through the memo (that'd be an email or viral tweet nowadays). The yellow house of Vincent van Gogh was actually a stately two-story provincial building along a street corner at 2 Place Lamartine in the heart of downtown Arles.

In 1888 Vincent rented out four rooms there with the financial help of his brother, Theo. He then set up his bedroom as shown in the previous painting, where he soon began to prepare for his close friend Paul Gauguin to join him, so they could create an art commune and artist's house that could represent the whole South of France. But that did not happen. Not even close. Nonetheless, Vincent's first impression of the green shuttered yellow house was a hopeful and positive one. He often ate late dinners at the café next door; the one with the bright pink awning. He could watch the handsomely dressed citizens of Arles stroll past down the street outside his 2nd story window as they took their nightly scrolls, arm in arm, every night. And his close friend, the local postman Joseph Roulin, lived only blocks away down passed the railway bridge seen in the painting above that Vincent would soon dare himself to paint in full luster. The yellow house in Arles is gone now, but you can visit its memory in this painting at the Van Gogh Museum in Amsterdam in the Netherlands.

The portrait of *Eugène Boch*, 1888.

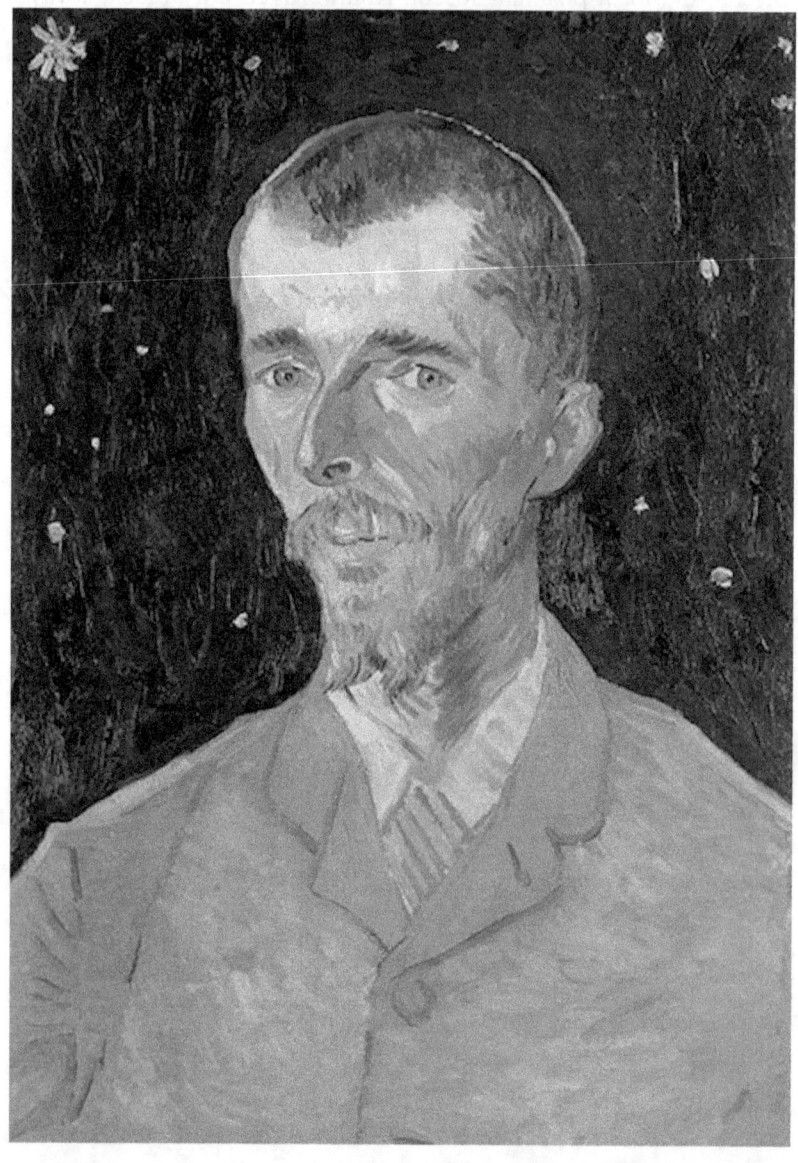

Portrait of Eugène Boch, 1888 with blue background and flower petals. Currently resides in the Musée d'Orsay in Paris, France.

The Lover (Portrait of Lieutenant Milliet). Late September-early October, 1888

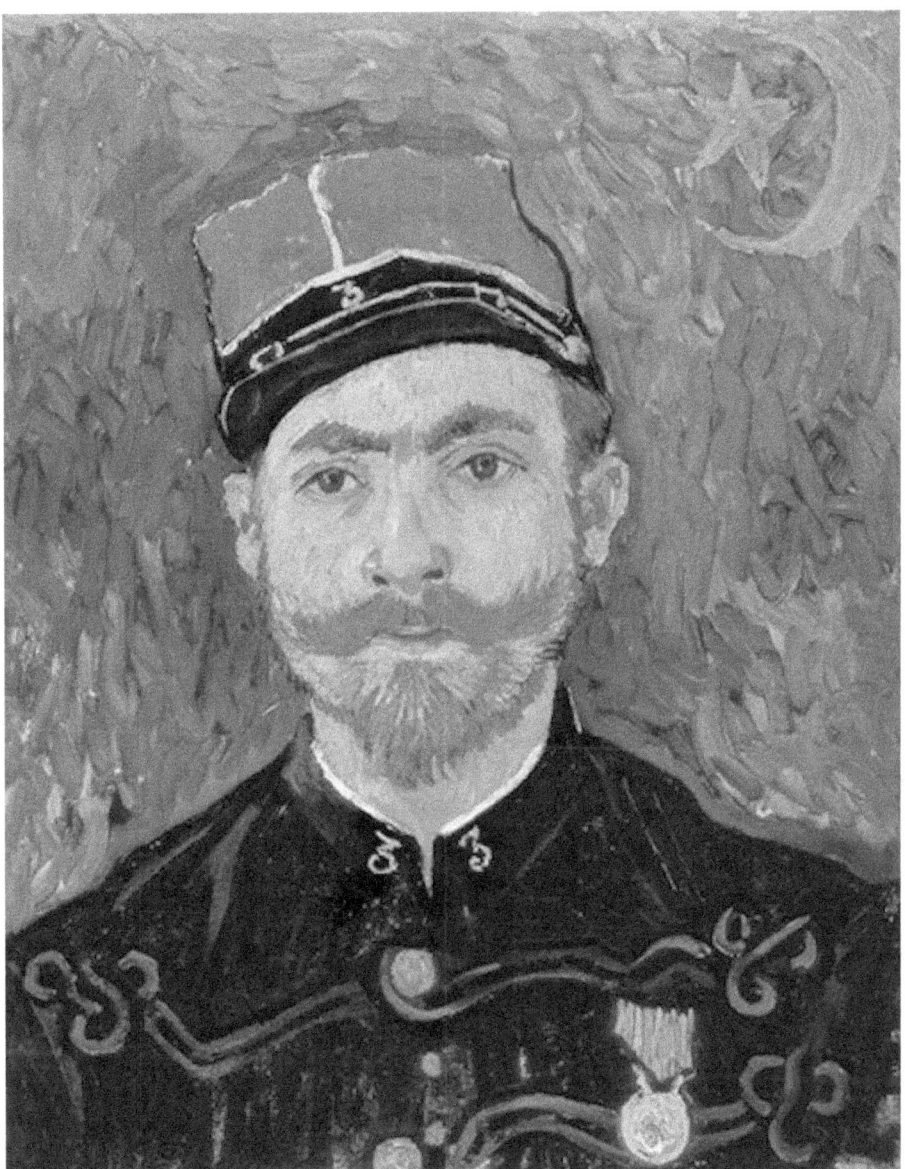

In stark contrast to the portrait of the artist Eugène Boch is the embodiment of masculinity and heroism that is depicted in the above portrait that van Gogh entitled *The Lover*. Its subject, Lieutenant Paul-Eugène Milliet, was a French Lieutenant in the Zouaves brigades that served at the bequest of the French Empire in North Africa. With his imperial moustache and goatee, steely brown eyes, red képi, navy blue frock coat with copper buttons, and silver metal all set against an emerald-aquamarine background the portrait is meant to represent the ideal of masculinity (during the late 19th Century anyway).

The Bedroom, No. 2, 1889

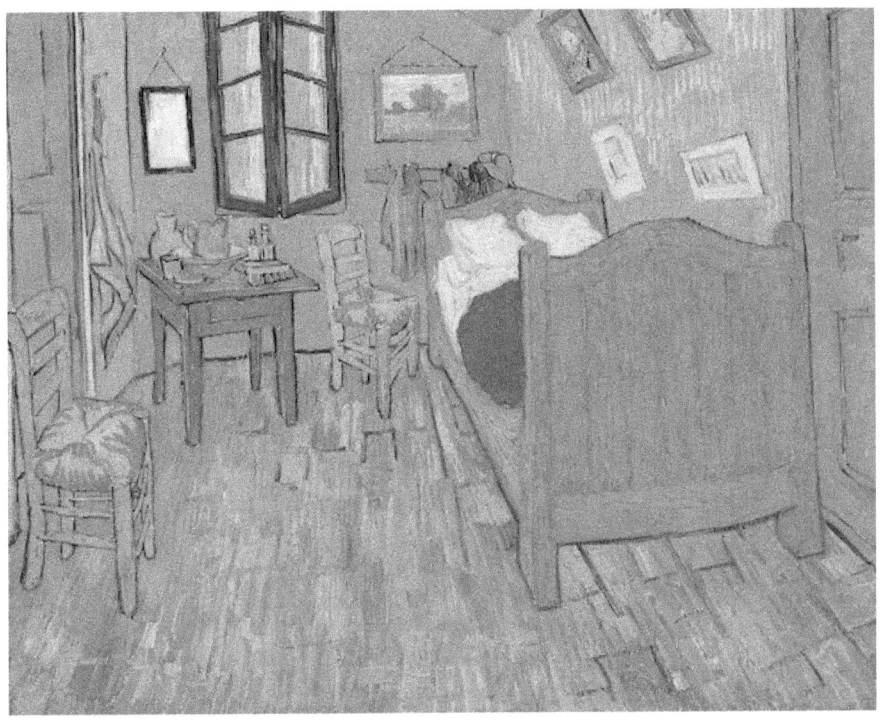

Note the portrait of van Gogh and a portrait of a woman with reddish-blonde hair that replace the two portraits of the two men in portrait No. 1.

The Bedroom, No. 2, 1889

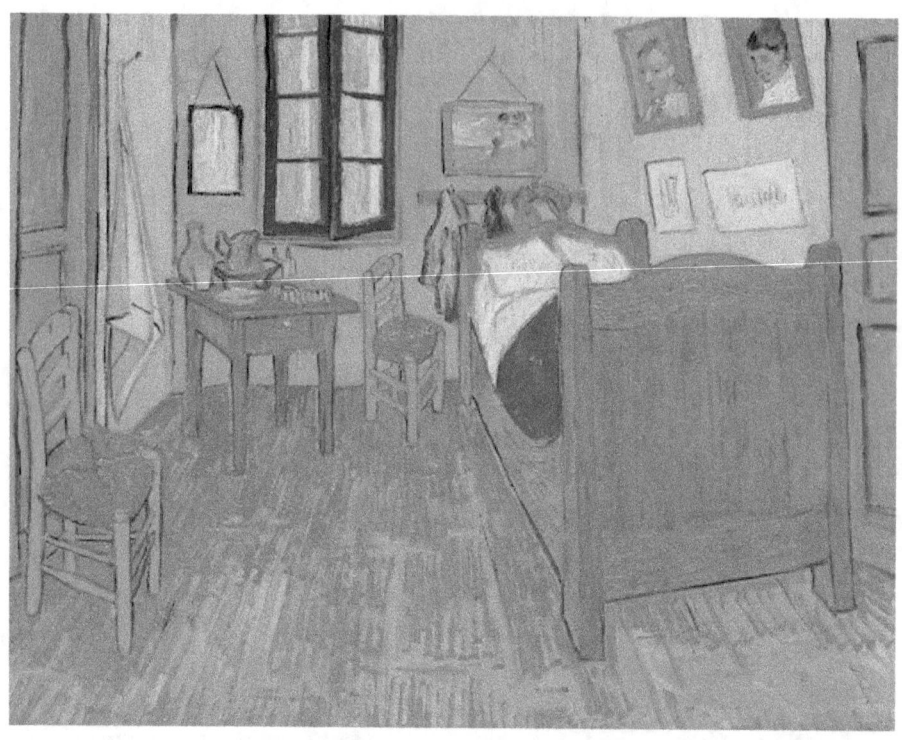

Note again note a more fleshed out portrait of van Gogh and the portrait of a brunette woman with a pinkish blouse that replace the two portraits of the same that hang on the wall in version No. 2. Also, the landscape behind the bed is quite different than versions 1 and 2 with a pinkish sky and without a bellowing wind-blown cypress.

The Bedroom, No. 1, 2, and 3 in comparison

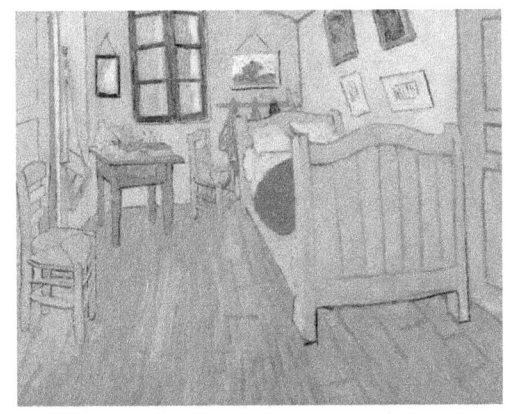

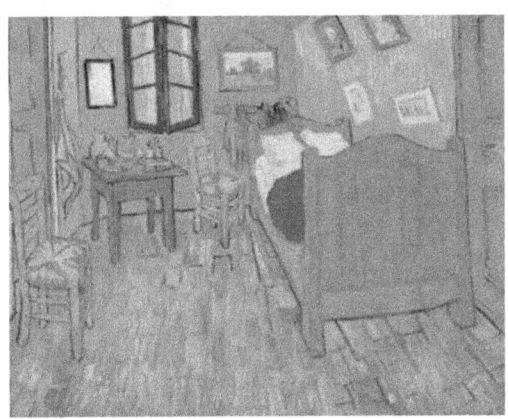

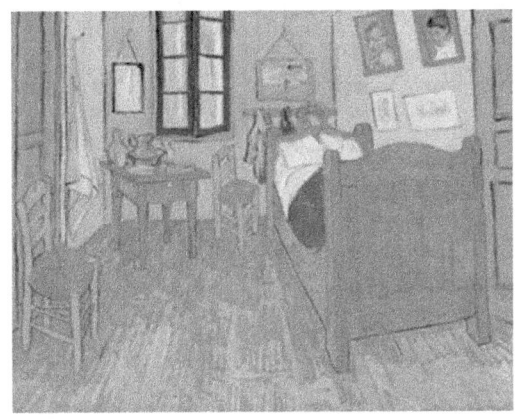

Stairway at Auvers, 1890

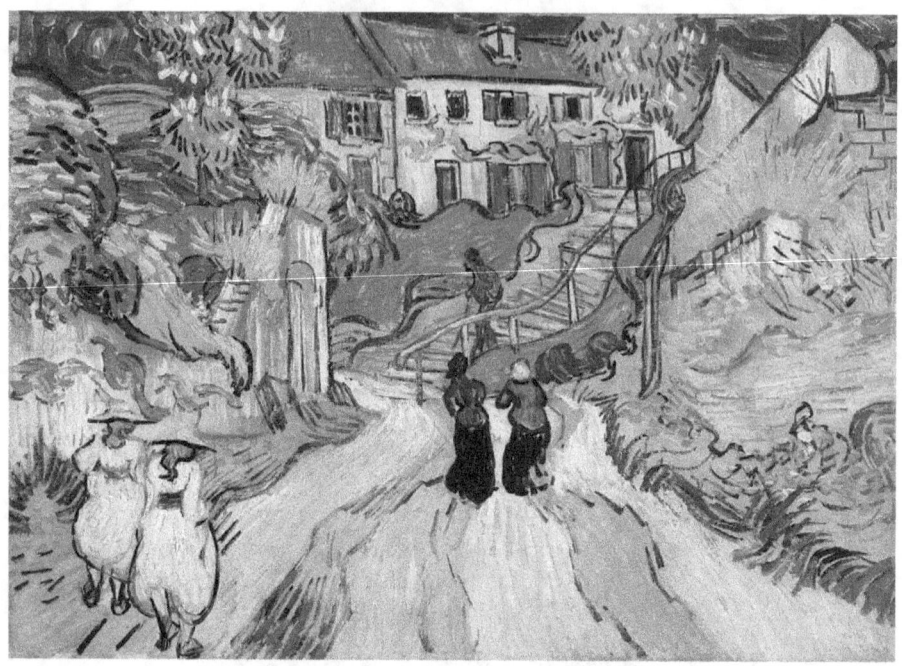

A beautiful line of cottages and houses dot Auvers-sur-Oise, Île-de-France that is centered by a golden coiling staircase that leads the men and women that stroll amid the well-worn pathway of the painting on up into the city center itself. Stairway at Auvers now rides at the Saint Louis Art Museum in St. Louis, Missouri.

Vase with Poppies, 1886

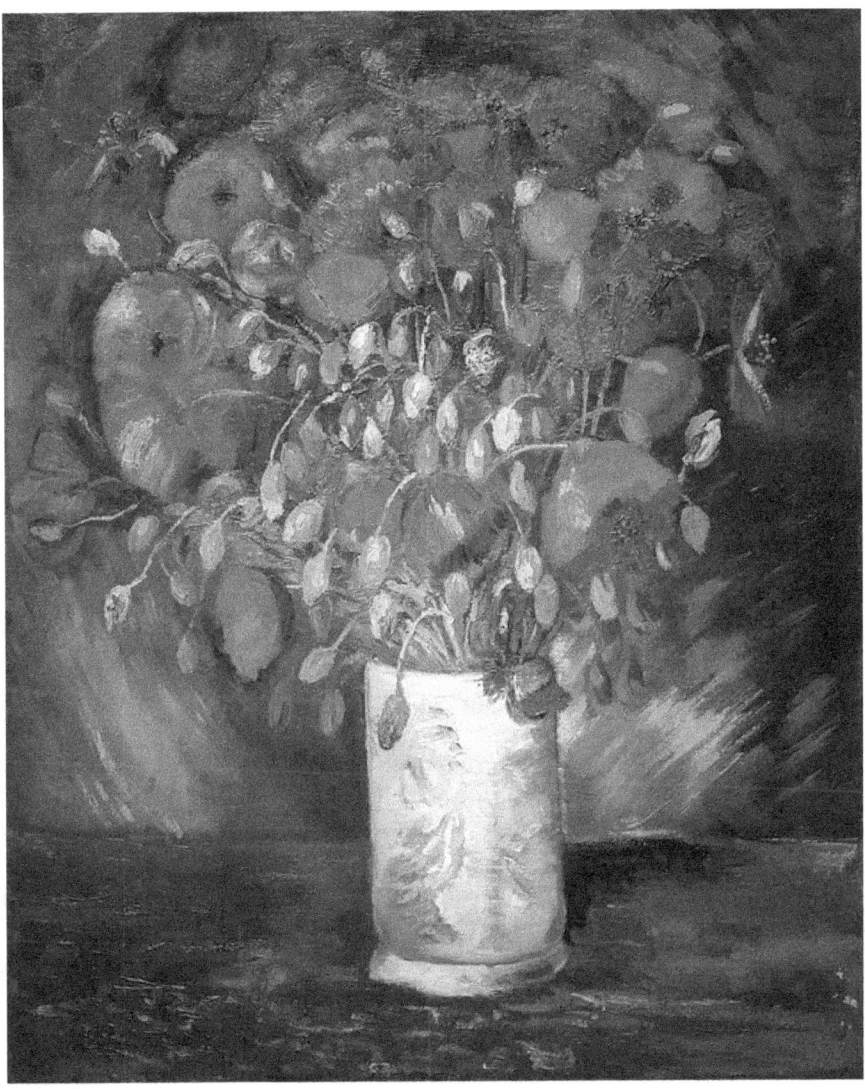

The 1886 still life *Vase with Poppies* would be a masterpiece if it had been painted by any other artists. Hints that it is a van Gogh abound within the brushstrokes of silver, green, and blue background, the broken brushstrokes that demarcate the top of the mahogany table, and the unique way the artist forms his flowers that a hallmark of many of his others portraits and landscapes that feature flower blossoms. It is currently on display at the Wadsworth Atheneum in Hartford, Connecticut.

The Siesta (La méridienne), 1889-90

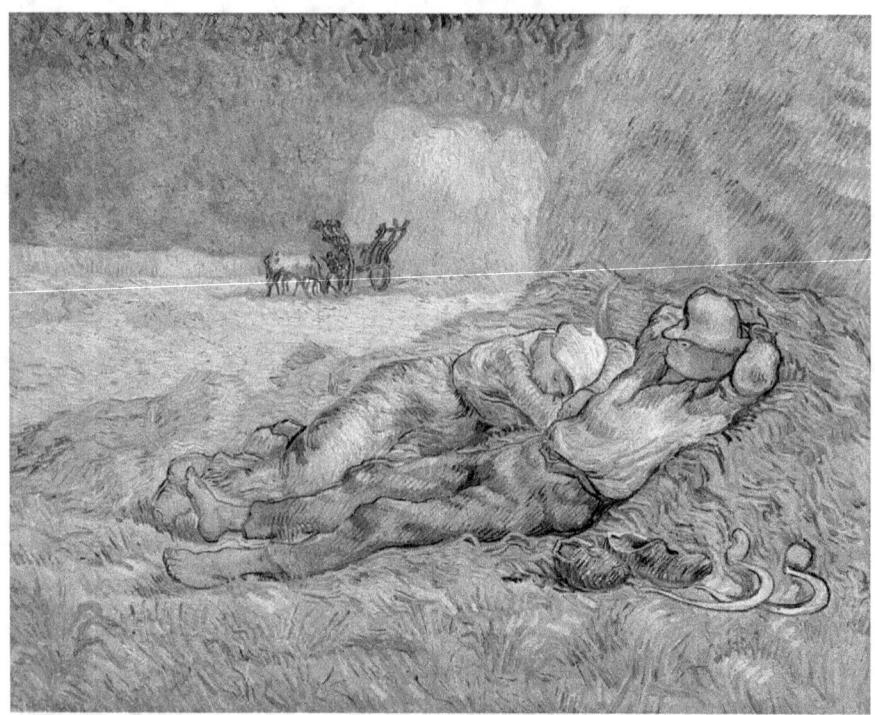

The Siesta (La méridienne) is another of the many oil on canvas works that van Gogh painted between December 1889 and January 1890 while at the mental asylum at Saint-Rémy-de-Provence. A couple with sickles rest in earlier afternoon against the tall haystacks of Provence after working all morning before the sun became too hot. It is a gentle, serene, and perfectly peaceful portrait when one looks out the framed in window of an asylum. Considered one of van Gogh's most superior works it now resides at the Musée d'Orsay in Paris, France.

The Langlois Bridge at Arles with Women Washing, 1888

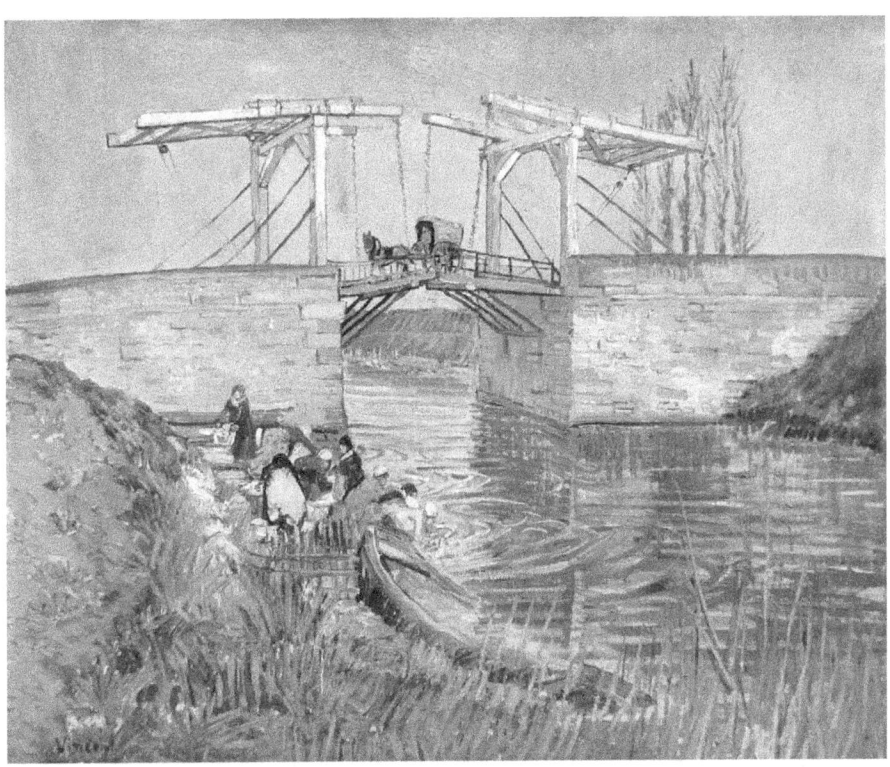

Of course, *The Langlois Bridge at Arles with Women Washing*, circa 1888, is considered one of van Gogh's most gorgeous and iconic works, because it is. The fieldstone work of his Provence countryside bridge is flawless and perfectly cut like a stonemason was in his head and upon the fingertips of his hand. The women have adorned themselves in smocks of different colors with caps to cover their heads from the morning sun. The river blue comes alive with ripples from the riverside labor being conducted while a mustard yellow horse cart strolls across the bridge with both its horse and driver peaking over the side of the bridge at the myriad of women down below just like they would have done in real life. Even the cattails along the side of the riverbank and the wash of brown, multi-varied greens of grass and the wildlife plant life have a tale to tell The sky is awash in a paler blue than the river below while its stillness is almost startling. Just a beautiful landscape that one can appreciate over and over until the end of eternity. The piece now resides at the Kröller-Müller Museum in Otterlo, the Netherlands.

Café Terrace at Night, 1888

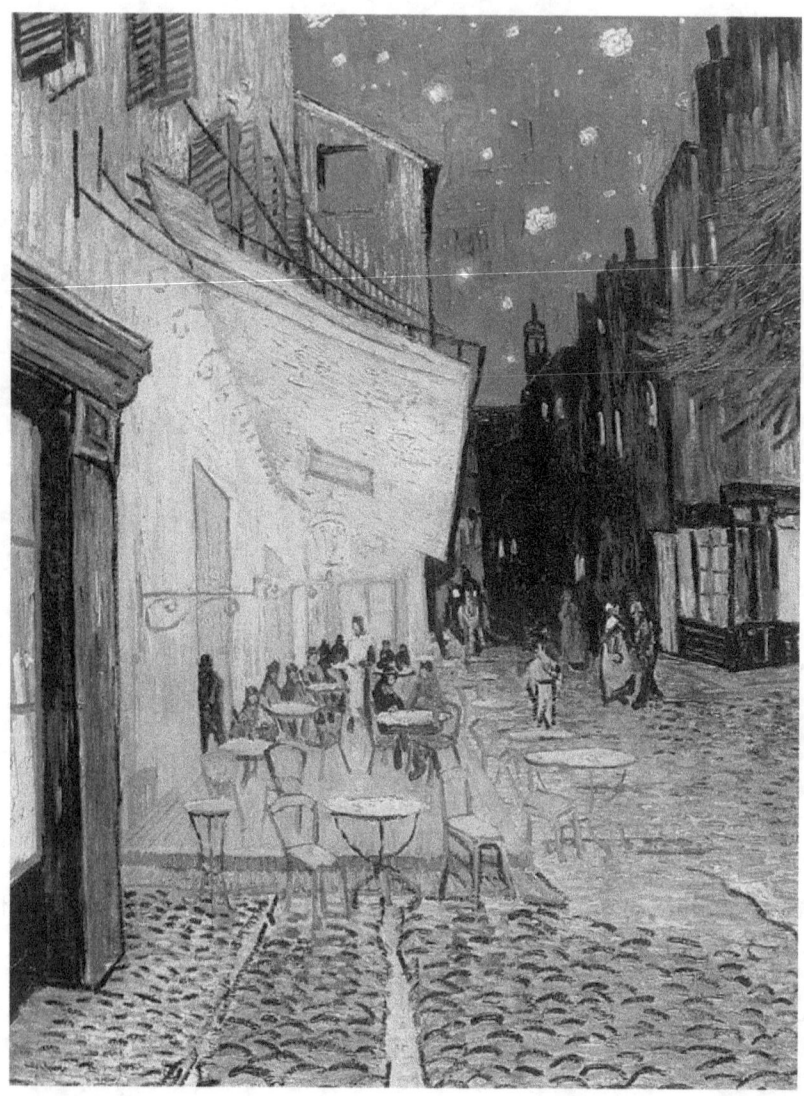

Twelve patrons gather together after sunset with a standing central figure, that of a long-haired young man who stands and wears a robe amidst the other patrons who are seated, while an ominous figure lurks in his own shadow just off the café with the same flower petals one sees in the portrait of Eugène Boch from the same year that dot the sky like heavenly stars. Is this da Vinci's *Last Supper* as some would suggest, one last sermon the younger van Gogh would have preached on his boyhood mission or just imaginative thought? Art is to be interpreted by the beholder of its beauty. You be the judge. *Café Terrace at Night* now resides both literally and spiritually (or not) in the Kröller-Müller Museum in Otterlo, Netherlands.

Wheatfield with a reaper, 1889

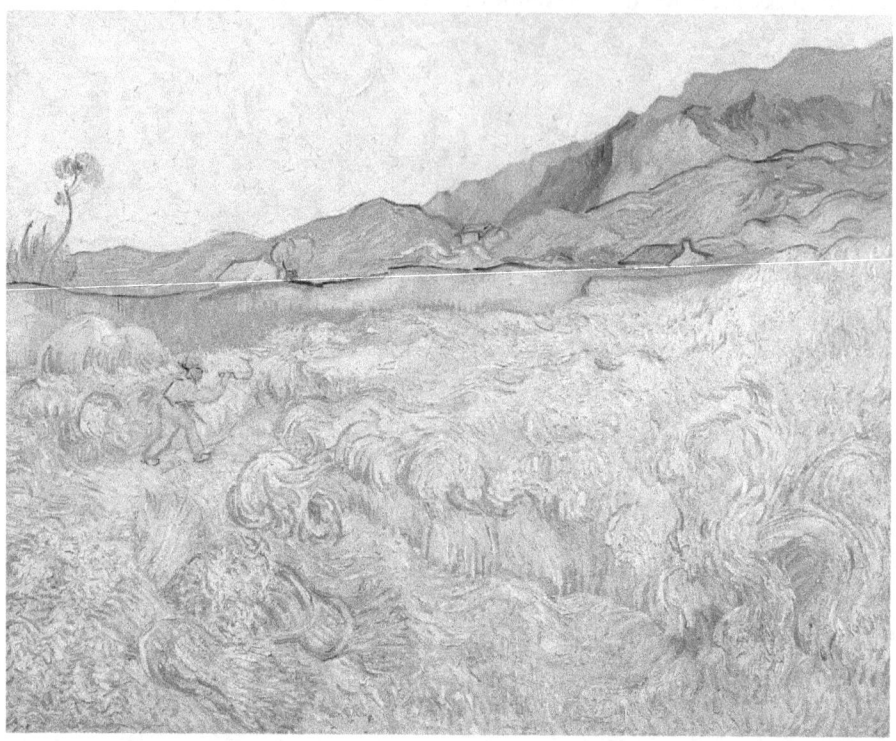

The eternal cycle of nature is featured in the work of Vincent van Gogh over and over again. To him nature is alive with the movement of the skies, the wind that blows across the fields causing the wheat to circle, shrug, and undulate. The ever changing colors of the seasons. Crops growing, harvested, fields furrow, asleep during winter, and then come spring alive again. His fields of gold are alive just as though you are standing right there 150 years ago. Not too shabby for a work of art that cannot move or act as some sort of virtual reality. Currently resides at the Van Gogh Museum, Amsterdam, The Netherlands.

Poppy Field, 1890

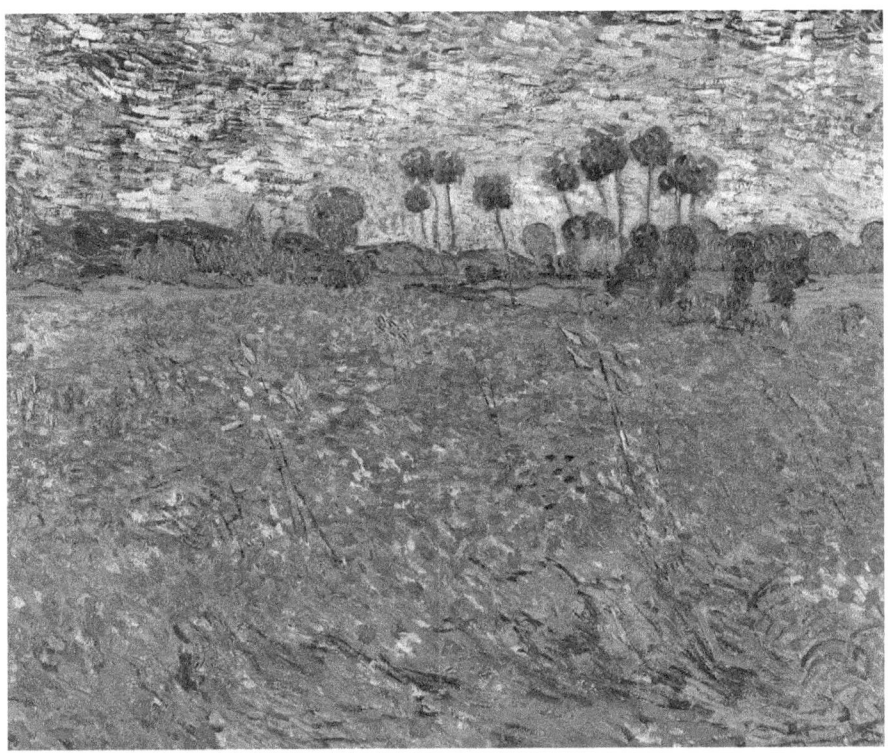

You can see the tip of van Gogh's healthy ego that was in there somewhere in 1890's *Poppy Field*. This is who I can be (if you just let me.) This is who I am. These are the red blood cells coursing through my veins, my sinew is full of blue and white lines of rapids and sky, here is the wind of my lungs that blows across the red poppies of Auvers, here are some beautiful trees. Please remember. Remember me, please. And try not to. I'll make it so you can never forget.

Van Gogh painted seven paintings during his lifetime that feature poppies. The flower spoke to him and he used it to speak to us too. This landscape was painted about one month before his death. The painting now resides amid the Kunstmuseum Den Haag, Cultural Heritage Agency of the Netherlands Art Collection in The Hague in the Netherlands.

Field with Poppies, 1889

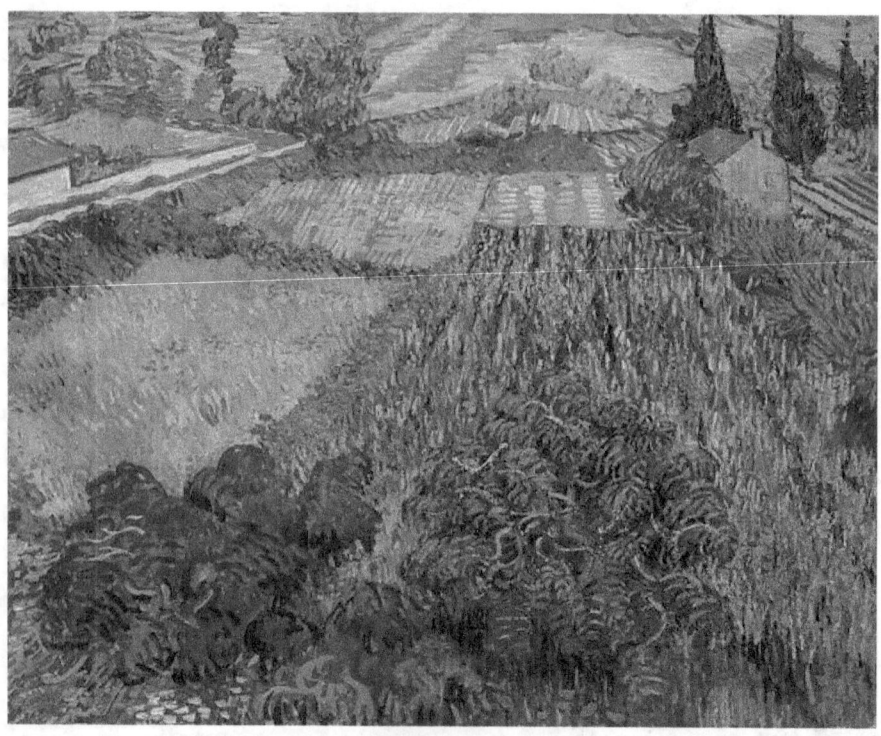

A lesser known work is *Field with Poppies* whose emerald greens pop in various shades in contrast to van Gogh's subtle poppy red. Tartans of other fields in various life stages fill in the rest of the landscape along with cypress and beautiful cedar. Currently on loan to the Metropolitan Museum of Art, Manhattan, New York City

Vineyards at Auvers, 1890

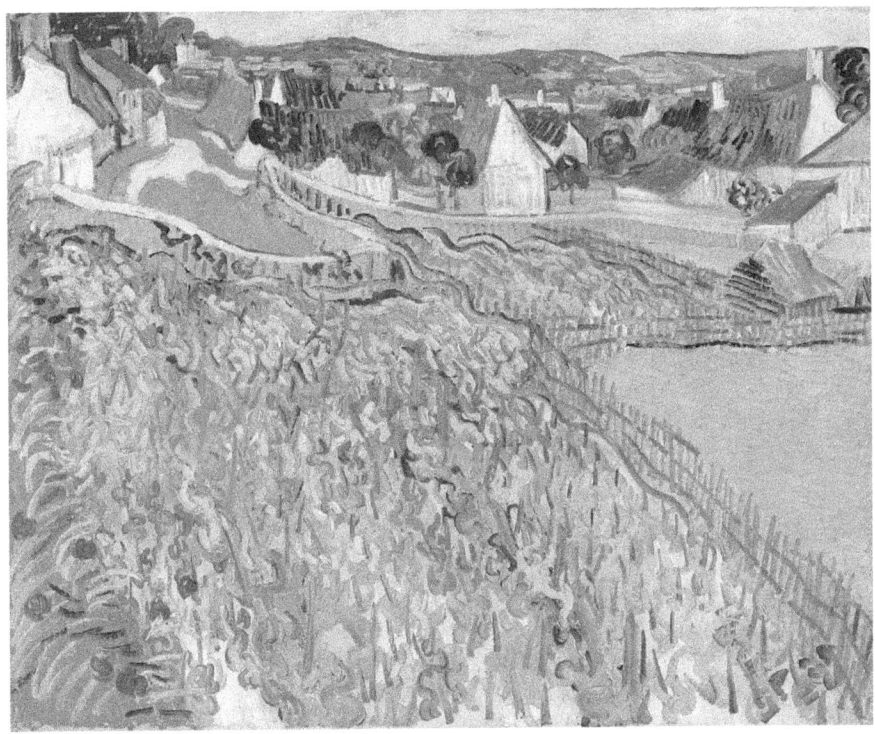

The beautiful setting of Auvers with vegetable gardens, grape vineyards, and red poppy with the rolling hills in the background. *Vineyards at Auvers* resides at the Saint Louis Art Museum, St. Louis, Missouri.

Enclosed Field with Rising Sun, Autumn 1889

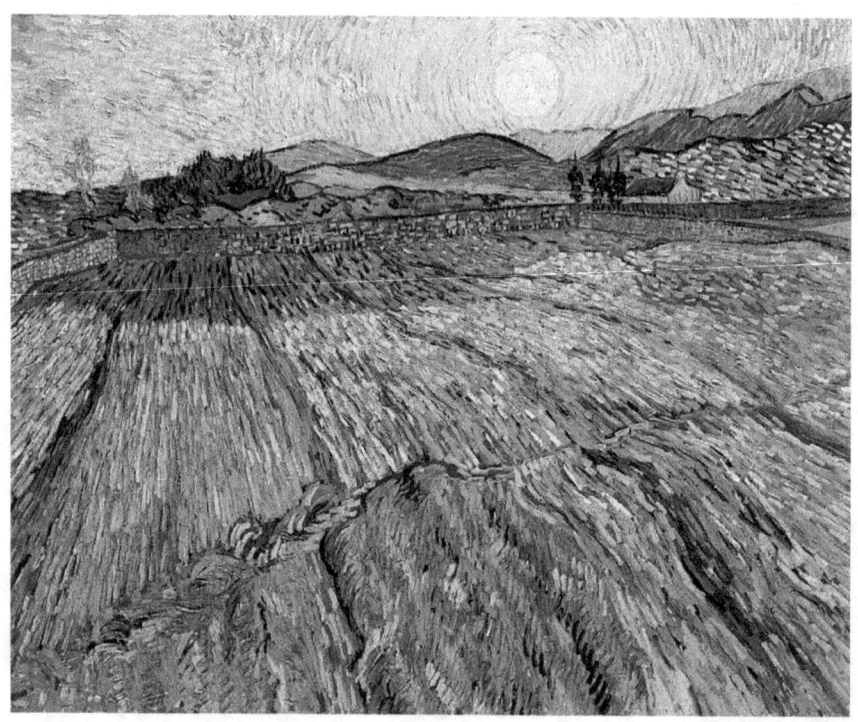

Enclosed Field with Rising Sun was painted sometime in the autumn of 1889 between November and December. A hopeful Vincent and Theo sent the painting to the 7th exhibition of Les XX in Brussels, where it was placed on display in the early months of 1890. The painting currently resides in the collection of Sammlung R. Oppenheimer in San Francisco, California.

Olive Trees against a Slope of a Hill, 1889

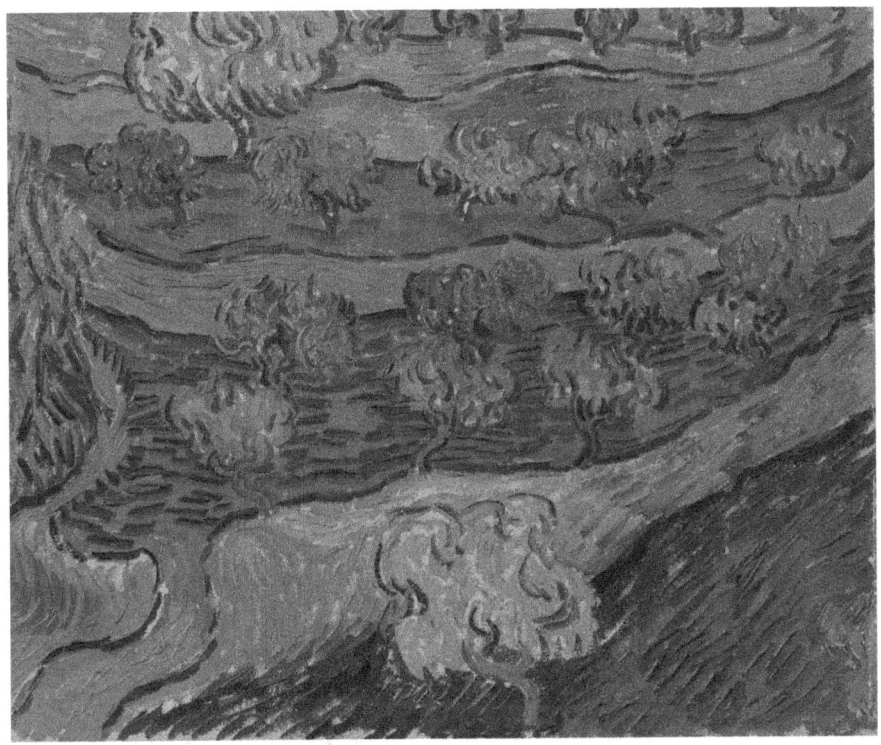

Olive Trees against a Slope of a Hill painted in 1889 in Saint-Rémy-de-Provence, France uses the same muted dark browns and greens that Vincent will use a year later in his more sweeping *Landscape with Bridge across the Oise* that shows the blue arched bridge, the meandering River Oise, and the farm and close by poplar trees. This painting here could be set anywhere in Sardinia; the olive rich rolling hills of Vieste of Foggia, Italy; or Tuscany for that matter. Nonetheless, I've never seen an ugly olive tree, so in my humble eyes the more olive tree paintings that exist in the world the better. This humblebrag-of-a-dessert painting resides in the Van Gogh Museum in Amsterdam in the Netherlands.

Girl in White in the Woods, 1882

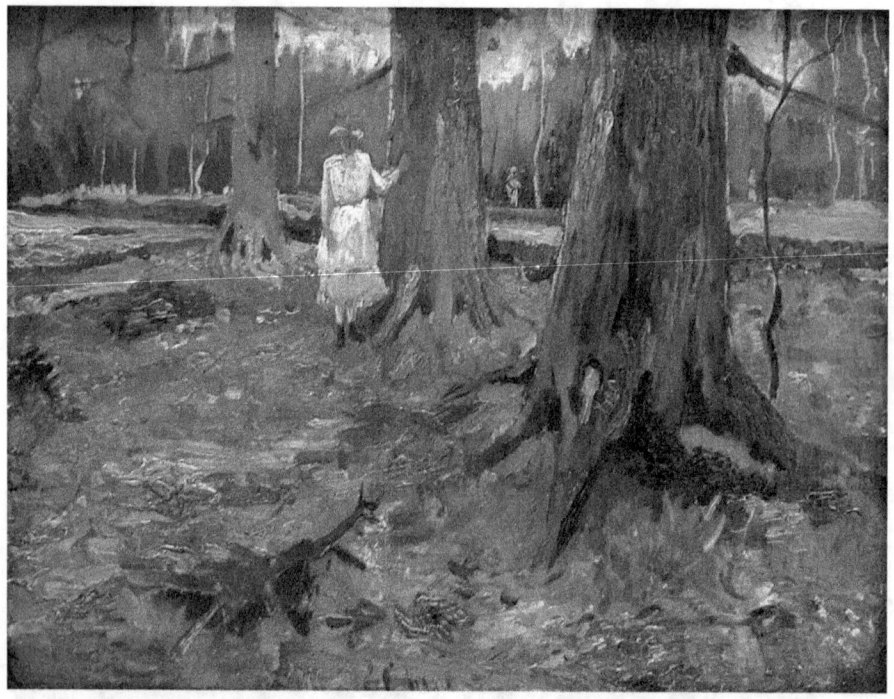

In Girl in White in the Woods, an early work painted in the Hauge from 1882, we can see where Vincent van Gogh may have taken his art work had he not had the influence of both the Japanese woodblock and Pointillism styles that he was exposed to later on in life, but luckily for us he took a different fork in the road and we all are the better for it for the later van Gogh works are much more euphoric and sublime. This haunting work currently resides in Kröller-Müller Museum in Otterlo in the Netherlands.

Dunes, 1882

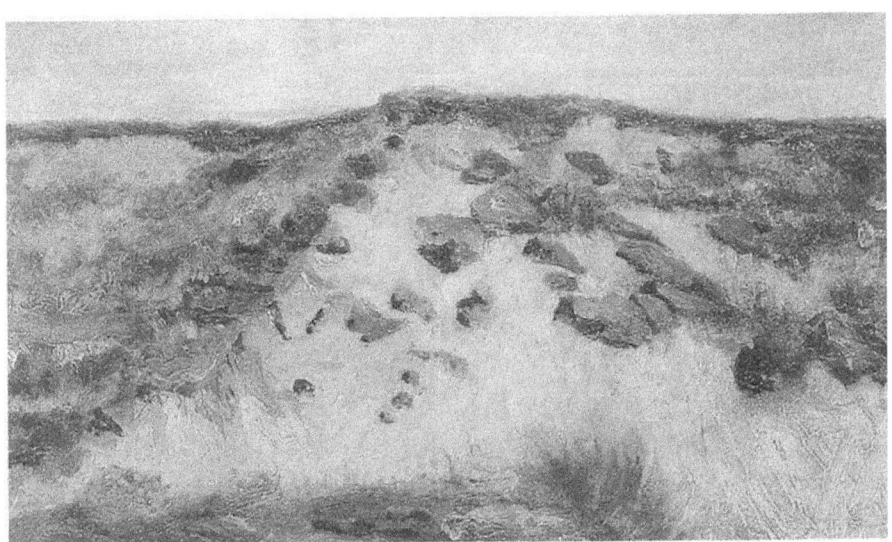

Painted in the municipality of the Hauge in 1882 in the typical realism style of the time it is steeped in beautiful rich golden-yellow with a cloud dappled sky in the background. It currently resides in a private collection in Amsterdam.

In the Dunes (In de Duinen), 1883

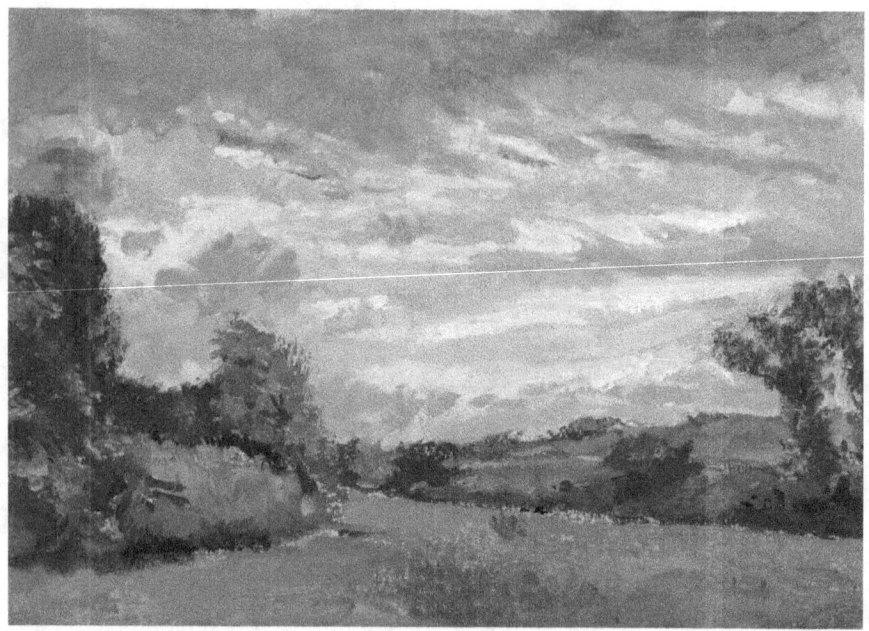

Painted in The Hague in September of 1883, In the Dunes is conceived in the typical realism style of the time, and although beautiful it is unremarkable from any other trained painter of the period, never mind hardly recognizable as a van Gogh.

Vincent wrote to his brother Theo in a letter dated September 5th, 1883 about the spot in the dunes that he painted in the Hague: "I received your letter just now when I came home from the dunes behind Loosduinen, soaking wet because I had spent 3 hours in the rain at a spot where everything was Ruisdael, Daubigny or Jules Dupré. I came back with a study of crooked, windswept trees, and a second of a farm after the rain. Everything is already bronze, everything is what one can see in nature only at this time of year, or if one stands before one of those paintings like a Dupré, for instance, and so beautiful that one's imagination always falls short of it."

The work is currently held in a private collection.

View of the Sea at Scheveningen, 1882; stolen December 7th, 2002

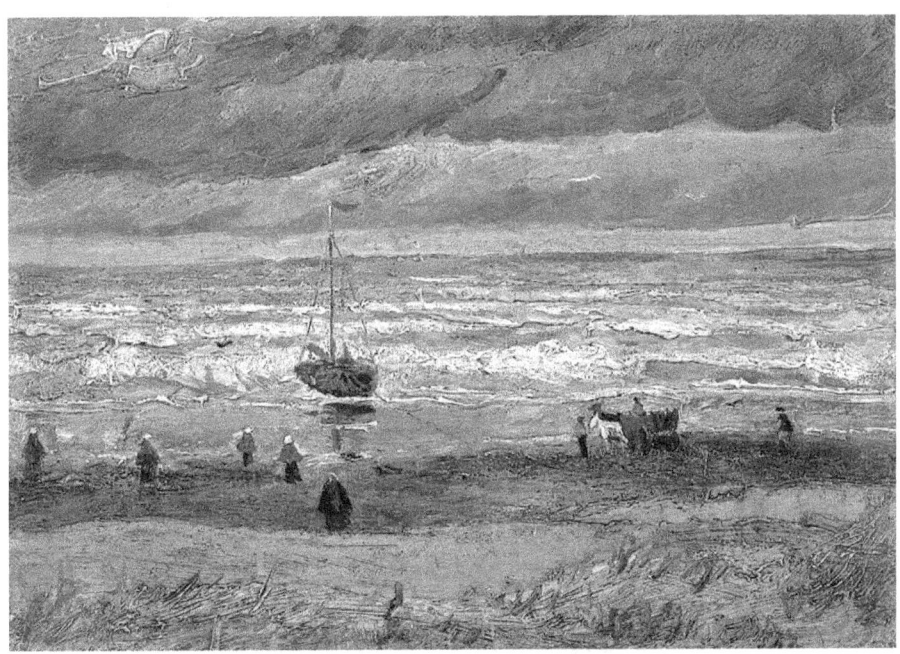

Painted in coastal Scheveningen, a seaside resort in one of the eight districts of the Hague in the Netherlands, View of the Sea at Scheveningen is renowned for having been stolen in 2002 along Congregation Leaving the Reformed Church in Nuenen from the Van Gogh Museum in Amsterdam. "The heist took about three minutes and 40 seconds," stated one of the underworld thieves, Octave Durham, who pulled off the heist the New York Times reported. "When I was done, the police were there, and I was passing by with my getaway car. Took my ski mask off, window down, and I was looking at them."

The two paintings remained missing for 13 years until they were recovered in Naples, Italy under the kitchen floor of a villa owned by Raffaele Imperiale, the man who bought the painting off the original thieves—he was a low-ranking mafioso associated with Camorra crime family. The painting had been cut out of its frame and had to be restored before it went back on display in March 2017 at the Van Gogh Museum in Amsterdam

Congregation Leaving the Reformed Church in Nuenen, 1884; stolen December 7th, 2002

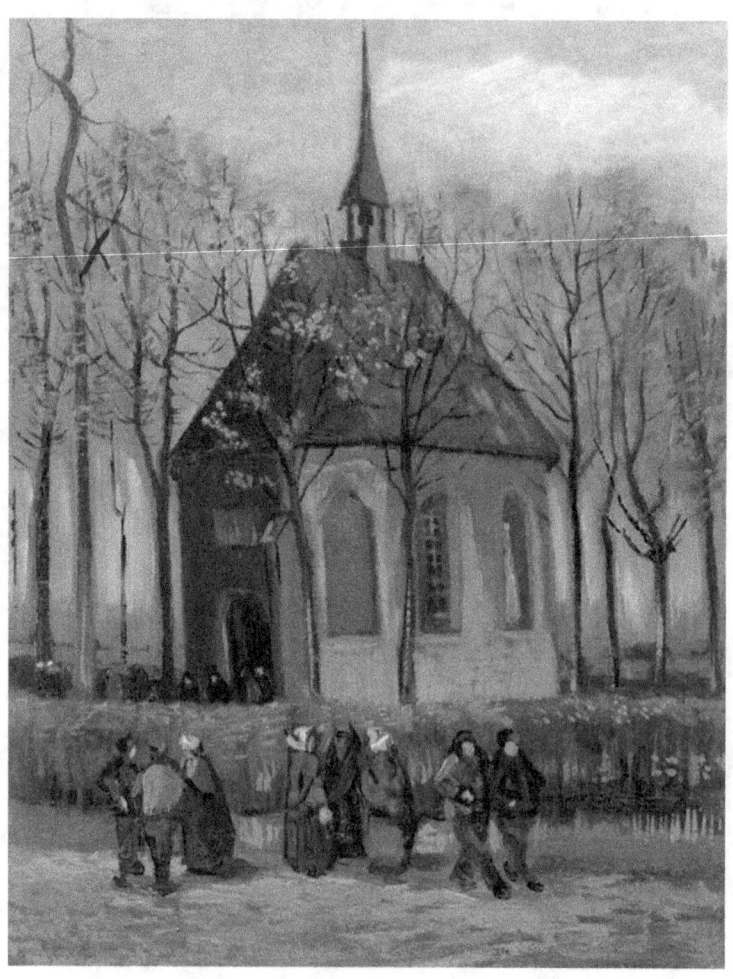

The other painting that was stolen from the Van Gogh Museum in Amsterdam on that fateful day in December of 2002, this portrait is a gorgeous rendition of the congregates of the church where van Gogh's father became pastor at Nuenen in 1882, and where van Gogh lived with his parents at the vicarage from December 1883 to May 1885. It was also returned to the Van Gogh Museum and put back on display in 2017.

Women Mending Nets in the Dunes, August 1882

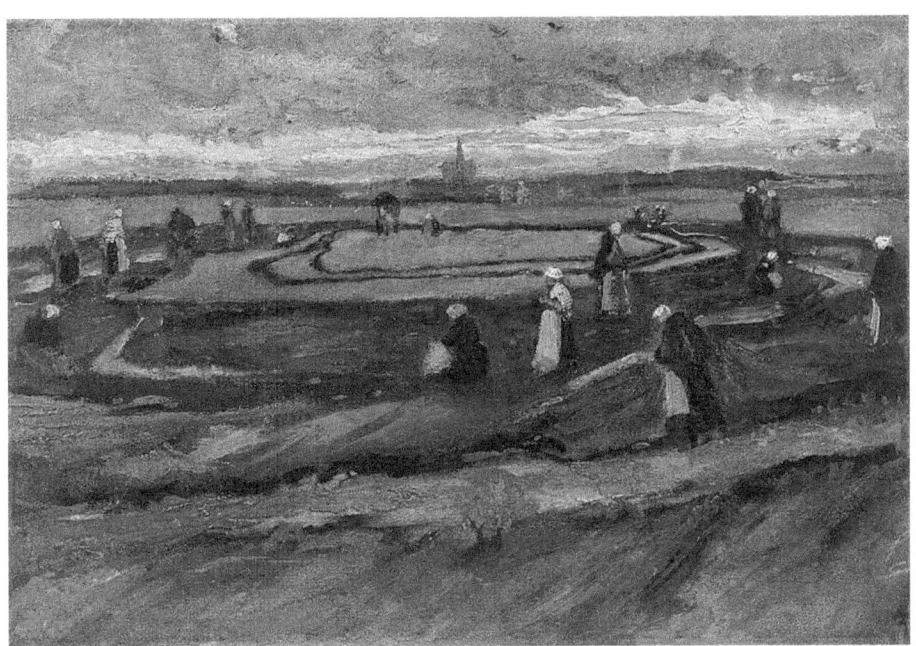

Oil on paper painted in 1882 along the coast in the municipality of at the Hauge in the Netherlands. The painting currently resides in a private collection.

Vase with Twelve Sunflowers, August 1888

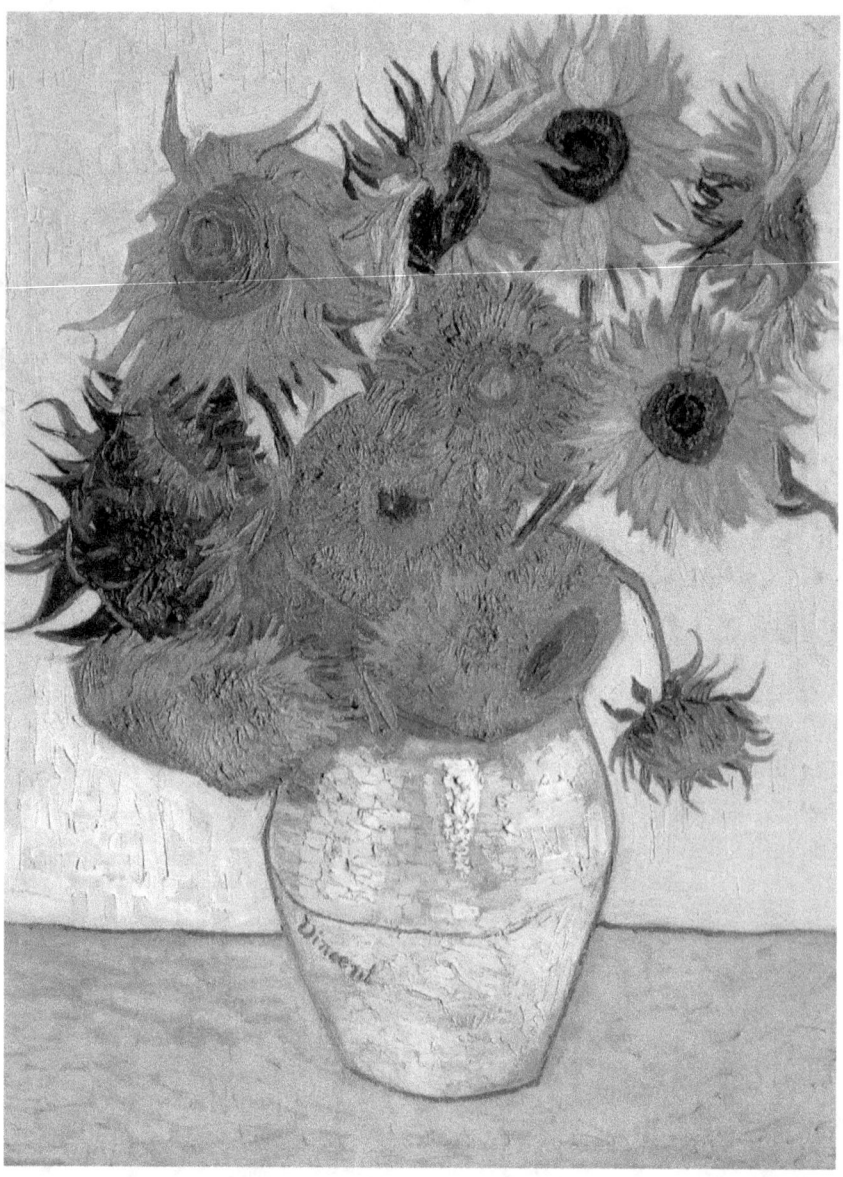

A symbol of life and hop this aqua background version of *Vase with Twelve Sunflowers* that was painted in Arles during August of the summer of 1888 features twelve gold-yellow and unripe green almost metallic looking blossoms. They sit in a gold mosaic vase with Vincent's omnipresent signature on the lefthand lower side of the earthen-clay part of the container.

In a letter to his friend Émile Henri Bernard who was also a French Post-Impressionist painter and writer, dated around late August 1888, Vincent noted about the portrait that he was planning to decorate the studio in his house before the arrival of his on-again, off-again best friend Paul Gauguin: "I'm thinking of decorating my studio with half a dozen paintings of Sunflowers [for Gauguin's arrival]. A decoration in which harsh or broken yellows will burst against various blue backgrounds, from the palest Veronese to royal blue, framed with thin laths painted in orange lead. Sorts of effects of stained-glass windows of a Gothic church."

What can be viewed in this particular portrait is exactly the picture van Gogh held in his mind that he shared with Émile Bernard. It is only the most extraordinary artist, writer, or musician that can form an artistic impression in the mind and execute it perfectly into creation. Most artists would give their right-hand to perform such great and astonishing feats.

Footbridge across a Ditch, 1883

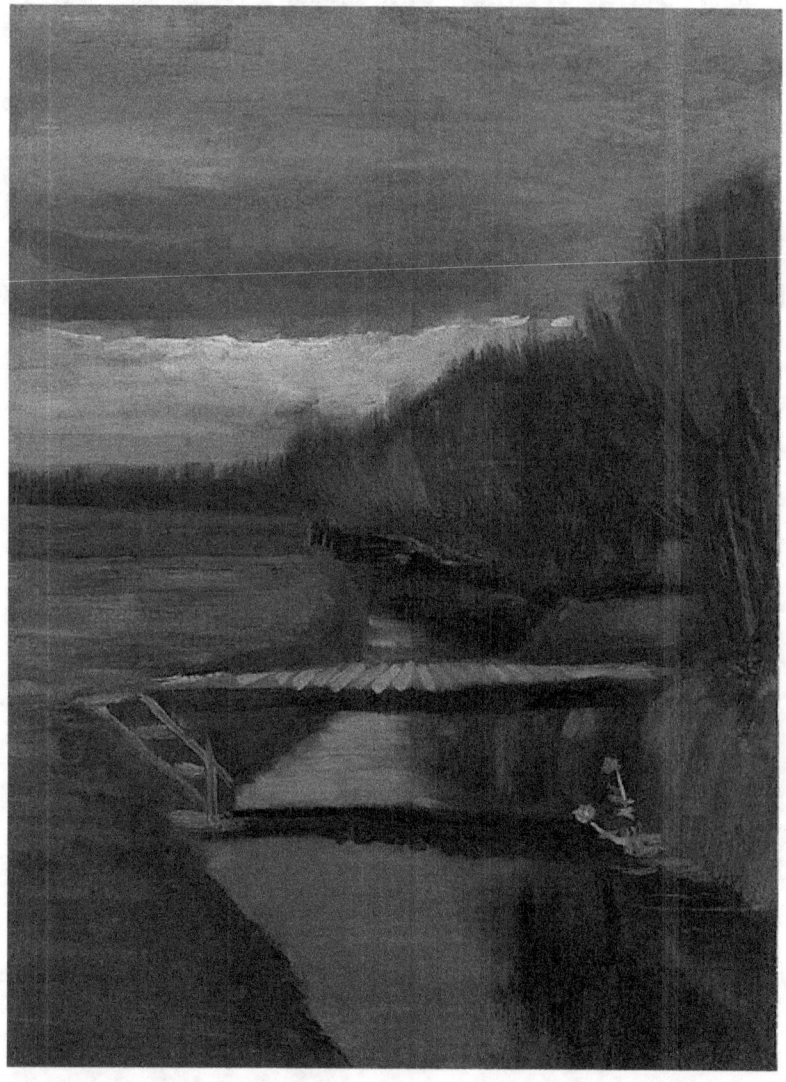

Painted along the coast of the Hague in the Netherlands, from August 1883 until September 1883 it, too, now resides in a private collection.

Peasant Burning Weeds, 1883

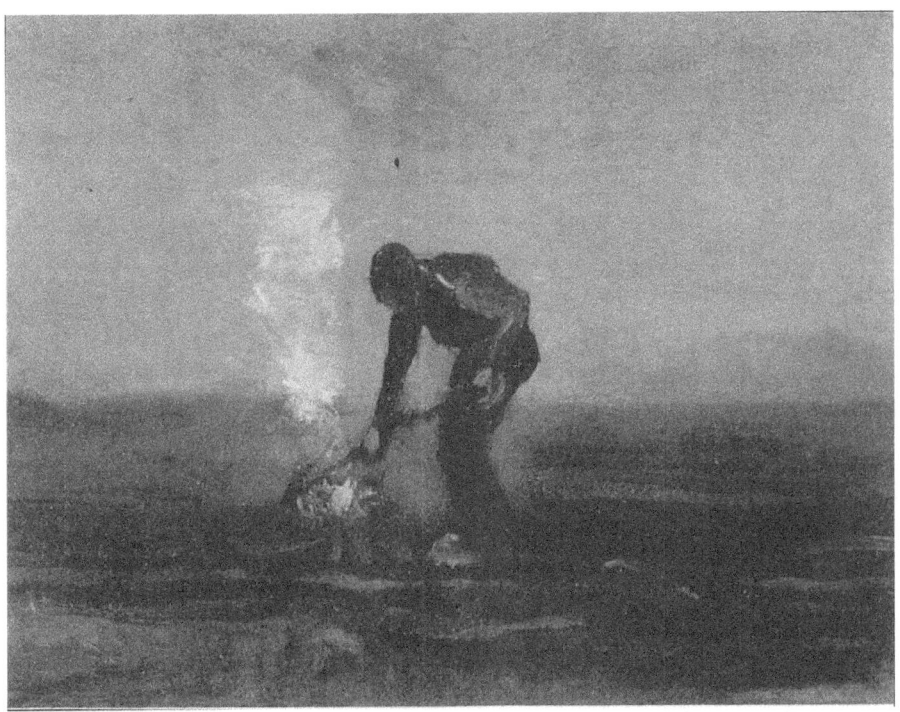

Painted by van Gogh in 1883 in Drenthe, a province of the Netherlands. It currently resides in the Drents Museum in Assen, Drenthe in the Netherlands.

Farmhouses Among Trees, 1883

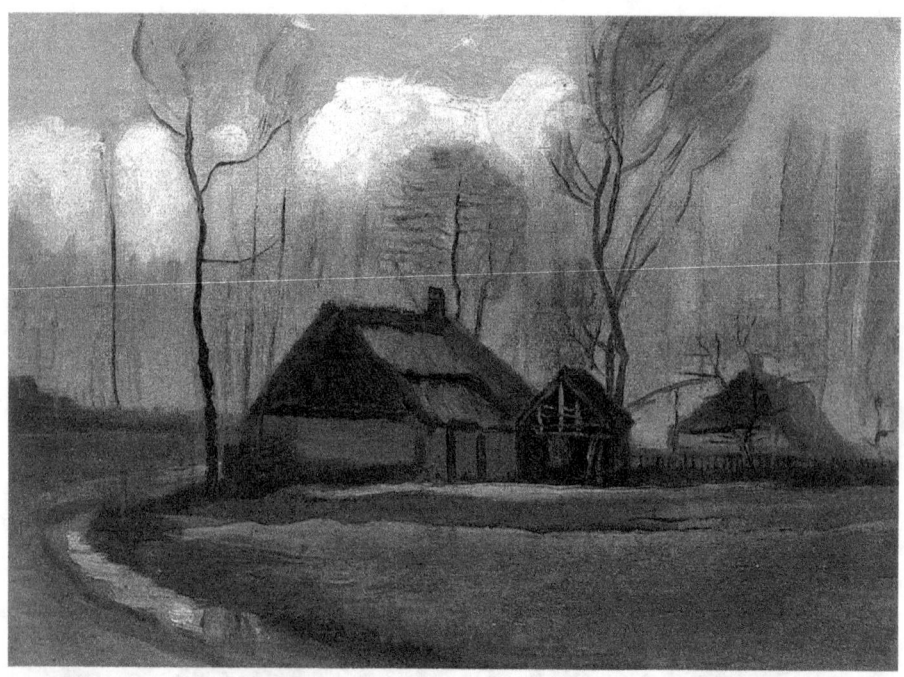

Oil on canvas mounted on panel, *Farmhouse Among Trees* is a work from 1883 that was painted in the area of the Hauge. Van Gogh stylistic clouds are recognizable in the blue sky, so too is the stroke of his notable brushwork visible amid the braid of silver stream. A beautiful landscape it currently resides in The Museum of Pope John Paul the 2nd in Warsaw, Poland.

Still Life with Pots, Jar and Bottles, November 1884

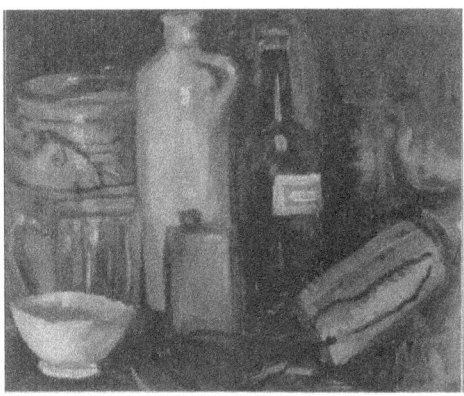

Still Life with Four Stone Bottles, Flask and White Cup, November 1884

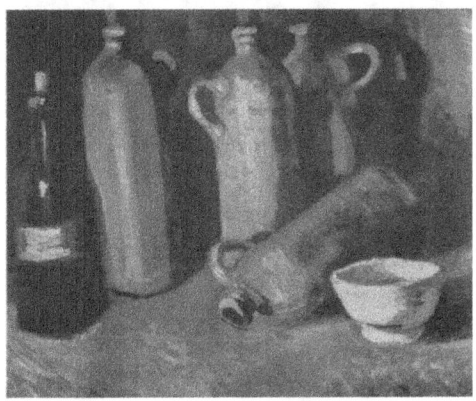

Still Life with Two Sacks and a Bottle, November 1884

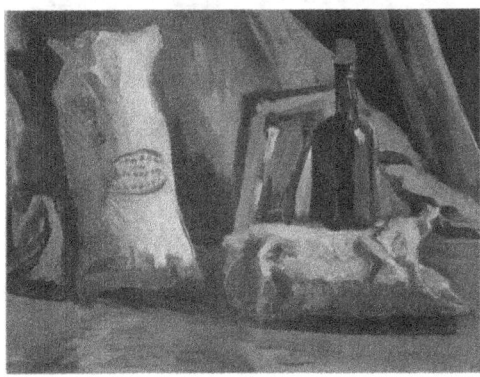

Still Life with Two Sacks and a Bottle, November 1884

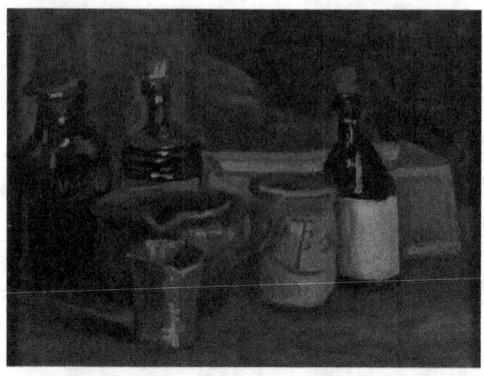

Beer Tankards, November 1884

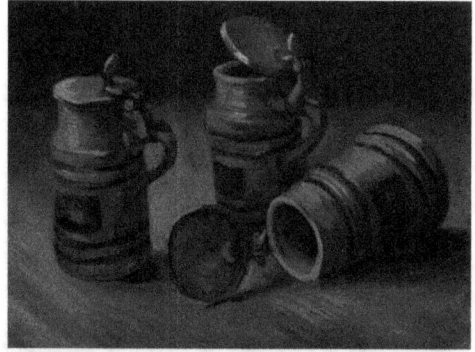

Still Life with Coffee Mill, Pipe Case and Jug, November 1884

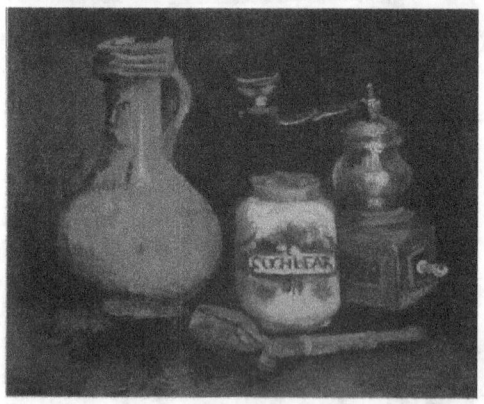

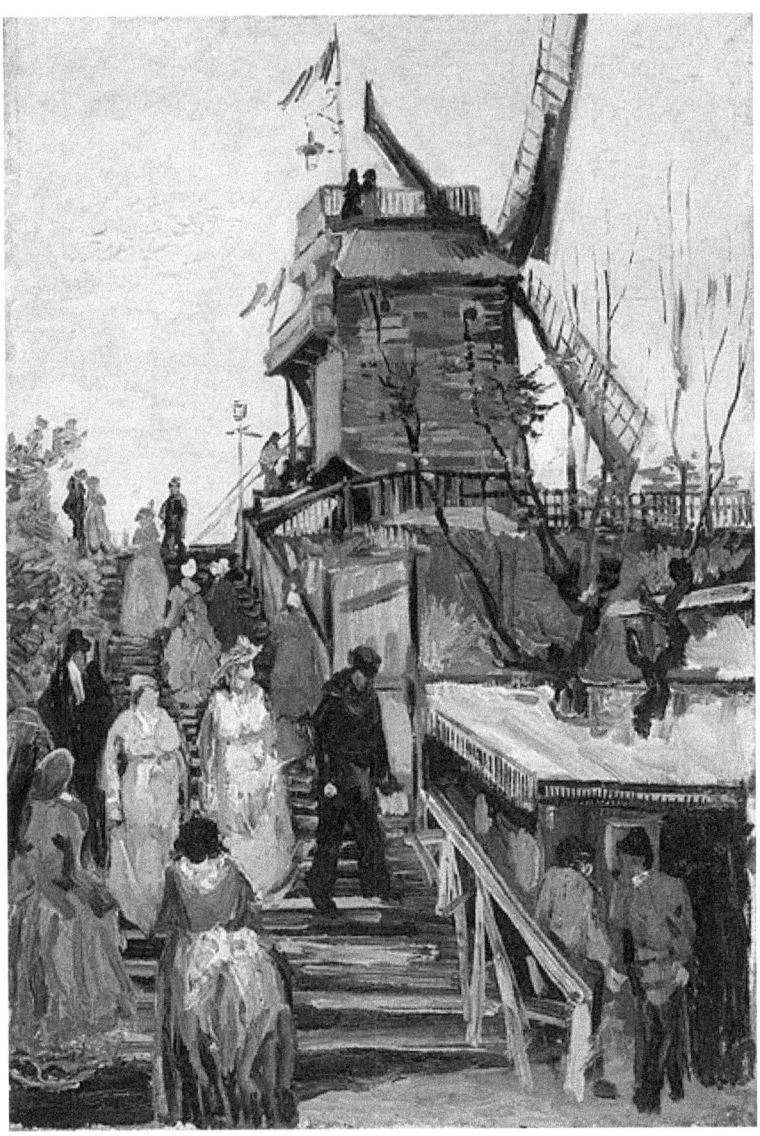

One of van Gogh's later Paris paintings, *Le Blute-Fin Mill* shows off the colorful life of Parisians going about the Moulin Blute-fin atop Montmartre even amid the gray autumn skies of the city of light. Only authenticated as a true van Gogh in 1995 after it was put through a series of extensive X-ray fluorescence spectrometry (XRF) and Scanning Electron Microscopy with Energy Dispersive Electroscopy (SEM-EDS) tests, all of which confirmed the pigments, paints, and canvas used was the same of what van Gogh used on his other paintings during 188. It should be noted that it is clearly evident that the work was never completed or was not to van Gogh's liking, because although this lovely work has been authenticated the fact remains van Gogh did not sign such an important work with his signature "Vincent" in the lower left-hand corner. The mystery remains, which is just lovely in the worlds of art and literature.

Fourteenth of July Celebration in Paris, 1886

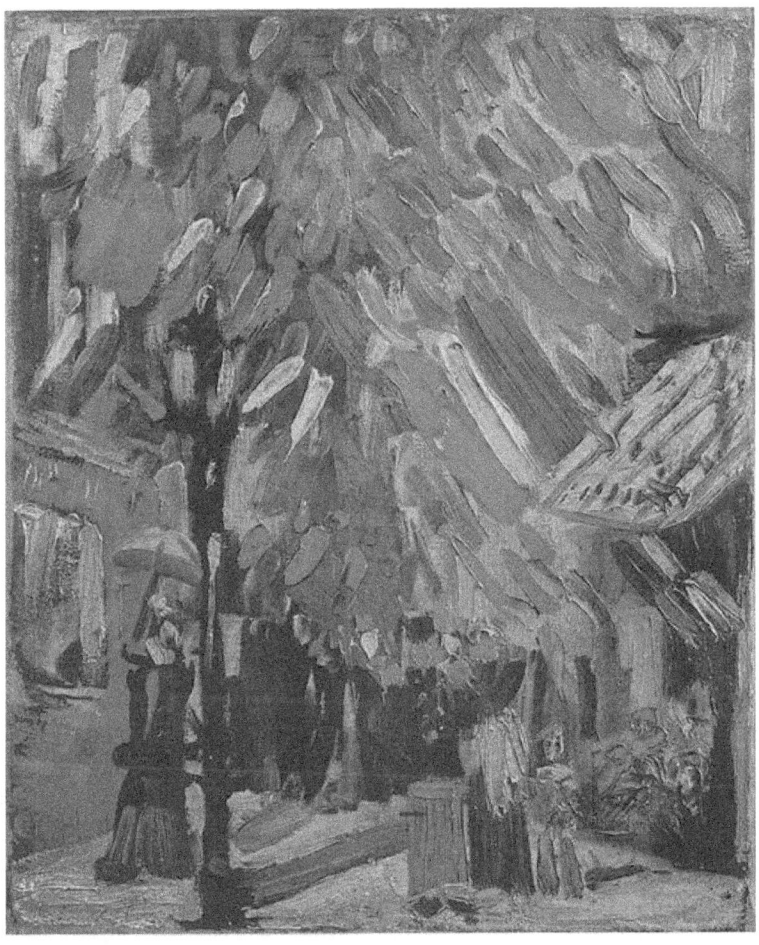

Another Paris era painting, *The 14th July in Paris* was painted during the summer of 1886 and celebrates the French revolutionary day Bastille Day in the city in commemoration of the storming of the Bastille back on July 14, 1789. Currently, located at the Hahnloser/Jaeggli Foundation in Winterthur, Switzerland.

View of the Roofs of Paris, 1886

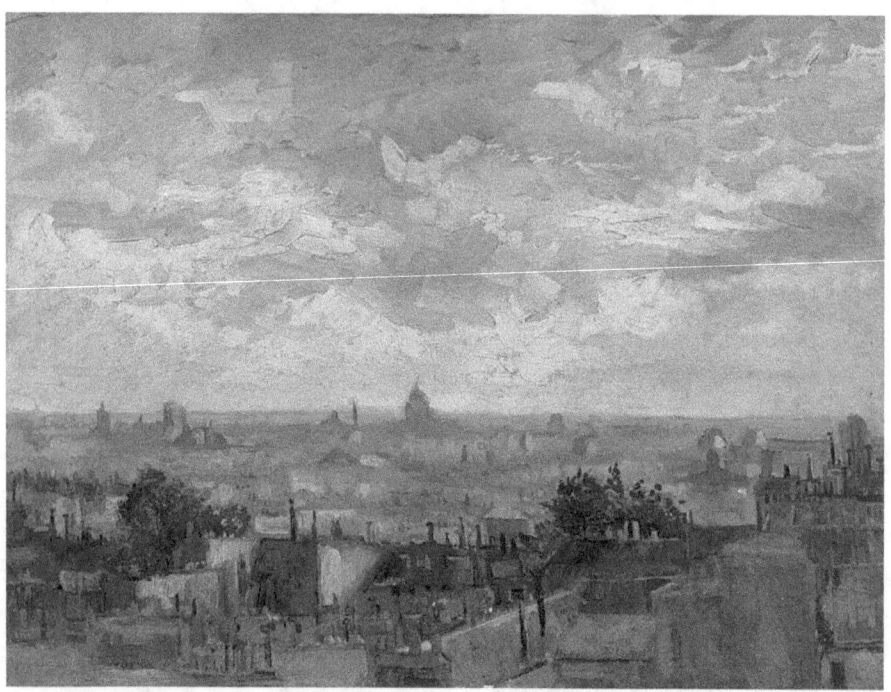

Cityscape of Paris circa 1886 entitled *View of the Roofs of Paris* was put to canvas by Vincent van Gogh from his eyes to yours for time immemorial. Currently resides at the Van Gogh Museum in Amsterdam in the Netherlands.

Montmartre: behind the Moulin de la Galette, 1887

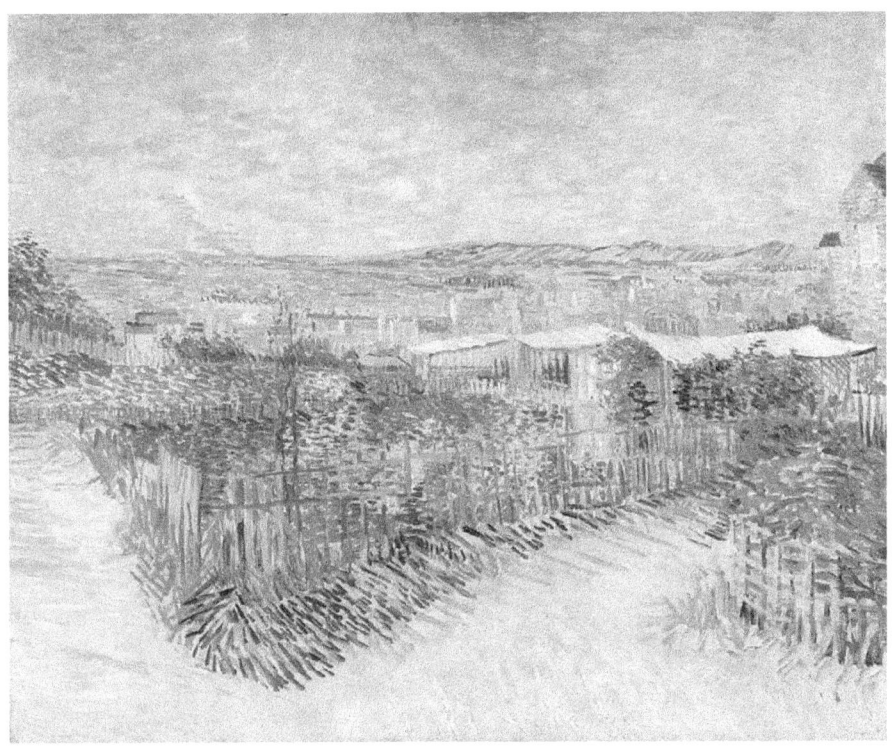

At nearly 40 inches by 32 inches *Montmartre: behind the Moulin de la Galette* holds the distinction of being one of the largest landscapes that van Gogh ever produced.

Painted in Paris in early 1887 it shows a rather pastoral northwest panoramic view of the city of Paris and the faraway hills of Meudon from atop the peak of Montmartre with fenced in allotment vegetable and communal gardens in the foreground and pale blue skies up above. It is currently housed at the Van Gogh Museum, in Amsterdam in the Netherlands.

Le Moulin de la Galette, Autumn 1886

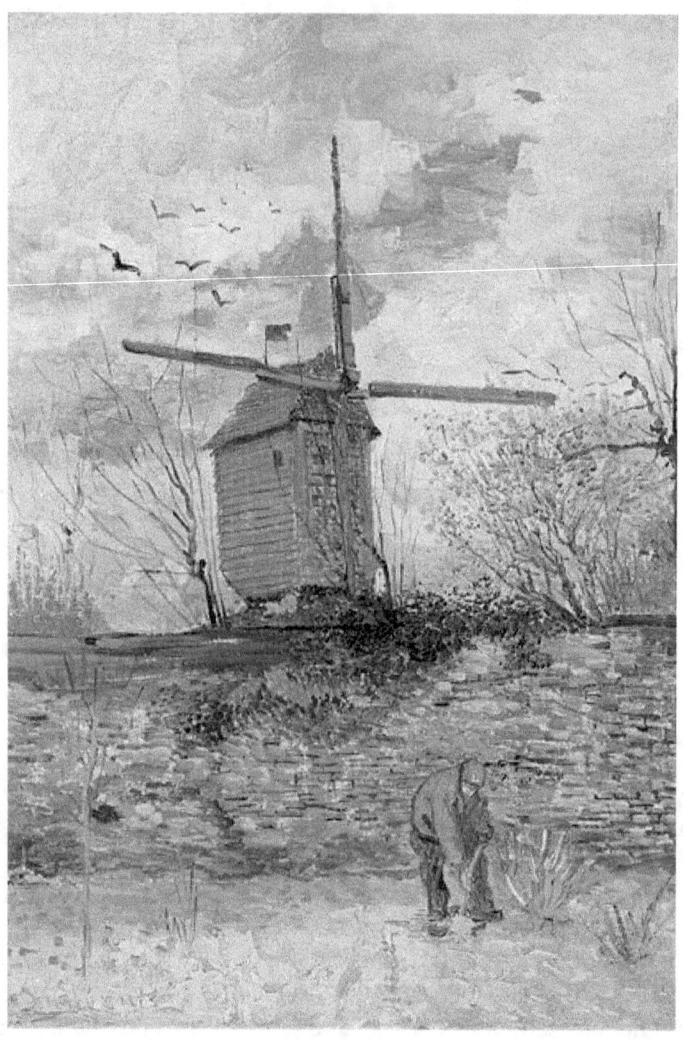

Nearby the Parisan apartment where Vincent and his brother lived after moving to France from the Netheralnds sat a stoic rural looking windmill named the Moulin de la Galette. It sat on the lovely butte that overlooked the bustling cityscape of Paris full of its cafés, dance halls, churches, bistros, and man arrondissements. In the autumn of 1886 Vincent created a series of windmill paintings using different vantage points of his beloved Moulin de la Galette, many of which evoke beautiful metallic blues, limes, emeralds, and greens within the serene melancholy of its subject matter. The above work now resides in a private collection.

Le Moulin de la Galette Windmill Series, 1886

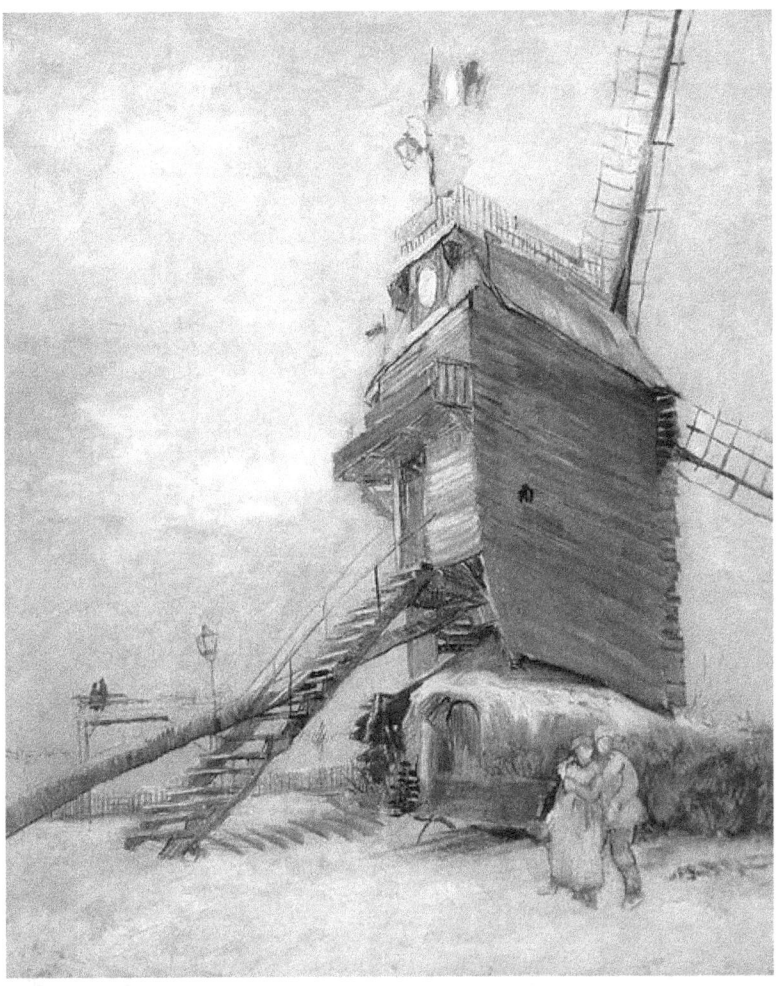

Another in the Windmill Series from atop Montmartre this landscape now resides in the Museo Nacional de Bellas Artes in Buenos Aries, Argentina.

Le Moulin de la Galette also The Blute-Fin Windmill, Montmartre, 1886

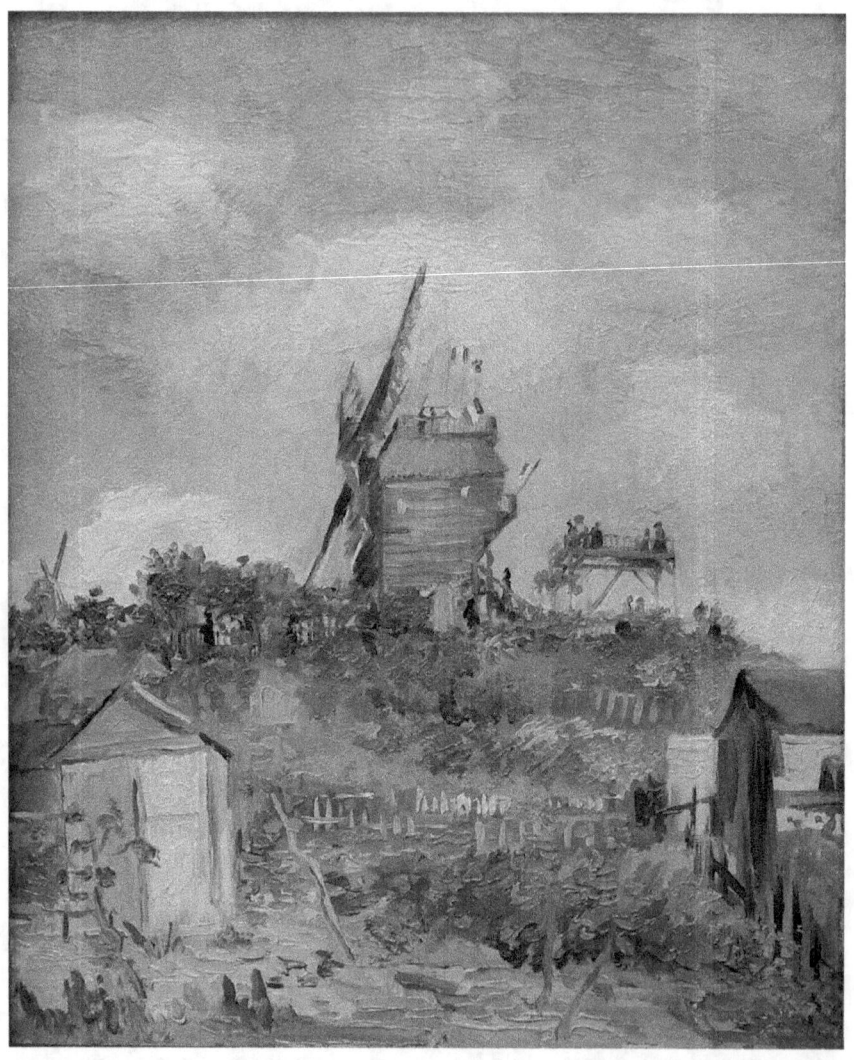

This variation in the Windmill series, *Le Moulin de la Galette also The Blute-Fin Windmill, Montmartre*, was painted during the summer of 1886 and currently resides in the Kelvingrove Art Gallery and Museum in Glasgow, Scotland.

Le Moulin de la Galette, Windmill Series 1886

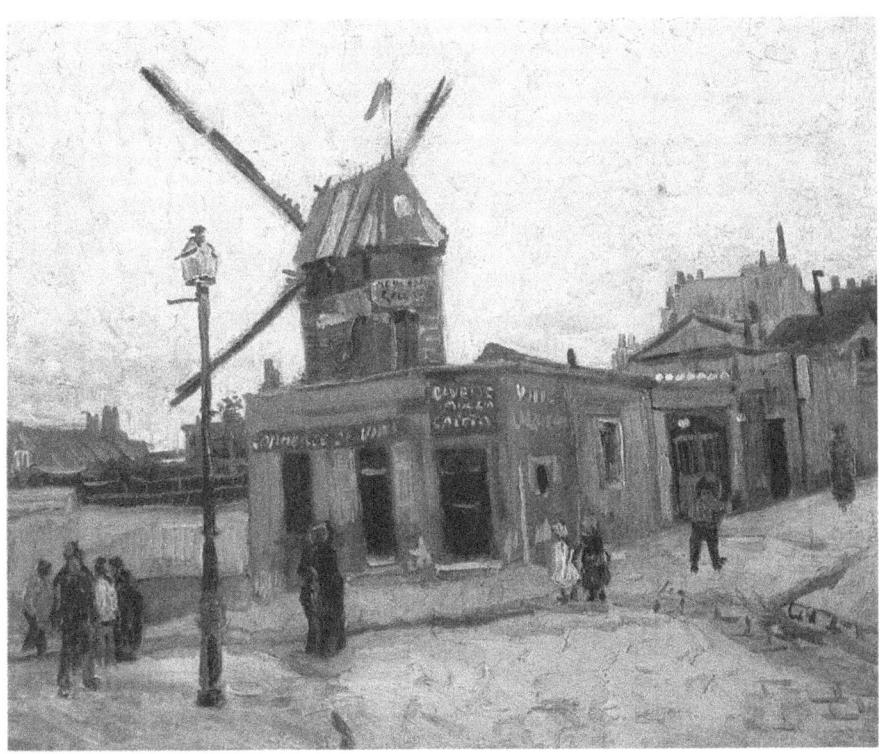

Van Gogh painted the same portrait of this version of Le Moulin de la Galette in three different versions. Each is exactly the same, but the tones of the paintings overall range from gold-yellow to blue to gray. This particular version, the blue version, resides at the Kröller-Müller Museum in Otterlo in the Netherlands.

The three different variations of Le Moulin de la Galette, Windmill Series 1886

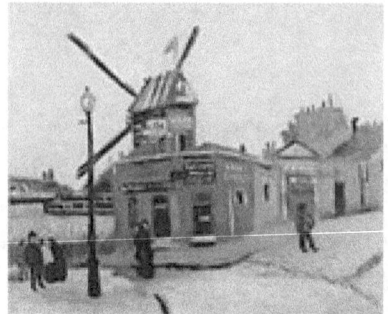 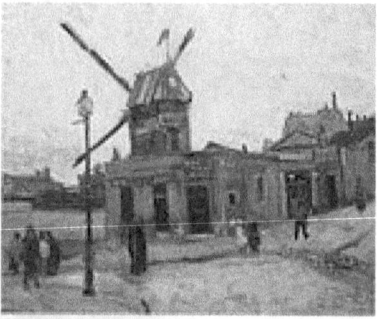

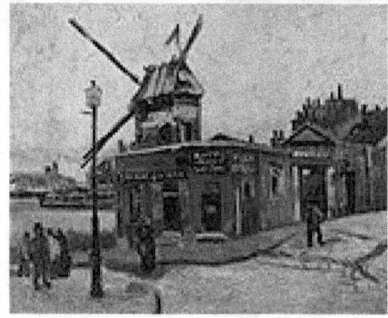

Le Moulin de la Galette, No. 1; now resides in the Stiftung Langmatt Museum, Baden, Switzerland

Le Moulin de la Galette, No. 2; Kröller-Müller Museum, Otterlo, Netherlands

Le Moulin de la Galette, No. 3; Neue National Gallery Museum, Berlin, Germany

Street Scene in Montmartre: Le Moulin a Poivre, 1887

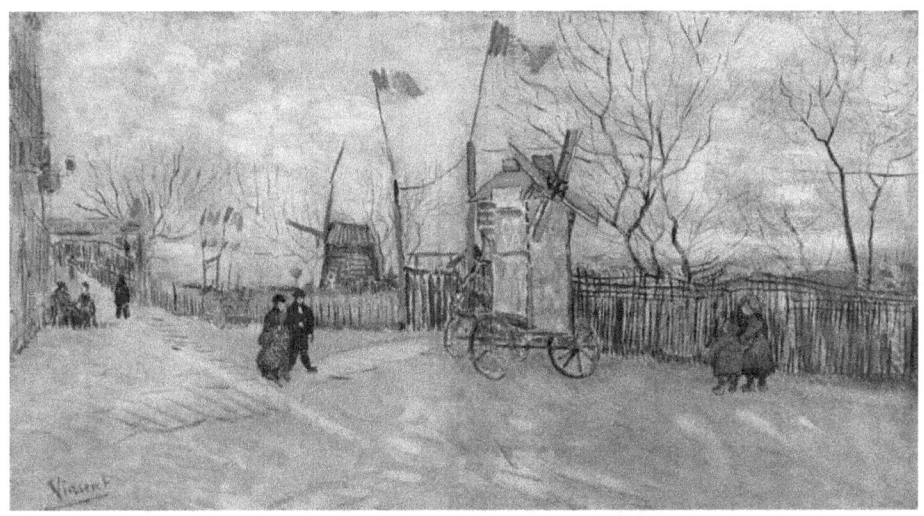

This street scene from atop the hill of Montmartre was painted in the spring of 1887 and shows off the colors of France like its own Bastille Day fireworks amid the flags and rolling windmill. It is currently on display at the Van Gogh Museum in Amsterdam in the Netherlands.

White Vase with Roses and Other Flowers, 1886

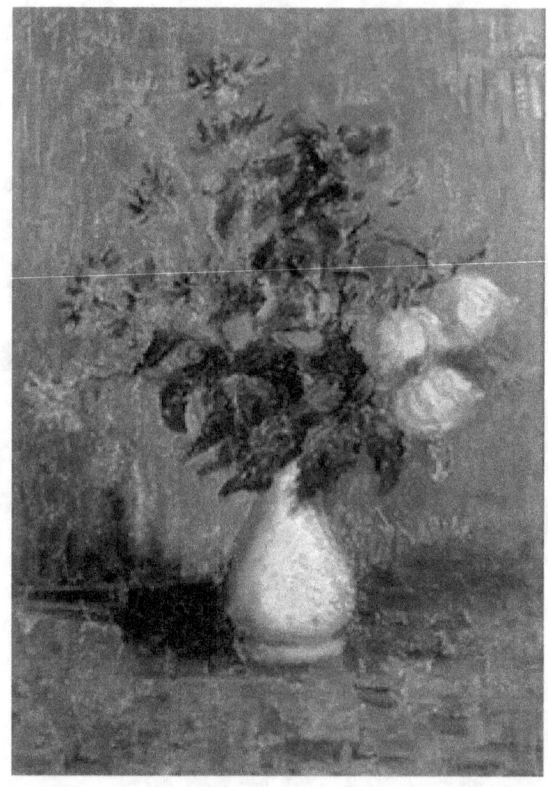

A beautiful floral roses in vase still life painted in Paris in 1886, *White Vase with Roses and Other Flowers* resides in the Yamagata Museum of Art in Yamagata, Japan.

Roses, 1890; looted from its rightful owner by the Nazi's in 1939

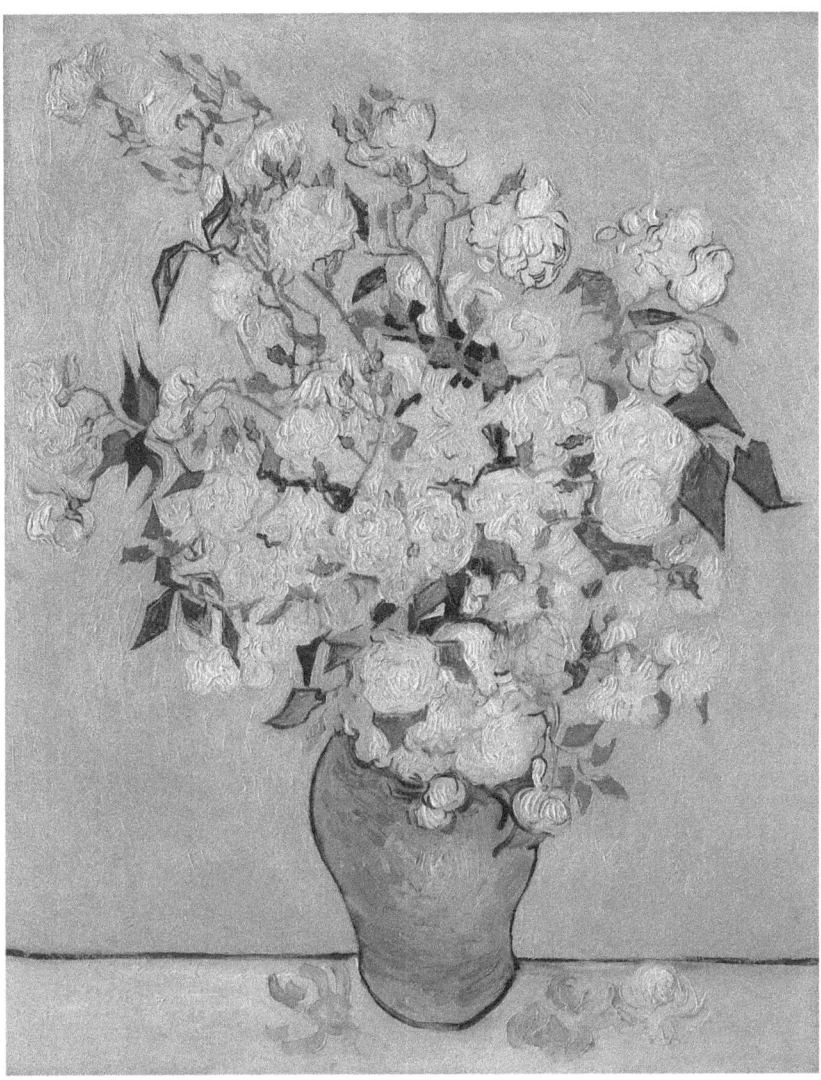

Novels and entire movies could be written about van Gogh's 1890 still life entitled simply *Roses*. This gorgeous painting was seized by the Nazis from Jewish businessman Georg Simon Hirschland in Essen, Germany in early 1939, following Hirschland's forced emigration to the United States one year earlier. The bank his grandfather, Simon Hirschland, started in 1841 was forcibly sold ("Aryanized") by the Reich, his home looted, and his precious works of art stolen by command of that miserable failure-of-an-artist himself, *Der Kommissar*, the pitiable Adolf Hitler himself. It was finally restituted to the heirs of Georg Simon Hirschland in New York City around 1950. The painting has faded considerable through time where the roses that were once pink, as well as the linen of the table top that it sits upon, have faded mostly white. But a white rose still life by van Gogh is better than any pink or white rose still life by anyone else. Plus the sniveling Hilter rots in hell, where this beautiful still life still lives and breathes as a stark reminder to all humanity about the perils of hubris and tyranny.

La Mousmé, Sitting in a Cane Chair, Half-Figure (with a branch of oleander), 1888

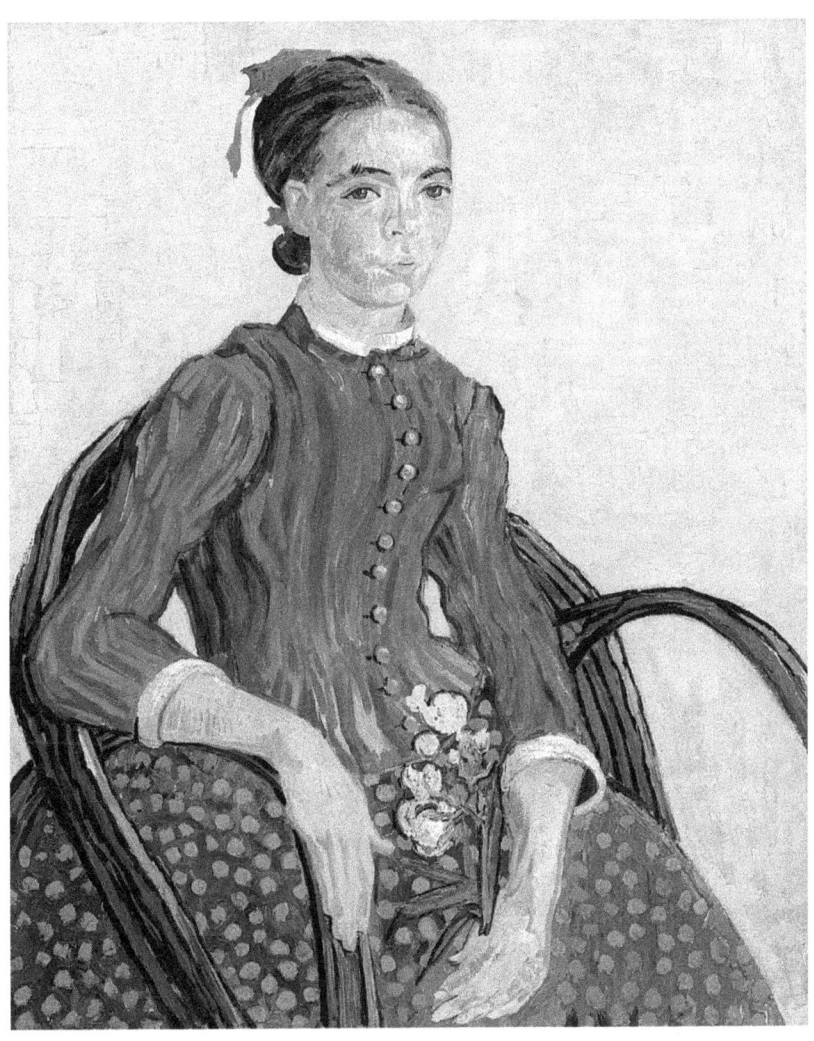

The beautifully brown-eyed La Mousmé with her crimson striped blouse and indigo orange blossom dotted skirt was inspired by a novel written in 1887 by Pierre Loti's entitled *Madame Chrysanthème* that was incredibly also the inspiration for Puccini's epic opera "Madama Butterfly." A young woman of Japanese descent, Vincent gushed to this brother Theo in a letter dated 1888 about his feelings for the beautiful seated still life:

"It took me a whole week...but I had to reserve my mental energy to do the mousmé well. A mousmé is a Japanese girl—Provençal in this case—twelve to fourteen years old."

The painting now resides at the National Gallery of Art in Washington, D.C.

The Cottage, May 1885

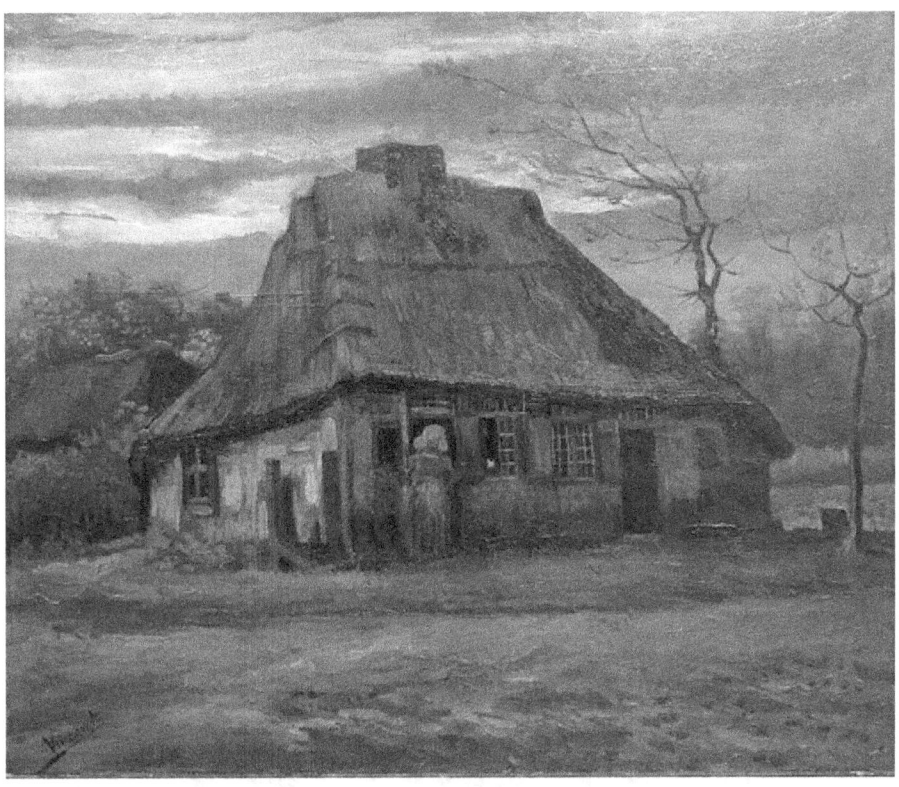

Painted in Nuenen in the Netherlands, May 1885, *The Cottage* shows the Dutch style dwelling that will appear in some later van Gogh works that are actually landscapes set in France, where this type of home with a thatch roof was not a part of the French experience. It is heavy, dark, and dreary with just a smear of red-orange sunset that opens like a portal halfway across the sky like perhaps that was the amount of light van Gogh felt inside himself during this period in the Netherlands from which he would soon leave behind.

If a visitor at a museum saw this painting today hung on its wall would they ever guess this was a Vincent van Gogh? Probably not simply for the reason none of the light, color, or joy found in his French paintings exist in this barren gray wasteland capture here on his 1885 oil on canvas. It now resides in the Van Gogh Museum in Amsterdam, the Netherlands.

Two Diggers among Trees, or The Diggers, 1889

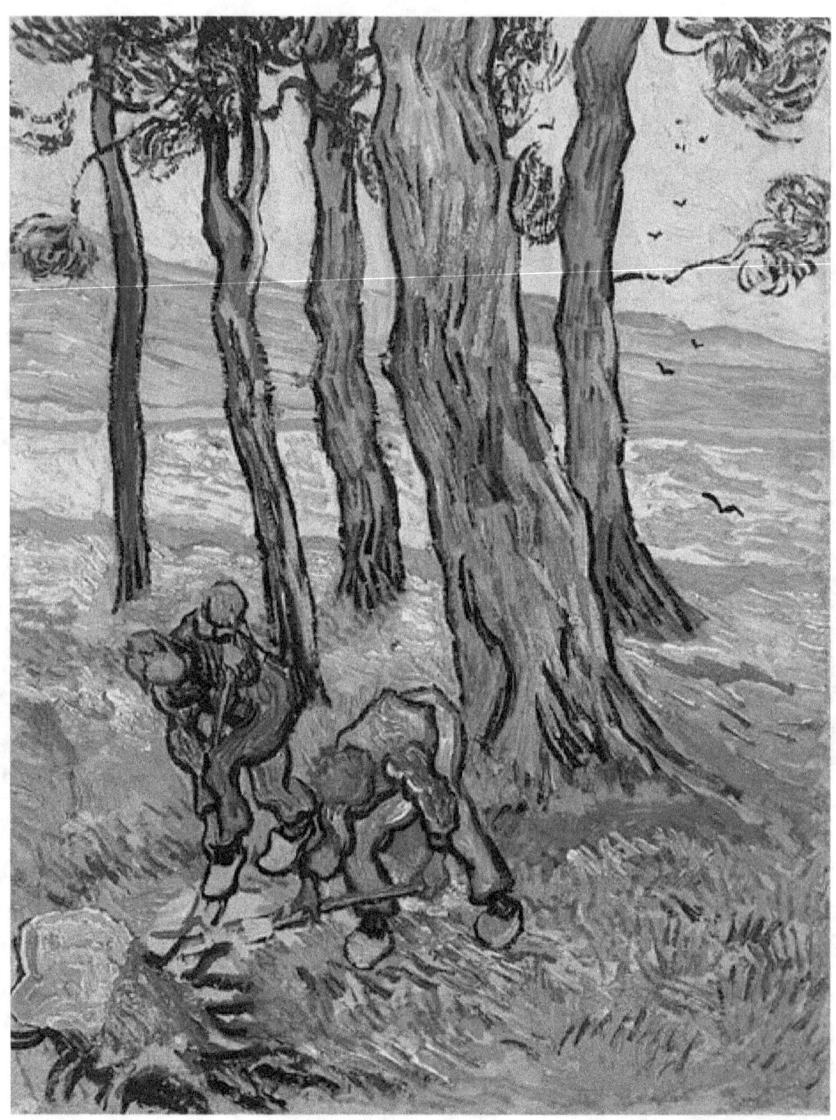

A beautiful oil on paper lined onto canvas that was painted in December 1889, *Two Diggers among Trees* was created in Saint-Rémy-de-Provence, France during that manic explosion of work that van Gogh had during the last two years of his short life. The Diggers was purchased in 1912 by Hugo Nathan, of Frankfurt, Germany, and then passed onto his heir, his wife Martha (Dreyfus) Nathan upon his death in 1922. Controversy surrounds the painting as 15 heirs of Martha Dreyfus put a calm on the painting in 2004 against the Detroit Institute of Arts that holds the portrait in their collection. They claimed that as a German Jew living in 1938 that Martha Dreyfus sold the painting under duress due to persecution from the Nazi regime who was going about looting all the Jewish art about the German state at that time. The claim was ultimately dismissed as Mrs. Dreyfus had taken the painting to Switzerland in 1930 on her own accord, three years before Hitler came to power, and sold the work in 1938 after moving to Paris for a price consistent with comparable prices of art work sold voluntarily during the years preceding WWII. Nonetheless, controversy still surrounds the old diggers. And the two blokes would not have it any other way!

Langlois Bridge at Arles, 1888

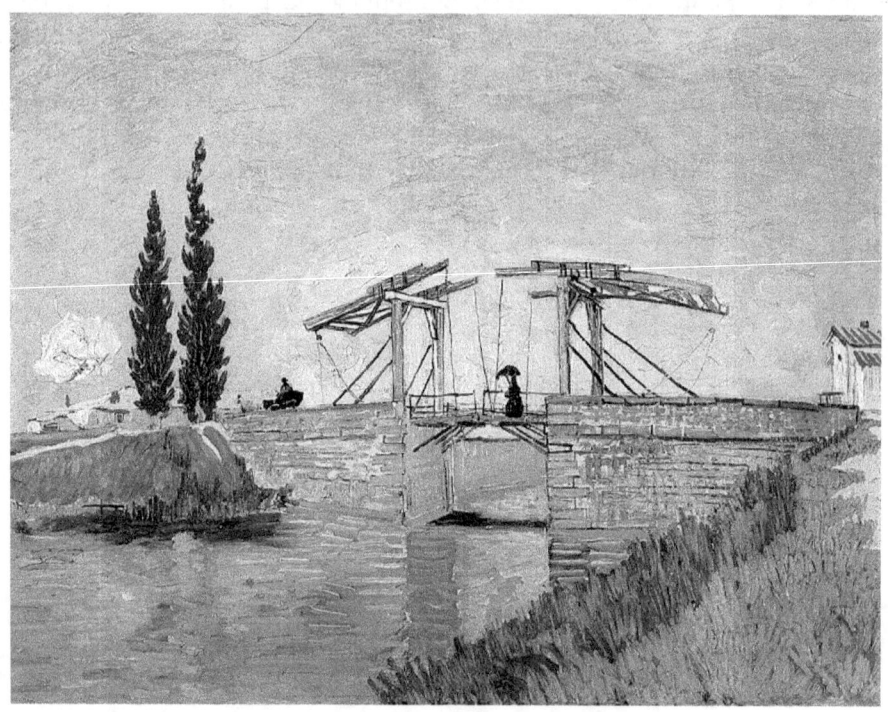

The Langlois Bridge at Arles, 1888, Wallraf-Richartz-Museum, Cologne

Van Gogh's Langlois Bridge at Arles (Mu. number 5805) was seized from the Rothschild collection by the Nazis, recovered by the Monuments Men and brought to the Munich Central Collecting Point

The Langlois Bridge at Arles, 1888, looted by Nazi Reichsmarschall Hermann Göring

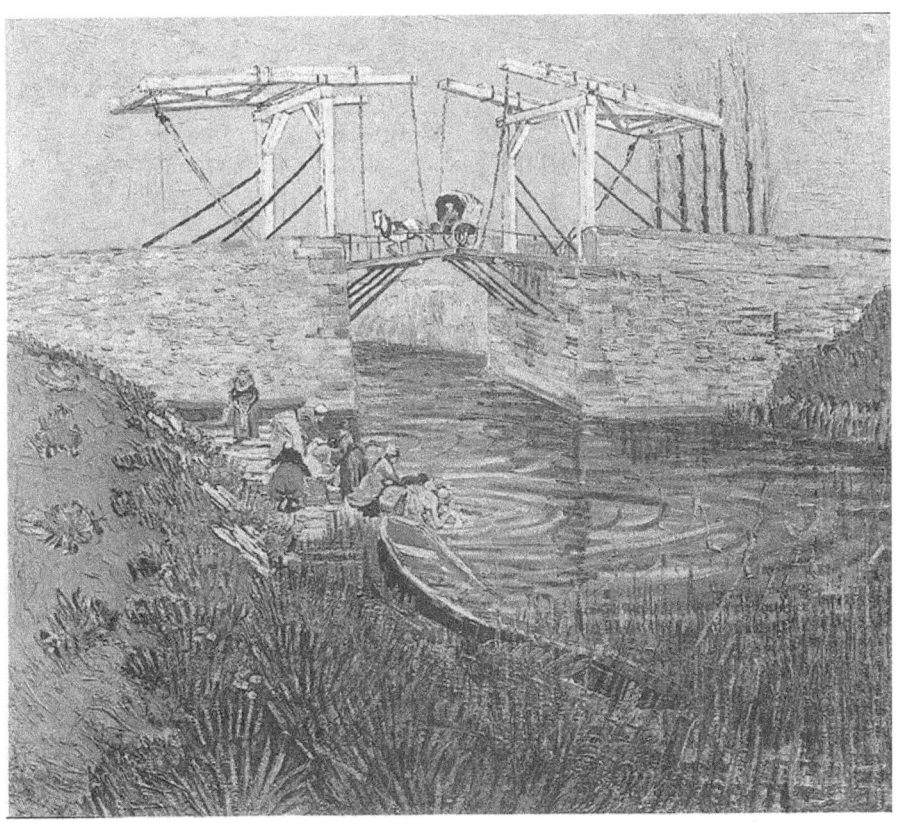

As previously stated this work of art was painted by van Gogh four times, but this particular version with a much darker and greener hue than some of the others was looted from Rothschild estate by the Nazi's and thus taken by Herman Goering for his Carinhall estate located in the Schorfheide Forest, in the north end of Brandenburg, between the lakes of Großdöllner See and Wuckersee during the purge of Jewish Germans out of Nazi Germany in the years leading up to WWII. It was known to be one of Goering's favorites and he bragged about it constantly to other Nazi brass. It is of note that he also stole another renowned van Gogh; that being one of the two Portraits of Dr. Gachet.

Portrait of Dr. Gachet, 1890, 1st Version; looted by the Nazi's in 1937

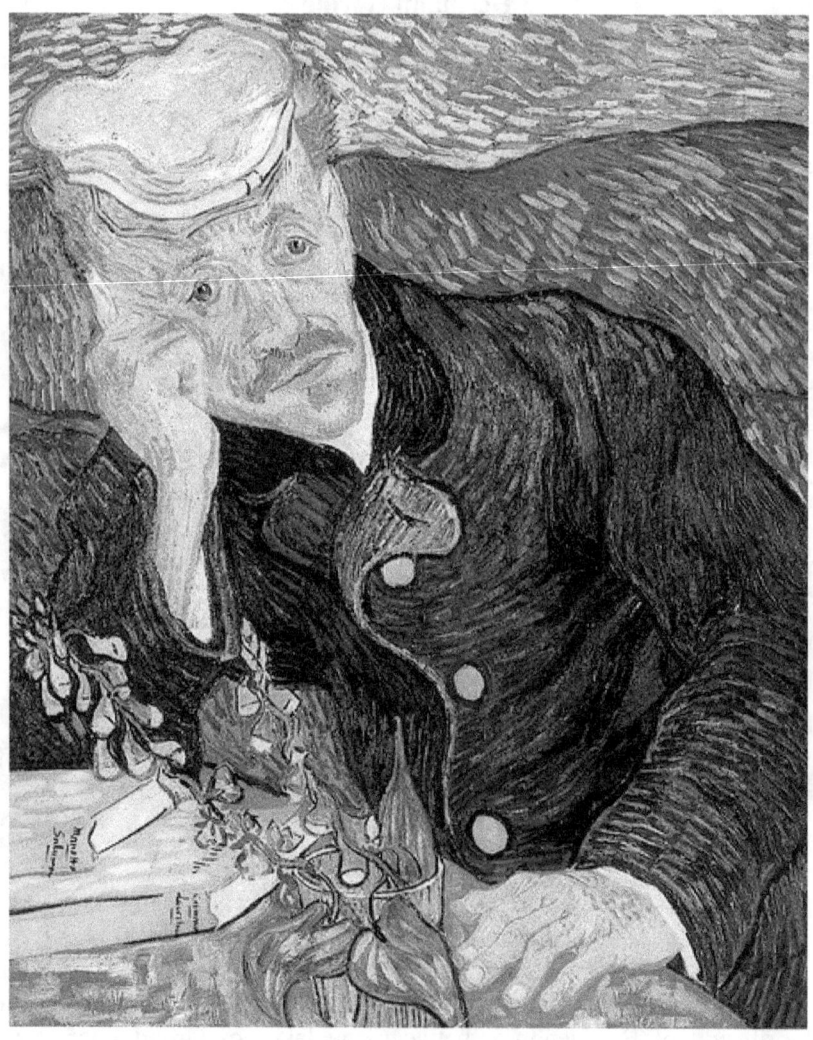

As he often did with many of his works that he could not sell right out of the gate, which was almost all of them, Vincent van Gogh painted two different versions of his famous Portrait of Doctor Gachet. In his final days it was Dr. Paul Gachet with whom van Gogh resided following another admission to the mental asylum in Saint-Rémy-de-Provence, the two men grew close and as he often did with those he took a liking to Vincent painted two portraits of Gachet who had become a confidant and close friend.

The above version was eventually sold after van Gogh died in 1911 to The Städel Art Museum of Frankfurt, Germany. In 1937, 77 paintings and 700 prints were confiscated from the museum when the Nazi regime declared the almost 800 paintings and prints "degenerate art". Much of this "degenerate art" was parted out to Nazi statesmen, such as those looted by Reichsmarschall Hermann Göring who hung it on the wall of his noted estate Carinhall. Oh, that degenerate art made the big, fate Nazi do it!

Eventually an allied platoon nicknamed the "Monuments Men"—an art historian, an architect, a museum director, and an art curator—were able to recover Dr. Gachet along with millions of other stolen Nazi art and loot and return them to their rightful owners, heirs, and countries.

In May 1990 the painting was sold to Japanese businessman Ryoei Saito $82.5 whose family in turn sold it again privately in 1997 after his death for an undisclosed amount. Dr. Gachet *numero uno* now rest peacefully under lock and key in the private estate of Austrian-born investment fund manager Wolfgang Flöttl.

Portrait of Dr. Gachet, 1890, 2nd Version

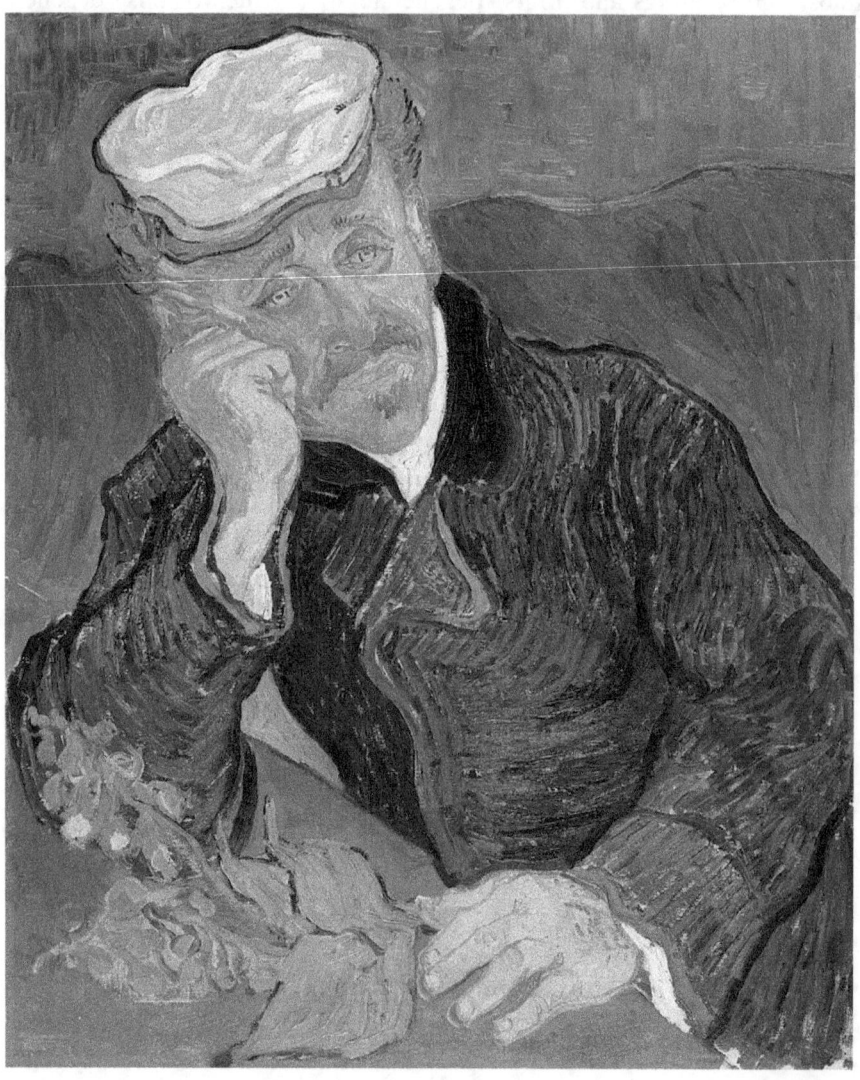

The I-wasn't-stolen-by-the-Nazi's version of *The Portrait of Doctor Gachet* was bequeath to Doctor Gachet himself and resided with his family for over half a century until they graciously donated it to the people of France in the 1950's. It currently hangs on display at the Musée d'Orsay in Paris, France. Of course, because several members of the Gachet family, including Doctor Gachet himself, painted themselves and often made copies of famous works which they always marked as copies it cast doubt on the authenticity of 2nd version of Doctor Gachet. Alas, science is king.

When tested in 1999 by the Musée d'Orsay it was found that the Gachet paintings were always drawn with outlines and then painted in, where van Gogh never used this amateur technique. Also, infrared, chemical, and ultraviolet analysis showed that the painting's pigments and canvas matched those of van Goghs and did not match any known Gachet knockoff. We can all sleep better now I guess. If not there is always absinthe or Xanax.

La cueillette des olives (Olive Picking), 1889; looted by the Nazi's during WWII

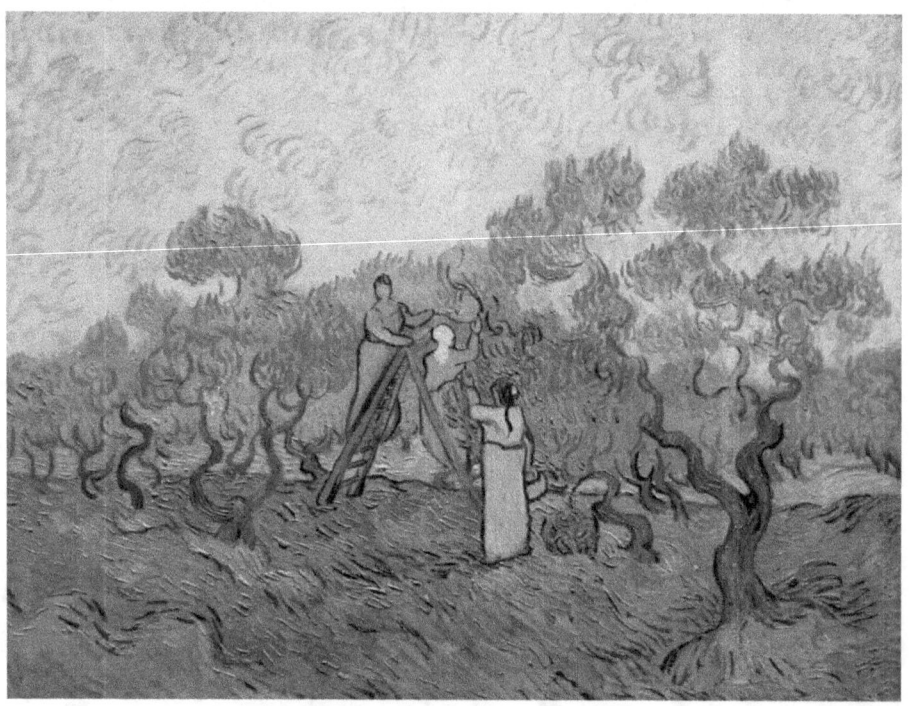

Owned by Hedwig Stern in Munich, Germany, the breathtaking *La cueillette des olives (Olive Picking)* that dates to 1889 at the Saint-Rémy mental asylum outside amid the olive groves inside van Gogh's memory it was seized by the Nazi regime in 1936 along with a Renoir that the Stern family owned when Mrs. Hedwig Stern fled Germany for the safety of American and Berkeley, California, along with her children and husband Fritz.

In 1938 the two stolen paintings that belonged to the Stern family were sold without authorization by the now "Aryanized" Thannhauser Gallery to a one Theodor Werner for $55,000 Reichsmarks. It was bought in 1972 by the Metropolitan Museum of Art in New York City from Italian industrialist Gianni Agnielli under a cloud of suspicion that has not gone away even to this day.

As of December, 2023 the Metropolitan stands by its decision to keep the painting as a part of the museum's illustrious inventory and the Stern family is left out in the cold without their pink twilight and olive grove trees that once looked down on them so happily in the parlor of their house in Munich. Such is life in the big city; isn't that right?

Sunflowers, 1888

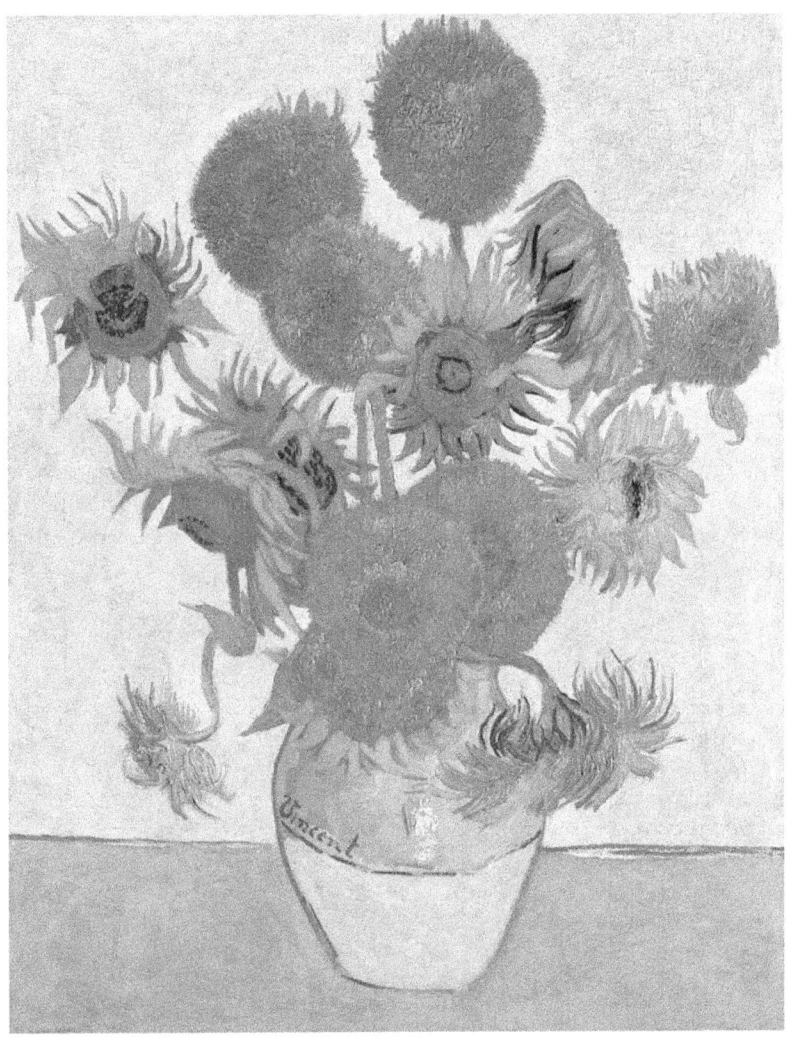

Sunflowers (with yellow-gold background) is yet again another amid many Vincent van Gogh works of art that German Jewish owners were forced to sell off during the 1930 era when the Nazi regime constantly harassed, harangued, and bullied Germans and Austrians of Jewish descent. It is a common story only validated by the 1938 pogrom *Kristallnacht*, or the Night of Broken Glass, in which the Nazi regime coordinated a wave of antisemitic violence throughout Germany and Austria: smashing the storefronts of German Jewish owned businesses, burning synagogues to the ground, beating up German Jewish citizens, on camera in the street no less (see YouTube).

In early November of 1938 more than 1,000 synagogues were purposely set on fire and burned to the ground while fire brigades stood by the burning synagogues with explicit instructions not to intervene. 7,500 Austrian and German Jewish businesses were ransacked and looted. 91 Germans of Jewish descent were murdered. 30,000 Germans of Jewish descent were summarily arrested. Even German Jewish cemeteries were desecrated. So, too, were Jewish homes, schools, hospitals, restaurants, and social clubs.

As for *Sunflowers* (with a yellow-gold background), its rightful owner, Paul von Mendelssohn-Bartholdy, sold it under duress during this volatile time period in Nazi Germany in order to use the money to protect his family, home, and his other assets. Decades later it was purchased by the Japanese firm Yasuda Fire and Marine for $39.9 million dollars. They quickly and proudly put it on display at the Sompo Museum of Art, where it still resides.

As of January 2023 the heirs of Mendelssohn-Bartholdy are currently in a court battle with Yasuda to try and have *Sunflowers* returned to the family. But we've seen this movie before haven't we? Get your popcorn ready. This should be a good one!

Madame Roulin and Her Baby, 1888

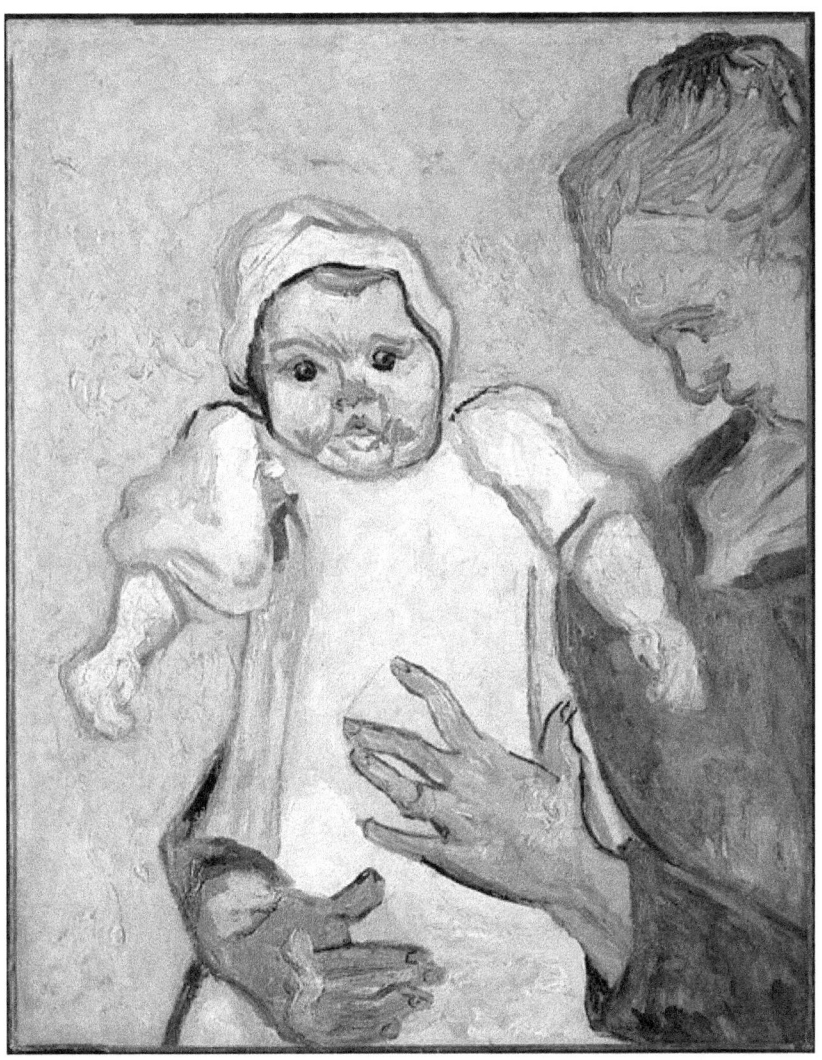

Painted in 1888 after van Gogh moved from Paris out to the countryside of Arles, *Madame Roulin and Her Baby* depicts Augustine and Marcelle Roulin, the wife and three-month old daughter of local postman Joseph Roulin who van Gogh would also famously paint many times as the two became close friends. This painting was another van Gogh of Nazi Germany that had been owned Paul von Mendelssohn-Bartholdy in which he was forced to sell under Nazi persecuted. It currently hangs in the Metropolitan Museum of Art, Manhattan, New York City.

Other portraits of the Roulin family, 1888

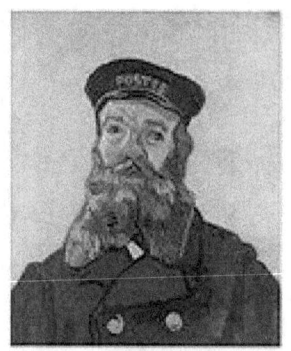

Joseph

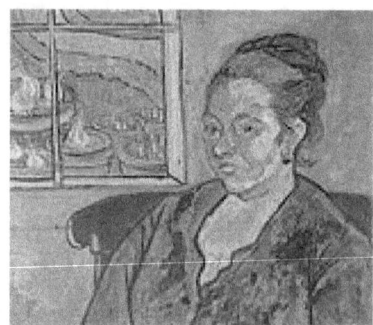

Augustine

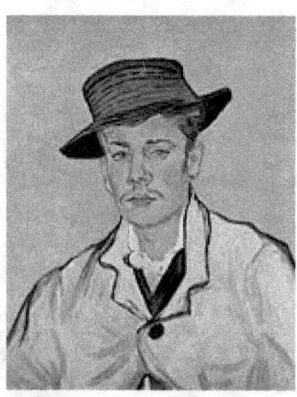

Armand

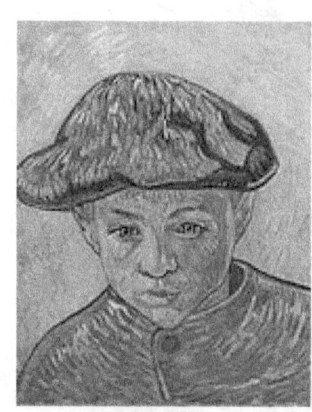

Camille

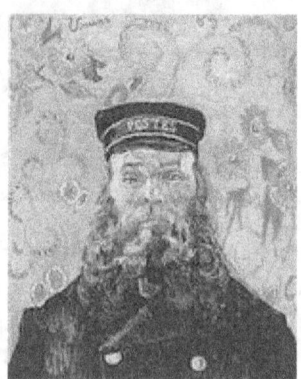

Another of Joseph

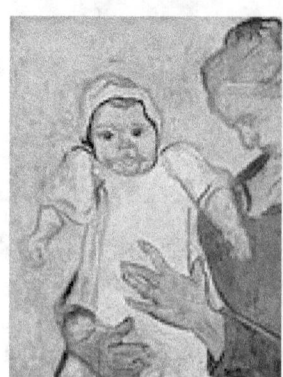

Augustine and Marcelle

View of the Asylum and Chapel of Saint-Rémy, 1889

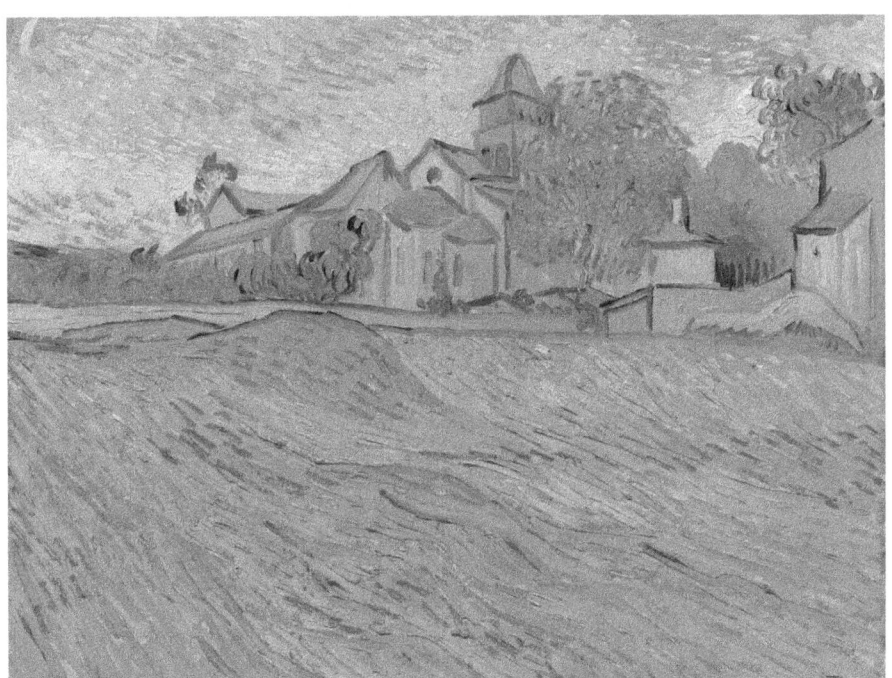

Painted in autumn 1889 at Saint-Rémy, France, where Vincent was convinced to voluntarily incarcerate himself at the mental asylum, *View of the Asylum and Chapel of Saint-Rémy* is a breathtaking example of the landscapes he painted while under doctor supervision inside the hospital. Pink-green brushstrokes of sky float against silver-blue with dotted and swirled clouds on the horizon. The cathedral and houses are blue. The fields of grass and wheat are blue. The entire countryside of Provence is blue aside for a few wisps of trees and scrub and a heap of golden hued hay raked up against a storehouse. It is truly a stunning masterpiece.

This work was owned by German art collector Margarete Mauthner. Due to some of her family having Jewish heritage she was targeted by the Nazi regime and constantly hounded by Hitler's minions. While she secretly helped many members of her family escape Germany as it invaded both Poland and Czechoslovakia, Margarete had little time to escape but with a suitcase and the close on her back. She was forced to leave her home and expansive art collection behind in late 1939 when she too escape Nazi Germany. Of course, her collection was sniffed out by the truffle noses of the likes of Hermann Göring where it disappeared into the colorless ether of WWII. Decades later Hollywood icon and movie star Elizabeth Taylor wound up owning *View of the Asylum and Chapel of Saint-Rémy*. When this came into public knowledge Elizabeth Taylor was sued by the heirs of Margarete Mauthner for return of the precious painting, but the lawsuit was dismissed because the court held that California's statute of limitations had expired. Afterwards, Elizabeth Taylor sold the painting for a cool 13 million. As good ol' Liz was once quoted as saying: "It's not the having, it's the getting." Nice.

Seascape near Les Saintes-Maries-de-la-Mer, 1888

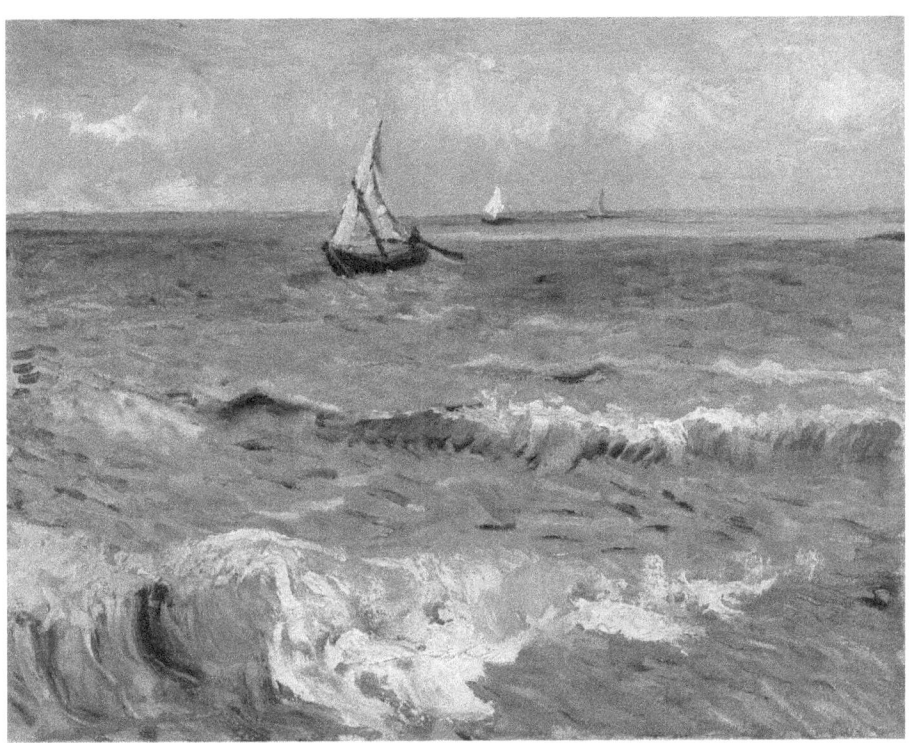

In June of 1888 Vincent van Gogh took a little sabbatical to the coastal fishing village of Les Saintes-Maries-de-la-Mer, where during the trip he was so moved by the beauty of the ocean and the sandy beach that he setup his easel on shore and painted *Seascape near Les Saintes-Maries-de-la-Mer*. How do we know he painted the seascape right there on the beach of Les Saintes-Maries-de-la-Mer? Quite simply really. Upon close examination almost one-hundred years after he painted this wonderful delight there was found to be grains of beach sand mixed in onto the canvas and within the many layers of blue, white, and emerald paint. I bet the bad boy didn't even wipe his feet when he came in the door home each night. *Tsk tsk.* The painting is currently housed at the Van Gogh Museum in Amsterdam in the Netherlands.

It should be noted that a van Gogh sketch of the above once was held amid the stolen collection of Margarete Mauthner. It was sold under Nazi persecution and now resides in the Am Römerholz Museum in Winterthur, Zürich, Switzerland.

Head of Man, 1886

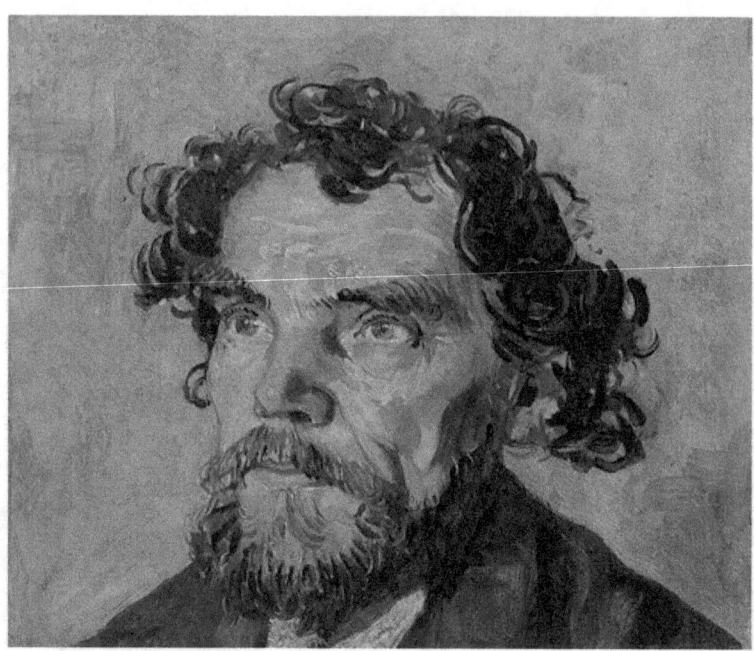

Vincent van Gogh liked to paint the heads of both men and women. Too much so. This once disputed van Gogh full of the unruly brown curls of a blue-eyed man, which has now been authenticated with the help and detective work of art enthusiast, actor, and all-around Renaissance man, Antonio De Robertis, after decades of controversy is of Ukrainian painter, Ivan Pavlovic Pokhitonov, who studied and lived across the street from the Académie Julian in Paris where van Gogh often visited with various contemporary artists of the day, such as Paul Sérusier; Paul Gauguin, and Pierre Bonnard. The portrait currently resides in the National Gallery of Victoria, in Melbourne, Victoria, Australia.

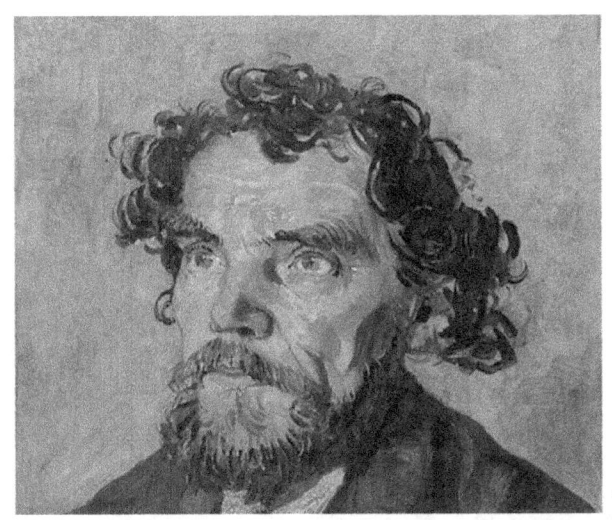

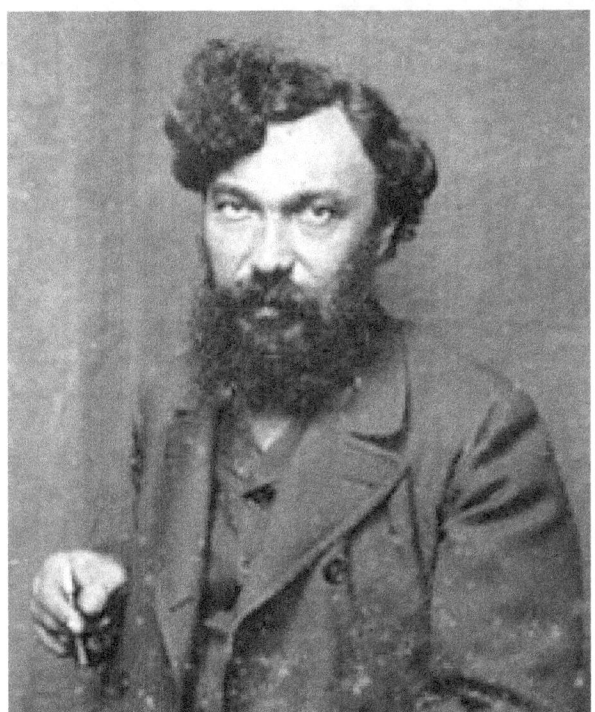

Ukrainian painter, Ivan Pavlovic Pokhitonov

The Green Vineyard, 1888

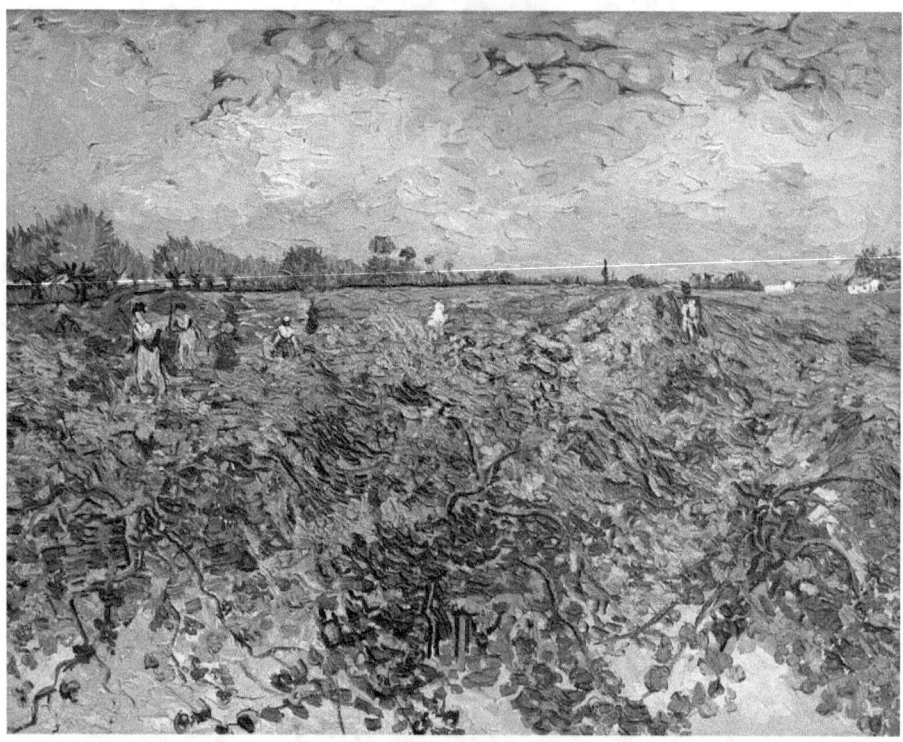

On 23 October 1888 Gauguin, after repeated requests, finally arrived in Arles to live with Vincent in the famed Yellow House. Throughout November 1888 the two painters lived and worked together. When the weather was bad — Gauguin had seemingly brought the rain with him from the north — they painted from memory, or de tête. After a stroll one Sunday evening, when they had been living together for 13 days, Vincent painted The Red Vineyard, having earlier painted The Green Vineyard.

Kröller-Müller Museum in Otterlo in the Netherlands

Vase with Carnations, 1886

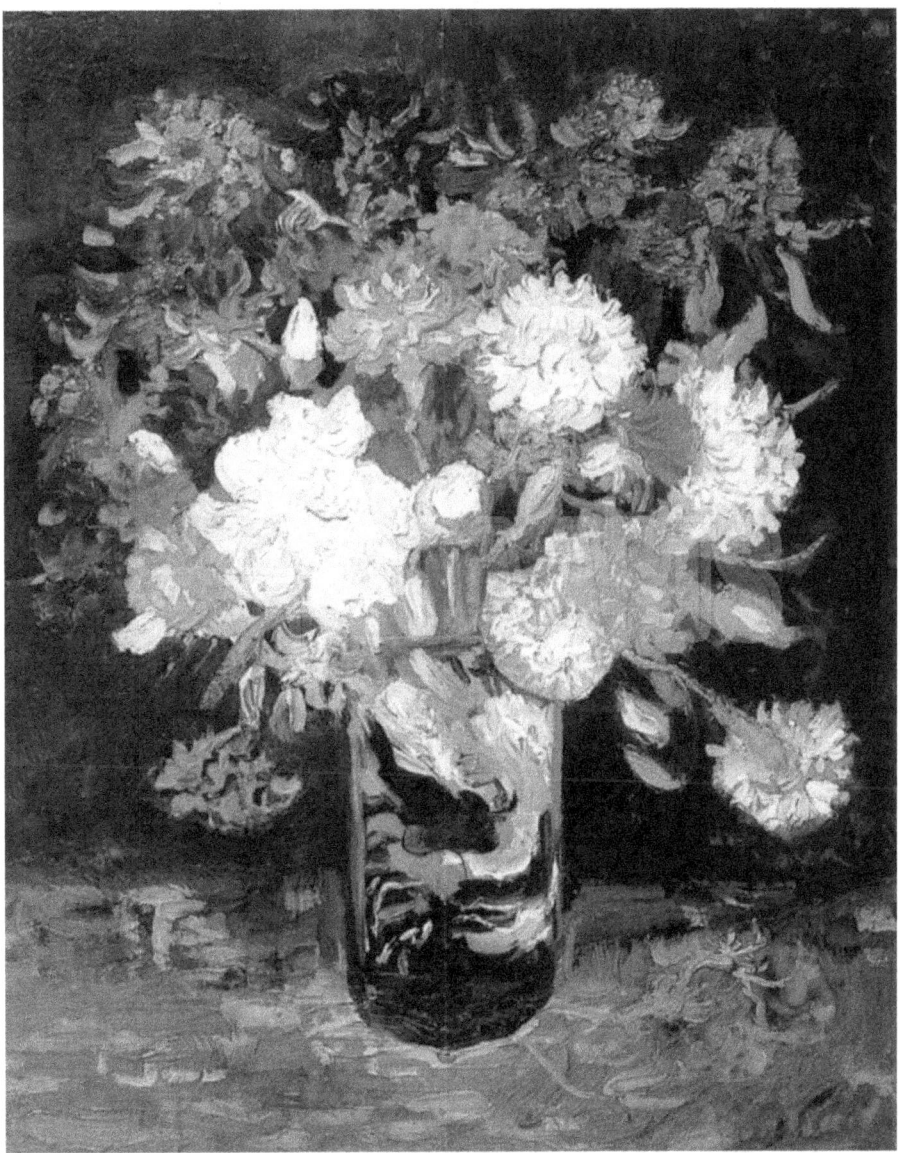

The elegant *Vase with Carnations* was painted in the 1886 time period. It shows pink plump carnations with red and in a blue-black swirled vase. Prior to WWII it became part of the collection of German Jewish art dealers Albert and Hedwig Ullmann. Like many others in their position they were forced to sell the painting at a reduced price before they immediately fled Nazi

Germany. The heirs of the family have requested its return, but it currently remains on display at the Detroit Institute of Arts in Detroit, Michigan.

Still life with Oleanders, August 1888

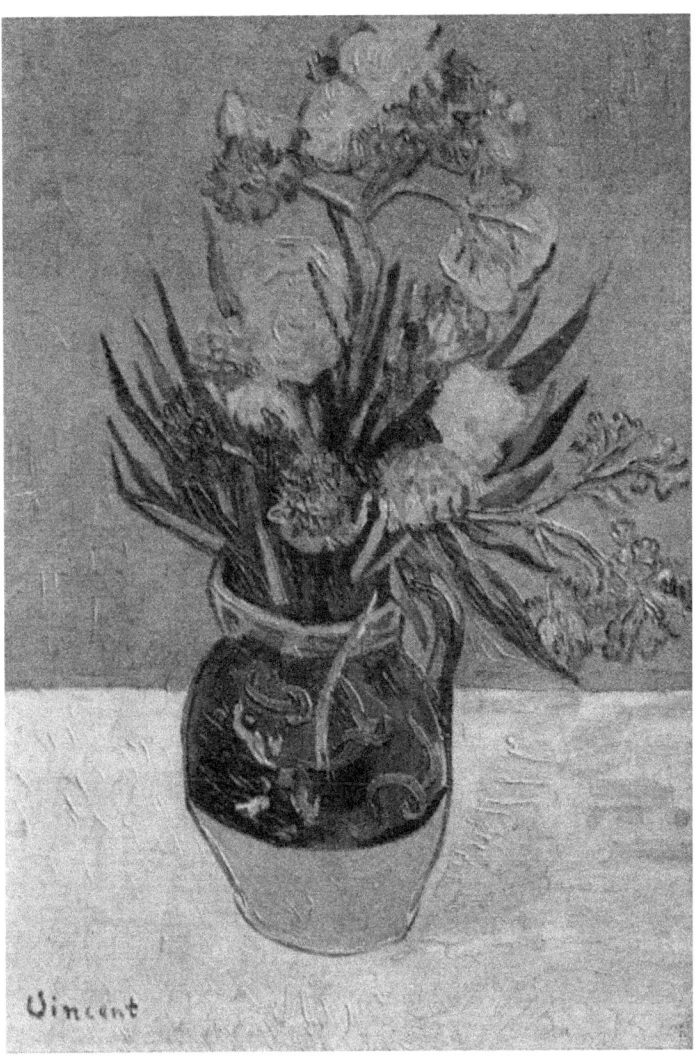

Painted the week in August 1998 as van Gogh's famous Sunflowers still life, Still life with Oleanders features the same pot as the sunflowers portrait he painted in the countryside of Arles. Vincent bequeath his work as a gift to his postman and friend Joseph Roulin that same summer. Almost two decades later the Bernheim Jeune family of France purchased the painting. With the Nazi's blitzkrieg rolling through France the family took the paintings and other works by Manet, Renoir, and Cezanne and remained them from their frames, rolled up the canvases, and hid them in a secret compart inside a trunk they hid in the attic it their château of Rastignac in the Dordogne in the southwest of France. Alas, the Nazi's found them out in March 1944 and five trucks arrived that they used to loot all the belongings of the Bernheim Jeune family before burning the château down to the ground. Still life with Oleanders has not been seen since.

Tree with Ivy in the Garden of the Asylum No. 1, May-June 1889

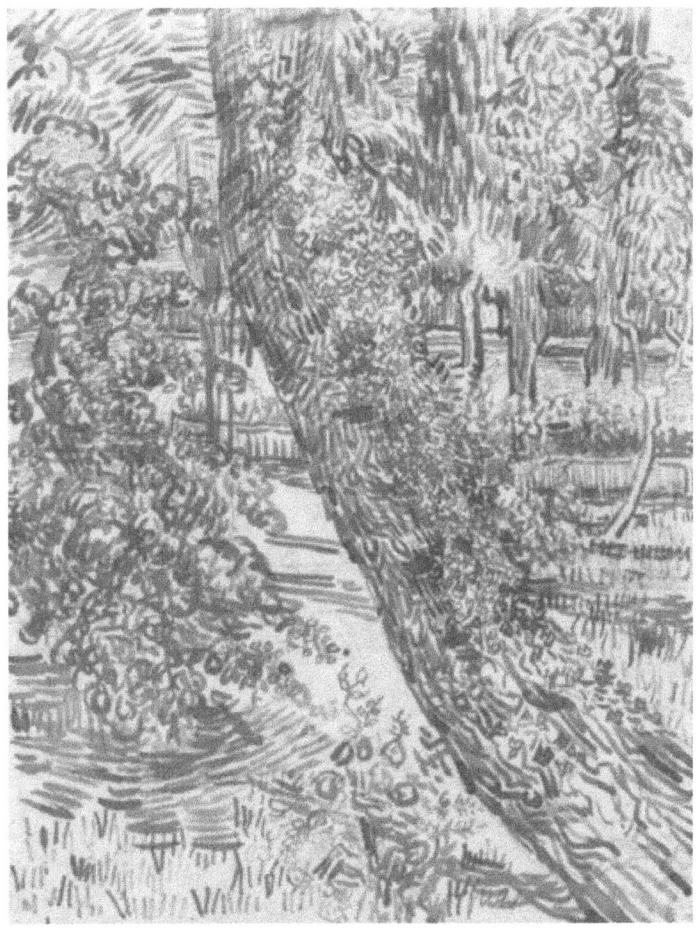

Concocted by van Gogh with reed pen, brush, pencil, ink on paper this drawing was 18 x 24 and created inside the hospital at Saint-Rémy-de-Provence. It depicts the asylum garden outside van Gogh's window that looks alive with movement and flora and fauna.

Trees with Ivy in the Garden of the Asylum, June-July 1889

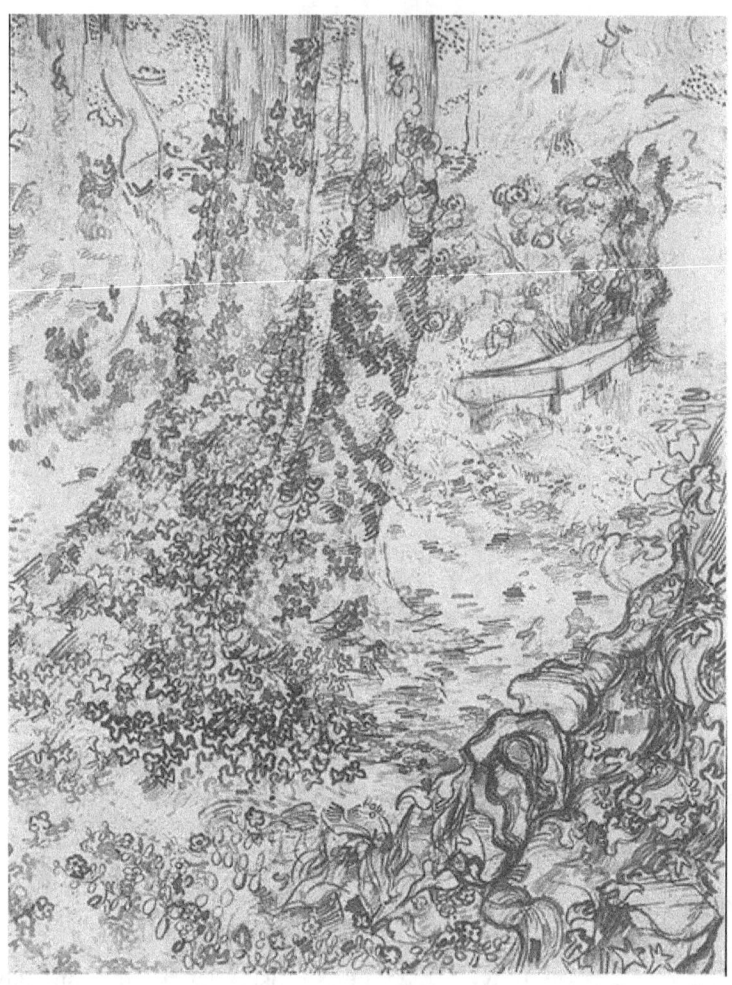

Also concocted by van Gogh with reed pen, brush, pencil, ink on paper the dimensions of this drawing are 18 x 24 as well. It too was created inside the hospital at Saint-Rémy-de-Provence. It depicts the asylum garden outside van Gogh's window that is lush wild ivy creeping up the trunks of the garden trees next to a granite bench he was quite familiar with from his stays at the asylum.

Vincent drew this sketch for his brother Theo to whom he wrote the following about his hospital stay and the above work of art:

"Here's a new no. 30 canvas, commonplace again, like one of those chromos from a penny bazaar that depict eternal nests of greenery for lovers.

Thick tree-trunks covered with ivy, the ground also covered with ivy and periwinkle, a stone bench and a bush of roses, blanched in the cold shadow. In the foreground a few plants with white calyxes. It's green, violet and pink.

It's just a question — which is unfortunately lacking in chromos from a penny bazaar and barrel organs — of putting in some style.

Since I've been here, the neglected garden planted with tall pines under which grows tall and badly tended grass intermingled with various weeds, has provided me with enough work, and I haven't yet gone outside.

However, the landscape of St-Rémy is very beautiful, and little by little I'm probably going to make trips into it. But staying here as I am, the doctor has naturally been in a better position to see what was wrong, and will, I dare hope, be more reassured that he can let me paint.

I assure you that I'm very well here, and that for the time being I see no reason at all to come and board in Paris or its surroundings. I have a little room with grey-green paper with two water-green curtains with designs of very pale roses enlivened with thin lines of blood-red. These curtains, probably the leftovers of a ruined, deceased rich man, are very pretty in design. Probably from the same source comes a very worn armchair covered with a tapestry flecked in the manner of a Diaz or a Monticelli, red-brown, pink, creamy white, black, forget-me-not blue and bottle green.

Through the iron-barred window I can make out a square of wheat in an enclosure, a perspective in the manner of Van Goyen, above which in the morning I see the sun rise in its glory.

With this — as there are more than 30 empty rooms — I have another room in which to work.

The food is so-so. It smells naturally a little musty, as in a cockroach-ridden restaurant in Paris or a boarding school. As these unfortunates do absolutely nothing (not a book, nothing to distract them but a game of boules and a game of draughts) they have no other daily distraction than to stuff themselves with chickpeas, haricot beans, lentils and other groceries and colonial foodstuffs by the regulated quantities and at fixed times."

Vincent, 1889

The painting was later part of the collection of the De Rothschild family that was located in Paris, France. After the German occupation of the city of light the work was looted from the De Rothschild estate and taken to the Nazi storage facility at the Jeu de Paume gallery, where, of course, it was one of those works truffled out by the Nazi nose of Hermann Göring as seen in the following photograph.

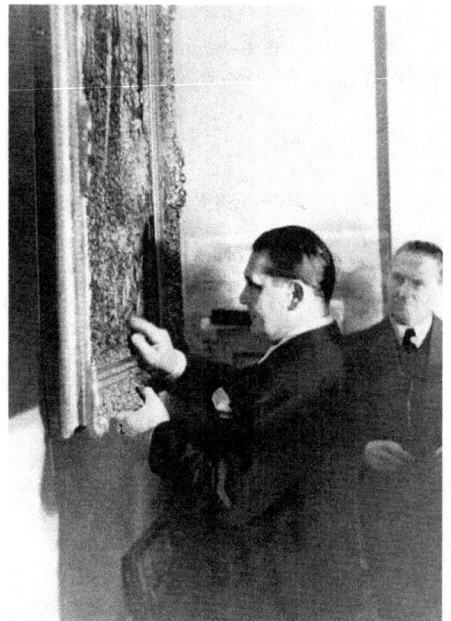

*Hermann Göring and his art advisor Walter Hofer
with van Gogh's Trees with Ivy in the Garden
of the Asylum No. 2, photographed by
Heinrich Hoffmann (1942).*

As previously noted, Hermann Göring was obsessed with the work of van Gogh and it has been said that he took this painting for his own collection. No trace of the painting has ever been found after WWII and it is quite possible that it is out there somewhere hidden in the underground of the art collector world, or more likely secret hung on someone's well decorated mansion wall.

Gesundheit dear *fräulein* Trees with Ivy!

Hospital at Saint-Rémy-de -Provence, 1889

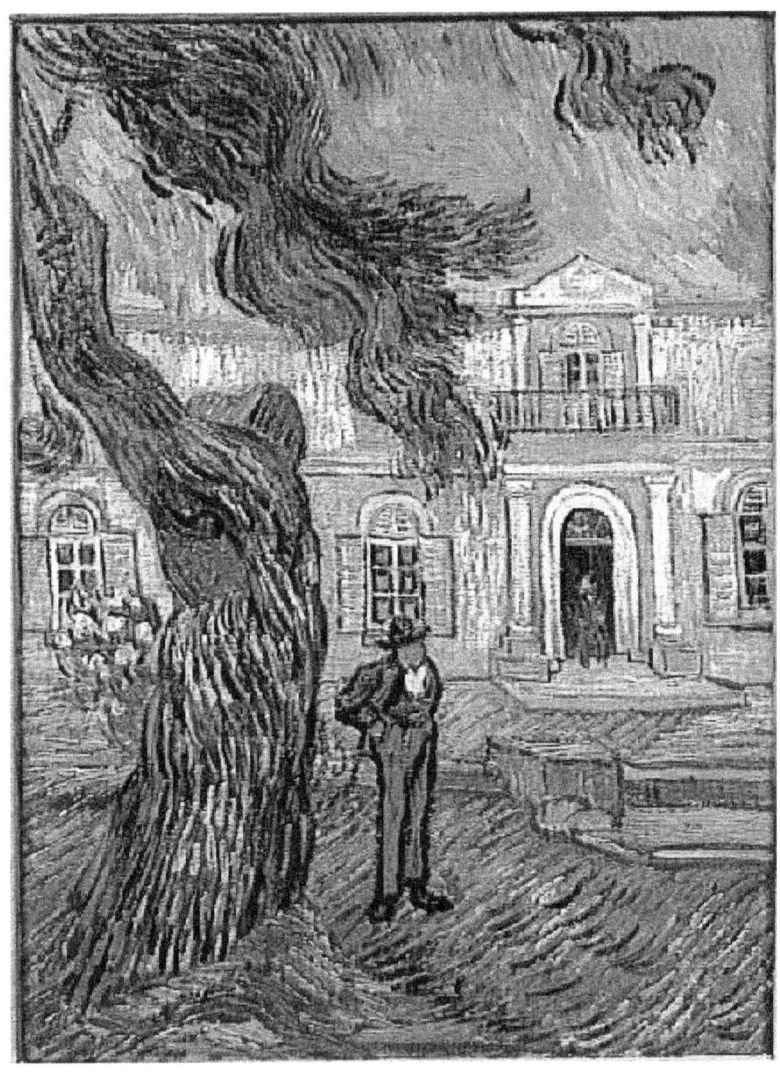

A smallish portrait of the Mental Asylum at Saint-Rémy that stands just 18 x 23 inches tall, *Hospital at Saint-Rémy-de -Provence* represents everything about the work of Vincent van Gogh that is spectacular. The swimming brushstrokes of blue sky, the way the wind seems to be shift and lift and blow the boughs and greenery of the gorgeous evergreen; not to mention the bejeweled light-emerald shutters and the gold and blood-orange motifs of the hospital façade. It shows a disturbed mind whose soul and eyes could still see and appreciate the beauty in the world ... even outside a mental hospital. Now that is gravitas!

The Garden of Saint-Paul Hospital October, 1889

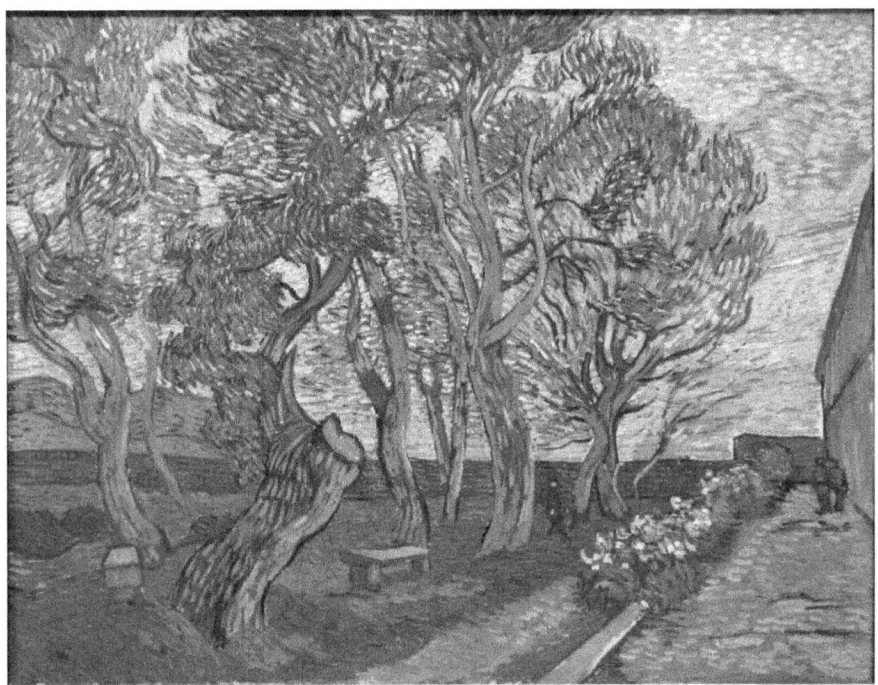

Van Gogh painted two landscapes corner of Saint-Remy hospital gardens while at the hospital in 1889. The best description of both is stated best by van Gogh himself in his letter to Émile Bernard about his latest two achievements:

"A view of the garden of the asylum where I am, on the right a gray terrace, a section the house, some rosebushes that have lost their flowers; on the left, the earth of the garden – red ochre – earth burnt by the sun, covered in fallen pine twigs. This edge of the garden is planted with large pines with red ochre trunks and branches, with green foliage saddened by a mixture of black. These tall trees stand out against an evening sky streaked with violet against a yellow background. High up, the yellow turns to pink, turns to green. A wall – red ocher again – blocks the view, and there's nothing above it but a violet and yellow ochre hill. Now, the first tree is an enormous trunk, but struck by lightning and sawn off. A side branch, thrusts up very high, however, and falls down again in an avalanche of dark green twigs. This dark giant – like a proud man brought low – contrasts, when seen as the character of a living being, with the pale smile of the last rose on the bush, which is fading in front of him. Under the trees, empty stone benches, dark box. The sky is reflected yellow in a puddle after the rain. A ray of sun – the last glimmer – exalts the dark ocher to orange – small dark figures prowl here and there between the trunks.

You'll understand that this combination of red ochre, of green saddened with grey, of black lines that define the outlines, this gives rise a little to the feeling of anxiety from which some of my companions in misfortune often suffer, and which is called 'seeing red. And what's more, the motif of the great tree struck by lightning, the sickly pink and green smile of the last flower of autumn, confirms this idea."

A Corner of Saint-Paul Hospital and the Garden with a Heavy, Sawed-Off Tree, 1889

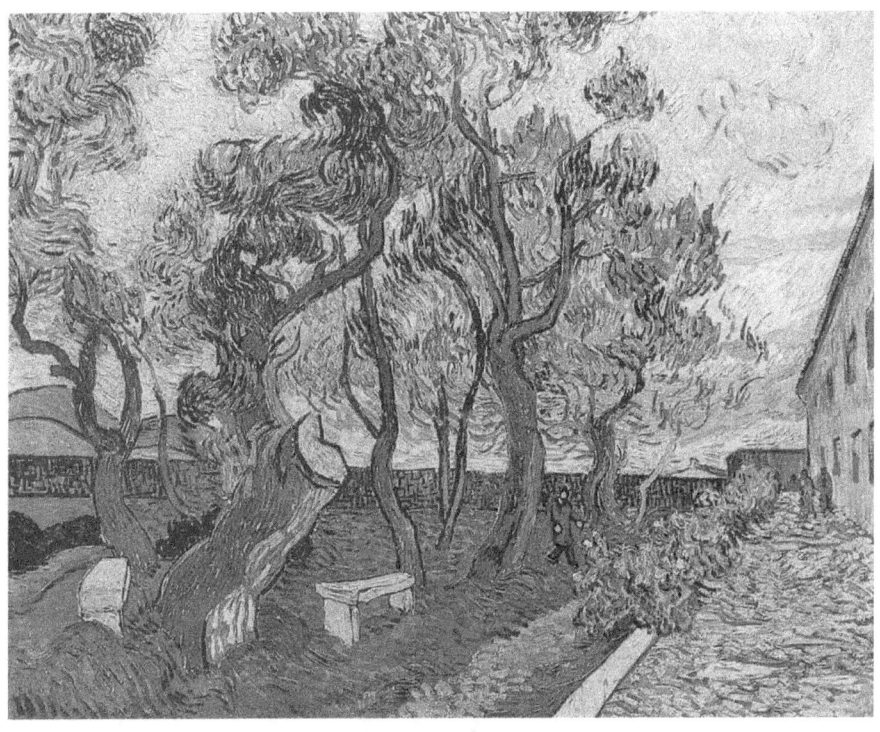

Great Peacock Moth (Death's-Head Moth on an Arum) 1889

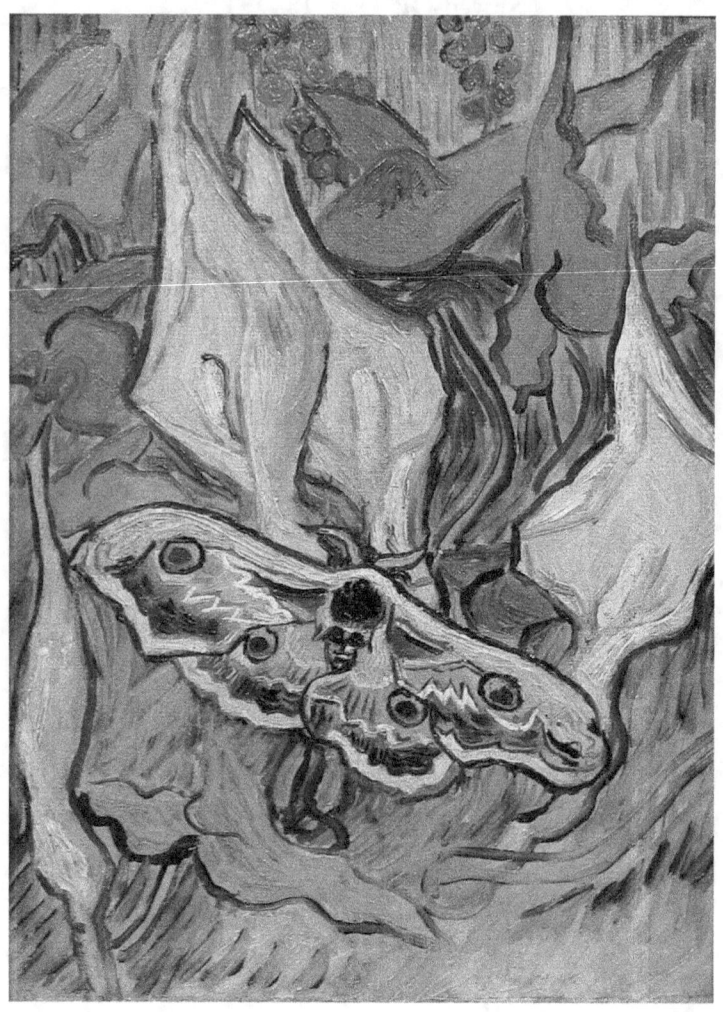

This beautiful portrait of an aquamarine colored great peacock moth amid garden calla lilies and bright red berries is a unique blend of old and new style van Gogh that he painted in 1889. As per usual, everything looks as though it is in transient motion, even the kaleidoscopic lightning bolts, hues of metallic blues that shift in height like tides, and those spotted circles on the moth that allow us to imagine its whole magnificence as though we might be standing right there beside van Gogh in the asylum garden painting this wonder amid the speckles of light and dust motes that shift and shrug and circle around back with us on the summer day of 1889.

Still Life of Oranges and Lemons with Blue Gloves, 1889

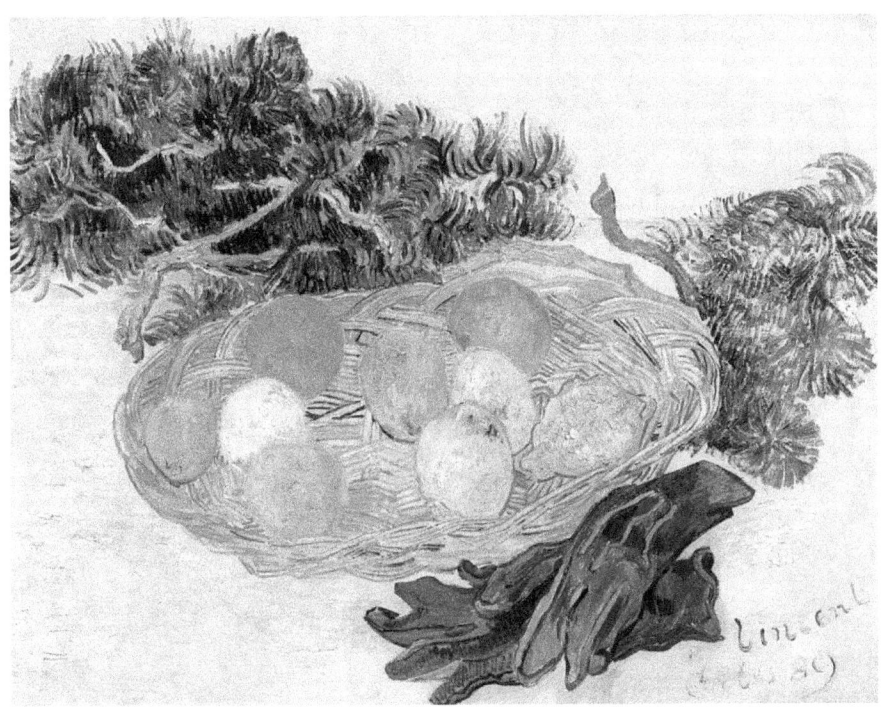

Still Life of Oranges and Lemons with Blue Gloves was painted in 1889 in between van Gogh's dual stints at the mental asylum following Paul Gauguin's brief but turbulent 63 days with him amid the four rooms Vincent rented at the Yellow House on the street corner of Place Lamartinein in Arles. The portrait is vibrant, colors spot on, but looks done in haste and without the usual broken brushstrokes Vincent later became so known for. This was a work to be sold for money, which is understandable since Gauguin is gone now, Vincent has half a left ear, and he's been locked away a while having no means to support himself. Some bright citrus in an oil on canvas with a pair of blue gloves just might do.

In a letter to Theo he describes this portrait as having an "air of chic" to it. Maybe this would have been true in the more cosmopolitan Paris, but alas he found himself in between hospital stays in Arles, where "chic" was probably considered a dirty word with a capital C. In his day the painting never sold. It currently belongs to the collection of the National Gallery of Art in Washington DC.

Enclosed Wheat Field with Rising Sun, May 1889

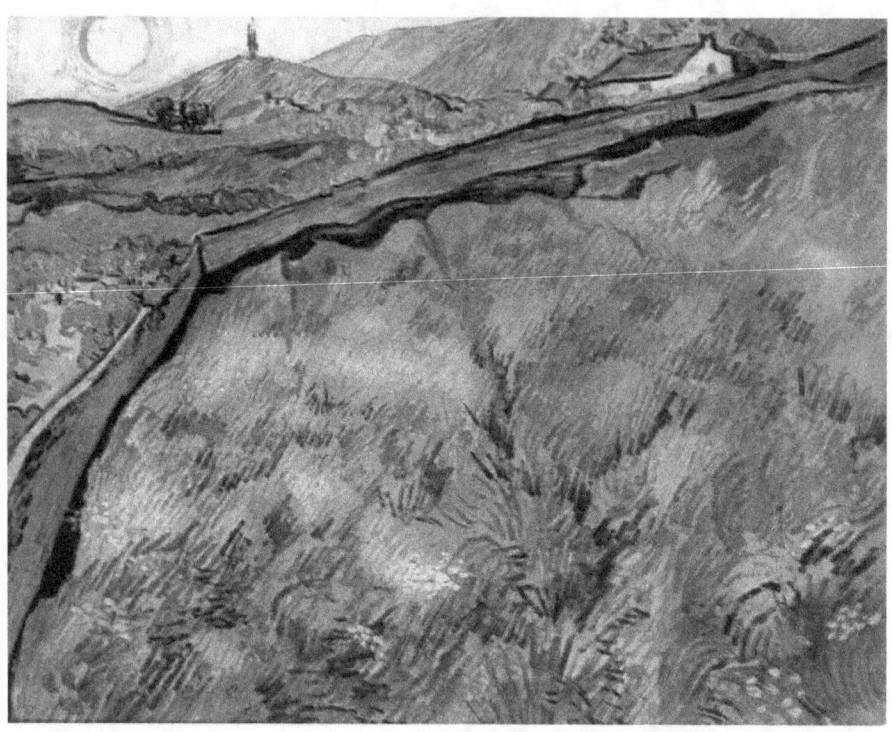

Red poppy, red tile roofed cottages, lush yellow and spring green wheat full of dew with the blue hills of the nearby mountains distinguish this beautiful landscape from May 1889. Enclosed Wheat Field with Rising Sun now lives at the Kröller-Müller Museum in Otterlo in the Netherlands.

Mountainous Landscape Behind Saint-Rémy, June 1889

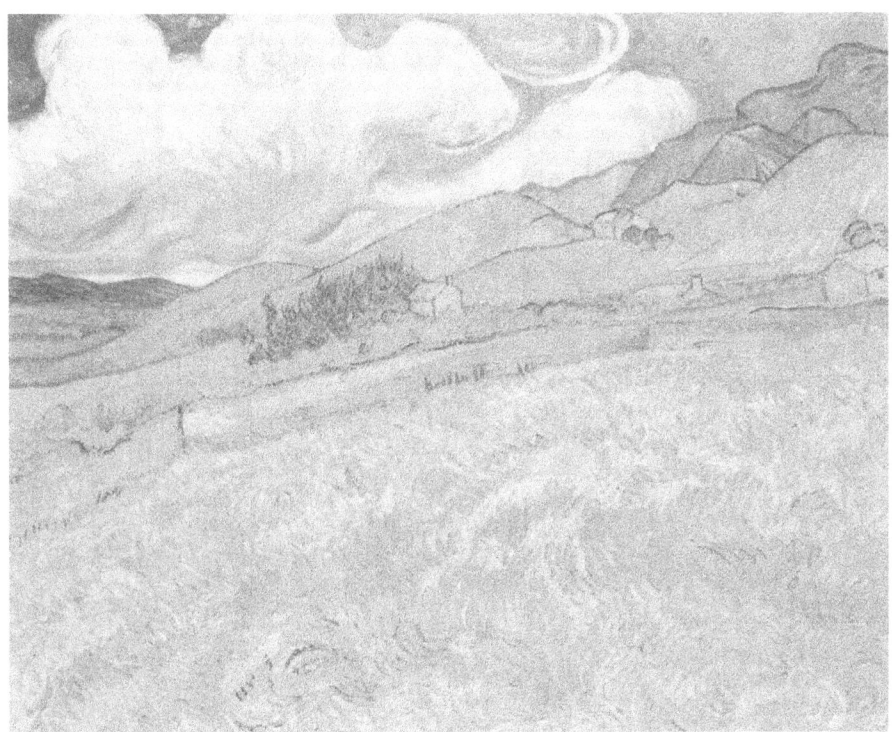

The blue rolling mountains of Saint-Rémy look harsher in noontime daylight compared with other landscapes of the alpines of the same time period. Noonday sun brightens the wheat fields, fades the red roofs of the nearby cottages to an almost opaque gray-red, and the sunlight washes out the fence of the fenced in wheat field. Schooled people of the 19th Century seemed to have more depth, more understanding of nature, time, and light than those of us who are currently living in the modern Internet age. Perhaps because they were learned from the great source of their day: actual books, which back in the 19th Century needed to be literate and written by studied experts who wrote in beautiful language, as opposed to someone locked in the basement of their parent's house while writing Steampunk fan fiction somewhere out on a 4CHAN thread.

Mountainous Landscape Behind Saint-Rémy, June 1889, now resides at the Ny Carlsberg Glyptotek Art Museum in Copenhagen, Denmark. It is very easy to look up directions to the museum out on the Internet. Just type its name in Google and press <Enter> "Oh, maybe just whistle. You know how to whistle, don't you, Steve? You just put your lips together and blow!"

Le Mont Gaussier with the Mas de Saint-Paul, 1889

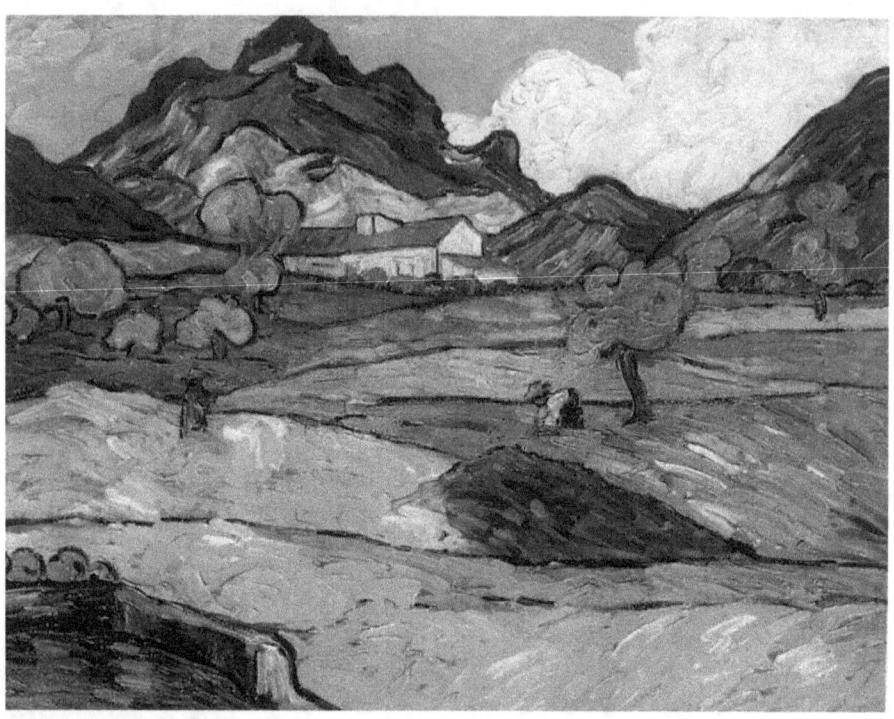

Twilight dim, ominous white and blue shouldered alpine mountains in the background, shifting shadows of various pigments of metallics and droll greens that rush in rapids that go moving forward across the rolling fields, *Le Mont Gaussier with the Mas de Saint-Paul* leaves us little Easter eggs all over the landscape with its lichen walls, a stark white farmhouse, its scattered olive trees, and a twilight green-teal sky with night clouds either rolling in or rolling out depending on the mood you are in that day.

A Meadow in the Mountains, 1889

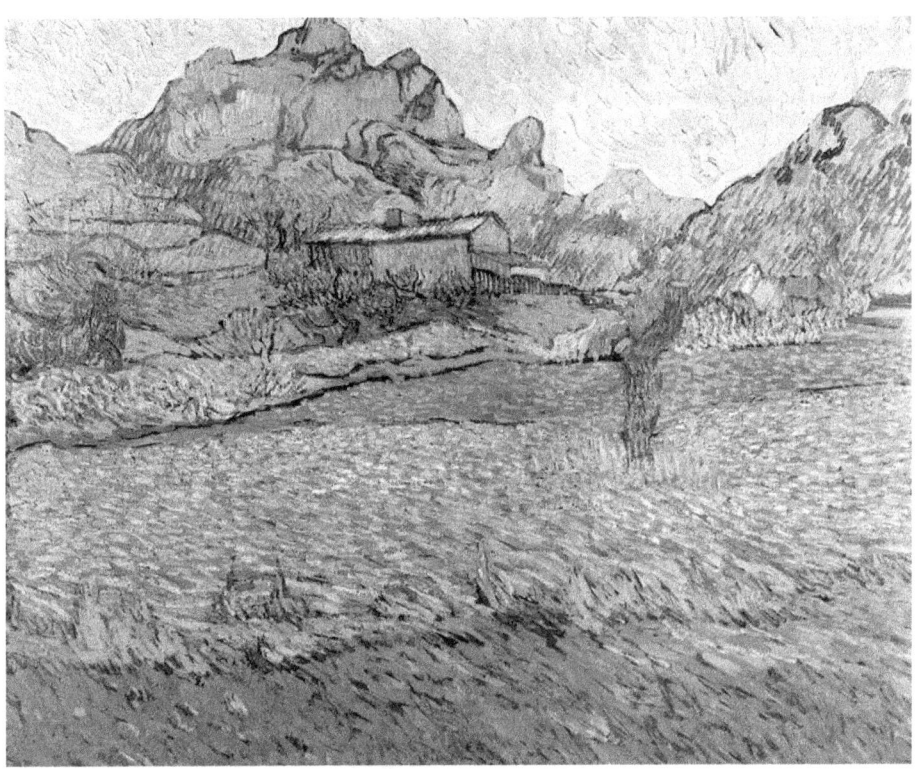

Another landscape van Gogh painted when he was permitted off the grounds of the asylum, A Meadow in the Mountains from December 1889 is one of the most beautiful and full of golden mid-day sunlight and sky. You can almost imagine yourself there amid the timothy and alfalfa as this area of Provence in France has not changed much since 1889. Thank heavens for minor miracles!

Vincent was so enamored with this Provincial landscape that he had it shipped back to his brother Theo the following month after having painted it. It now lights up and sparks the white of the walls of the Kröller-Müller Museum in Otterlo in the Netherlands.

The Trinquetaille Bridge, 1888

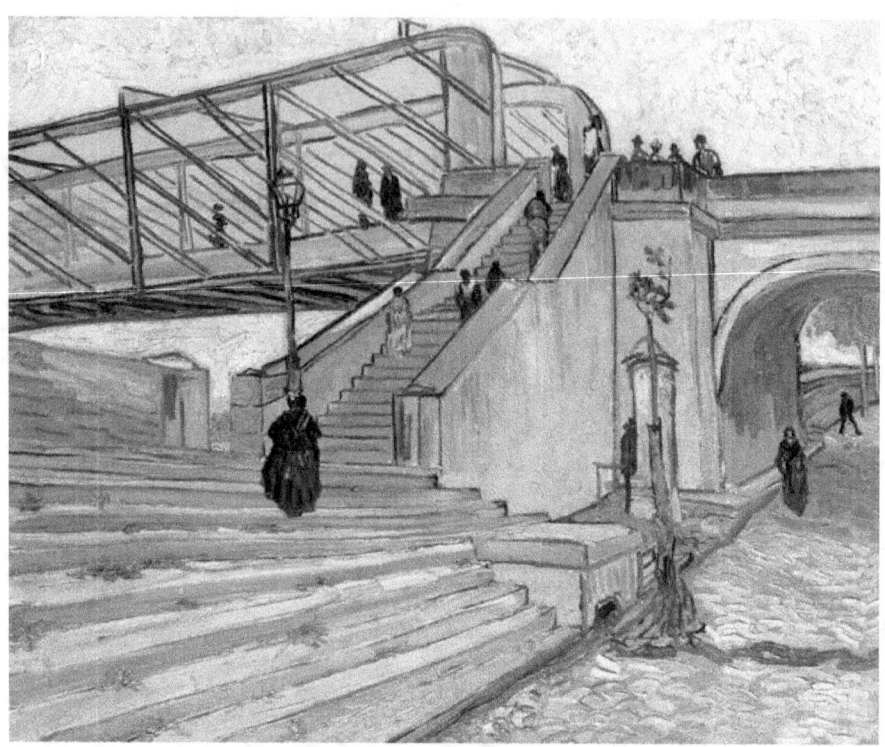

The more things change the more things stay the same. Could the Trinquetaille City Bridge at the delta of the Rhône look any less different than it does now in 2023-2024? The glass façade is no longer overhead and the public art deco urinal beside the bridge right off the street has been removed, but otherwise this still looks exactly as it did more than a century ago. There is something reassuring about such lesser monuments that most do not even take note of everyday unless it had once been painting in a masters repertoire.

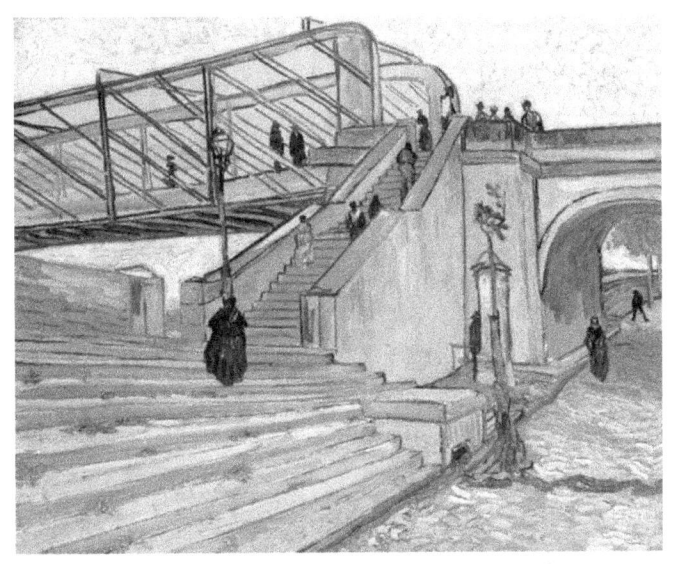

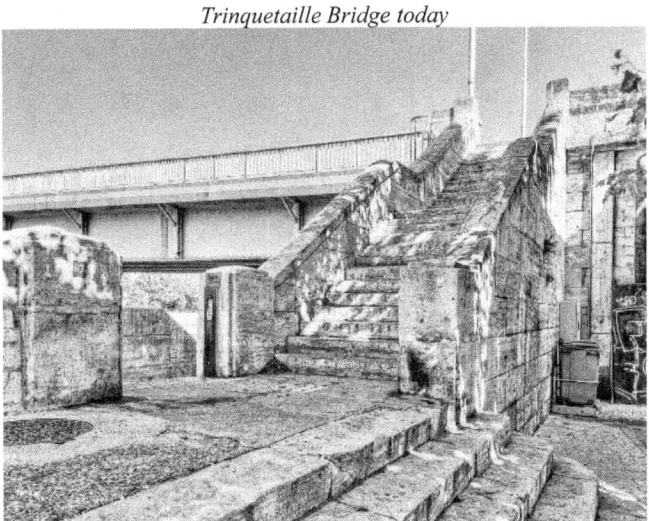

Trinquetaille Bridge today

Lilacs, May 1889

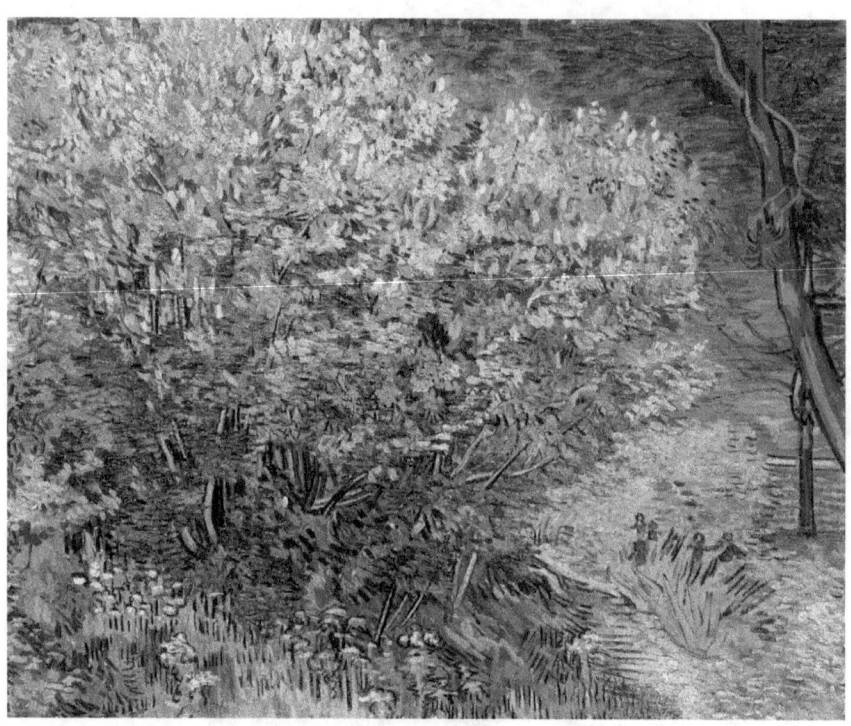

The simplicity of garden *Lilacs* from May 1889 exudes a supreme confidence and the appreciation of beauty by van Gogh in the subtle nuances of the height of the competing flowers of iris, forsythia, yarrow and marigolds all framed in by a dark purple sky and a brick and mortar stone wall all the while the earthen colored trunk of a cypress grows out of frame as though to tell us in a little whisper that there is so much more to the world than our trivial, pathetic little lives. Ain't that *not* a shame. *Lilacs* resides at the Hermitage Museum in St. Petersburg, Russia nowadays.

The Iris, May 1889

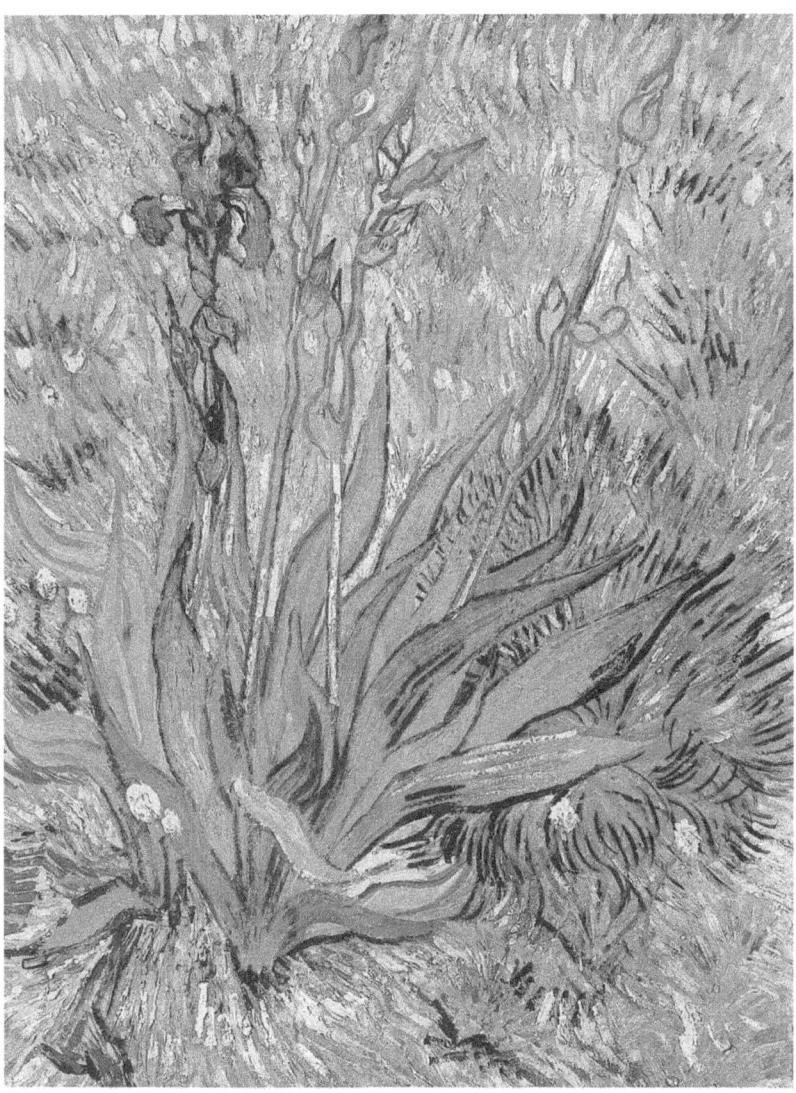

The only thing better than the portrait of *Irises* from May 1889 is this beautiful single iris featured in *The Iris* of the same time period. It seems more alive, more stately, and more blue than its big brother Irises and if a Sophie's Choice had to be done I'd personally take this one. But then again that won't be something any of us have to worry about. Unless you have a cool one-hundred million you can lend about. *The Iris* currently resides in the National Gallery of Canada in Ottawa, Canada.

Bowl With Sunflowers, Roses, And Other Flowers, 1887

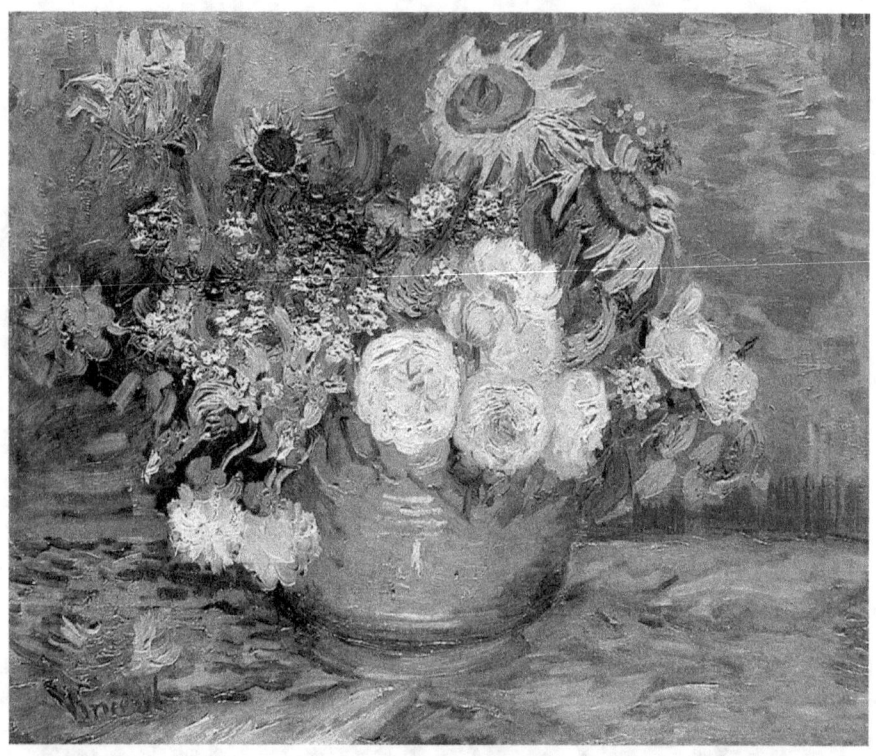

1887's *Bowl With Sunflowers, Roses, and Other Flowers* is a harbinger to what is to come. While still a still life portrait of flowers the vibrant broken brushstrokes of Vincent's later landscapes at Auvers are on full display here in muted reds and silver-whites along the right backdrop while purple rapids along with crimson and citrus orange hues decorate the whole of the white table cloth.

The vibrant colors and that bursting waterfall of the cut flowers that spills out the olive vase speak to the soul that "you must have me;" or at the very least: "you must lust after me (even if just a little)." And isn't that what every great paintings wants to say to us? These are the colors a paintings wants to dream in. And for a van Gogh it seems only fitting. The portrait is on display at the Kunsthalle Mannheim Museum of Modern and Contemporary Art located in Mannheim, Germany.

Undergrowth with Ivy, July 1889

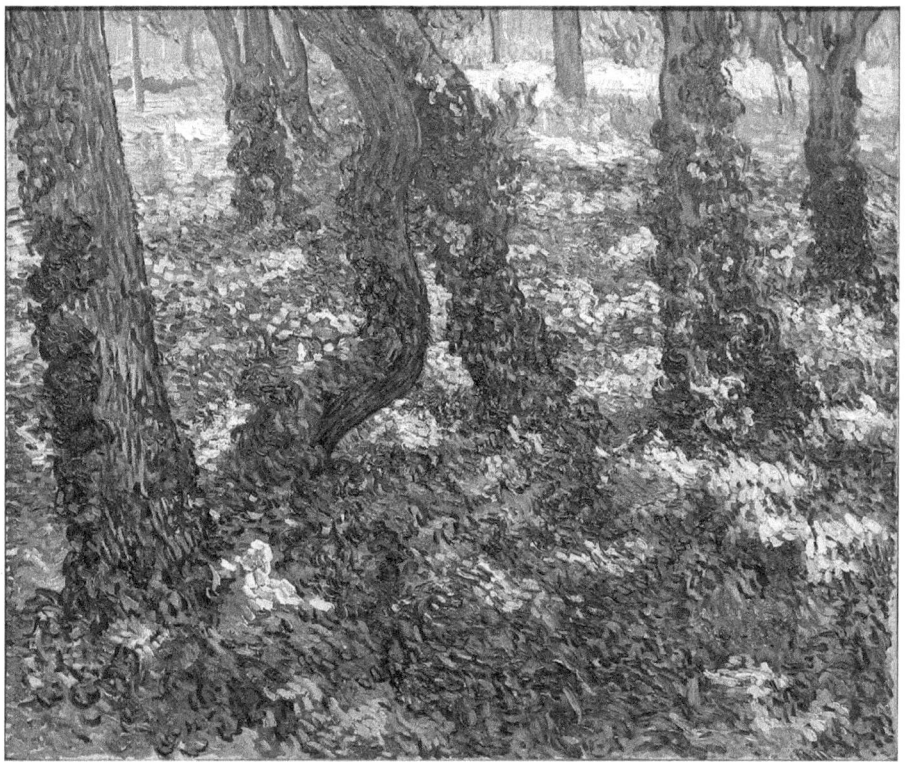

God and van Goth both seemed to adore the color green. Vincent uses it in so many different shades and hues, some hues that he seemed to manufacture out of the barbiturates of green he had stored in his own head like he had his own little Apothecary full of different bottles of green somewhere in his cerebellum that he could pull out and use on in a landscape or portrait simply by mixing and matching and dabbing the new connotation down on canvas. The above is one of the finest examples of this treatment of various shades of greens there ever was constructed. *Undergrowth with Ivy* from July 1889 now resides at the Van Gogh Museum in Amsterdam in the Netherlands.

Pine Trees and Dandelions in the Garden of Saint-Paul Hospital April, May 1890

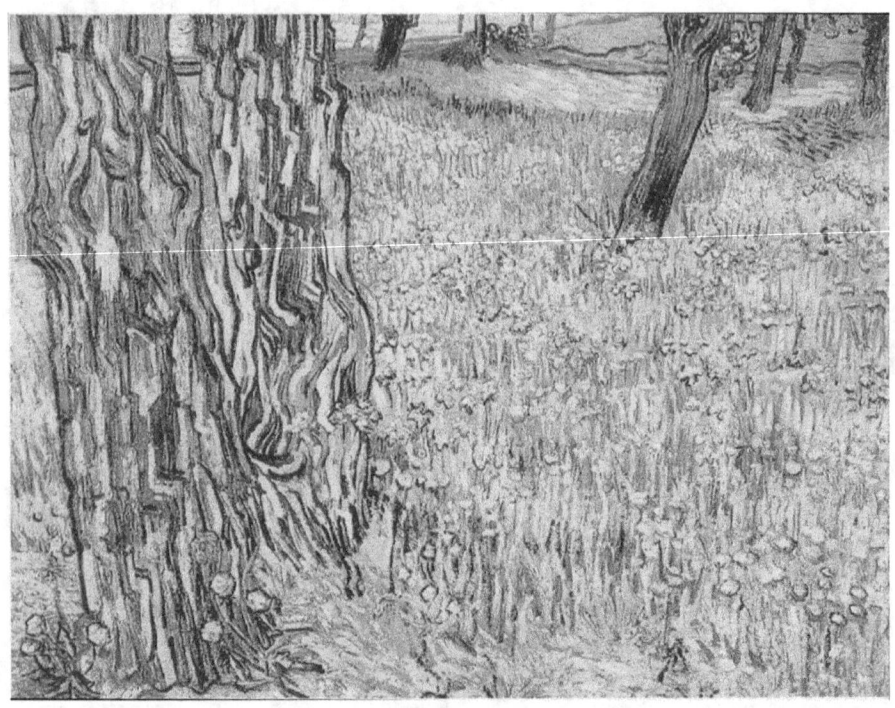

If one has ever been lucky enough to visit Blithewold Mansion, Gardens & Arboretum along the coast of Narragansett Bay in Bristol, Rhode Island then would can understand the ethereal beauty of springtime flowers, in the case of the 33 acres at Blithewold, some 40,000 white and yellow daffodils during the month of April each spring, that grow amid deciduous old-growth trees as seen similarly with the dandelions and wildflowers in van Gogh's created in April and May of 1889 called *May Pine Trees and Dandelions in the Garden of Saint-Paul Hospital, April*. It looks as though a moment from a poem or great romantic novel or perhaps a David Lean movie has been captured of man-made painted flowers amid the forest like in a fever dream. One can visit this figurative Eden of Vincent van Gogh's at the Kröller-Müller Museum in Otterlo in the Netherlands.

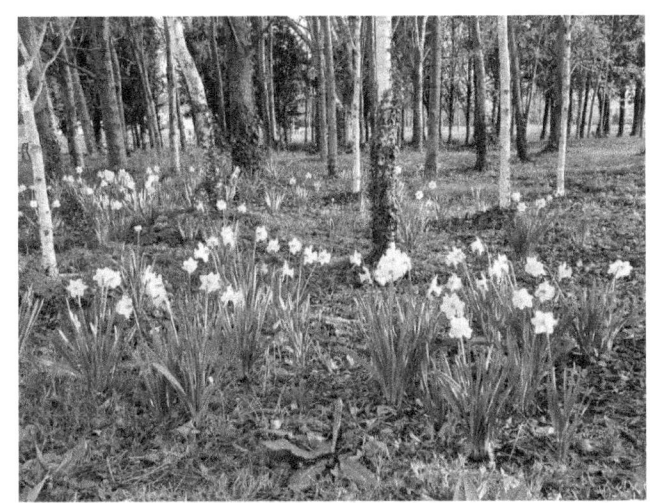

The Lovers, October 1888; looted by the Nazi's

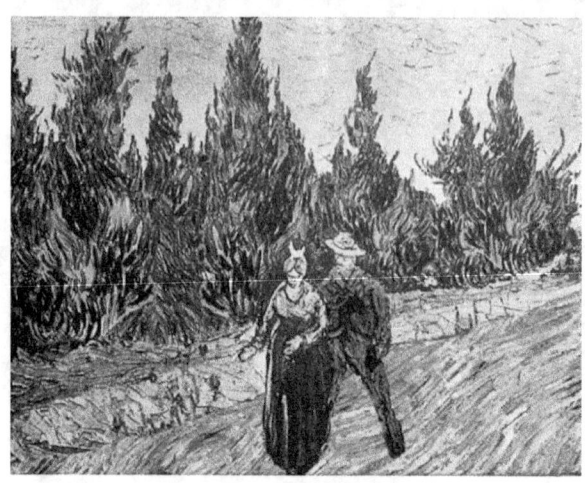

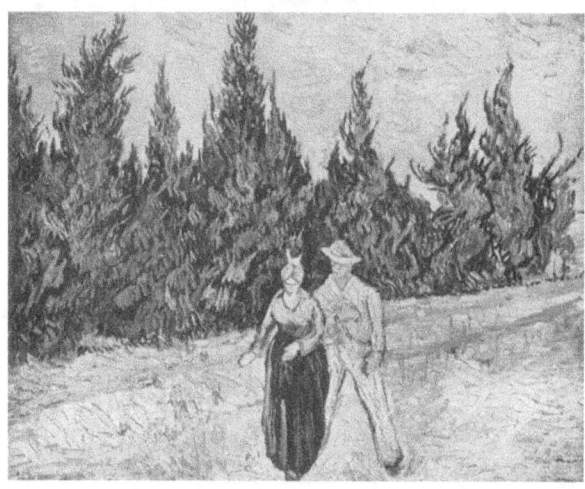

In autumn 888 Vincent sketched a new proposed painting entitled *The Lovers* using pencil on paper. In a letter to his brother Theo he wrote about what he was going to paint the sketch into: "A row of green cypresses against a pink sky with a pale lemon crescent moon. Foreground a piece of waste land, and some sand and a few thistles. Two lovers, the man pale blue with a yellow hat, the woman has a pink bodice and a black skirt."

He then created the same image using oil on canvas. Each shows the young couple, obviously one of them Vincent who wears his trademark yellow straw hat, as they stroll along a pathway lined by evergreens and cypress that must have been inspired by the park not far from the Yellow House where he lived.

189

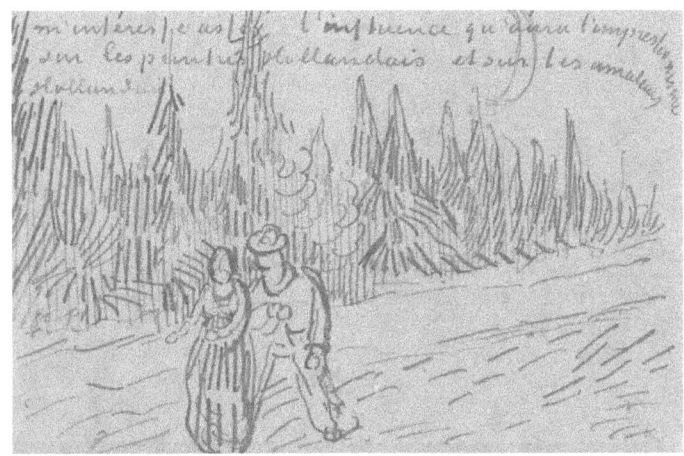

The painting was purchased by the National Gallery in Berlin during 1929. In 1937 it was stolen by the Nazi regime by which Hermann Göring took possession of it, but sold it off surreptitiously, and it has never been seen again. *Thanks Hermann! You dummkopf!*

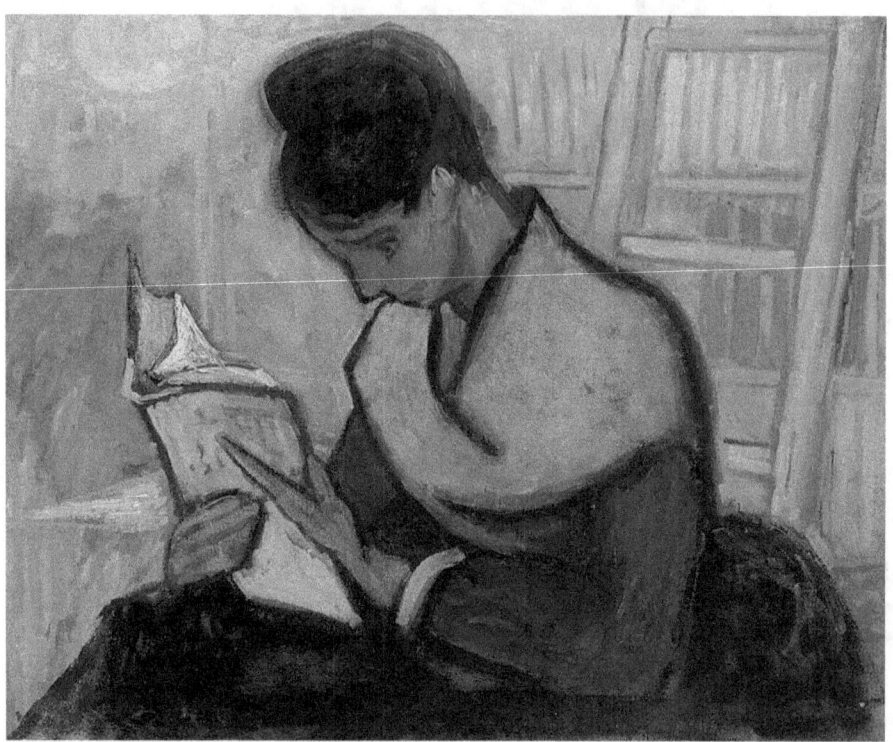

Painted in Arles in November 1888 this illustrious portrait show a raven-haired woman engulfed in the throes of the pages of a yellow novel amid a handsome study with library and bookshelf ladder. Her blouse is oxblood red, her hands tightened in a strong grip, her gaze looking almost seduced, if not afraid from the narrative unfolding before her.

Current ownership of the painting is in dispute, but ownership and title to the painting belongs to Brazilian art collector Gustavo Soter who recently filed suit in 2023 for its immediate return to him.

Self-portrait, 1887

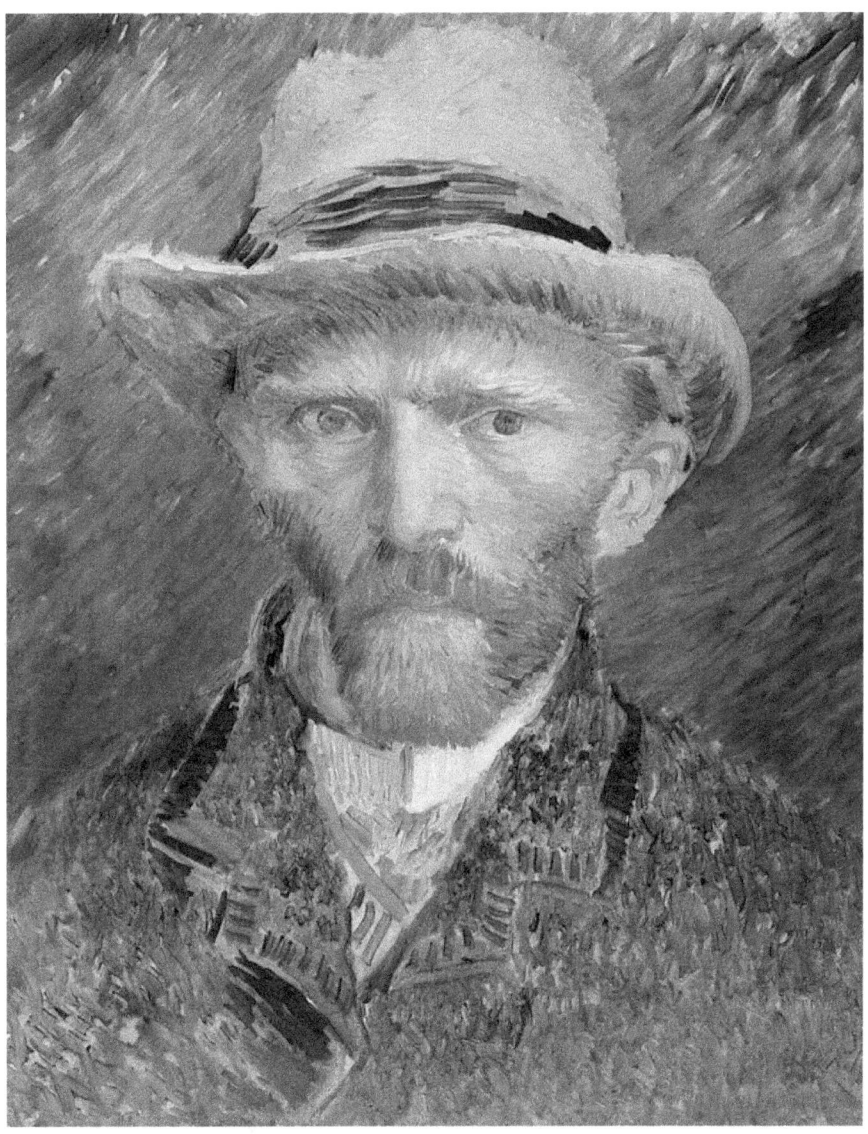

One of the most beautiful van Gogh self-portraits this magnificent still life was painted in a manic phase during 1887. Van Gogh's penetrating green eyes stare off-camera, his faze firm, frustrated almost, his red beard brushed perfectly, his colorful dream-coat screaming for us to pay attention to the artwork in front of us. Just magnificent. *Muy bueno señor! Muy bueno!*

Shoes, 1888

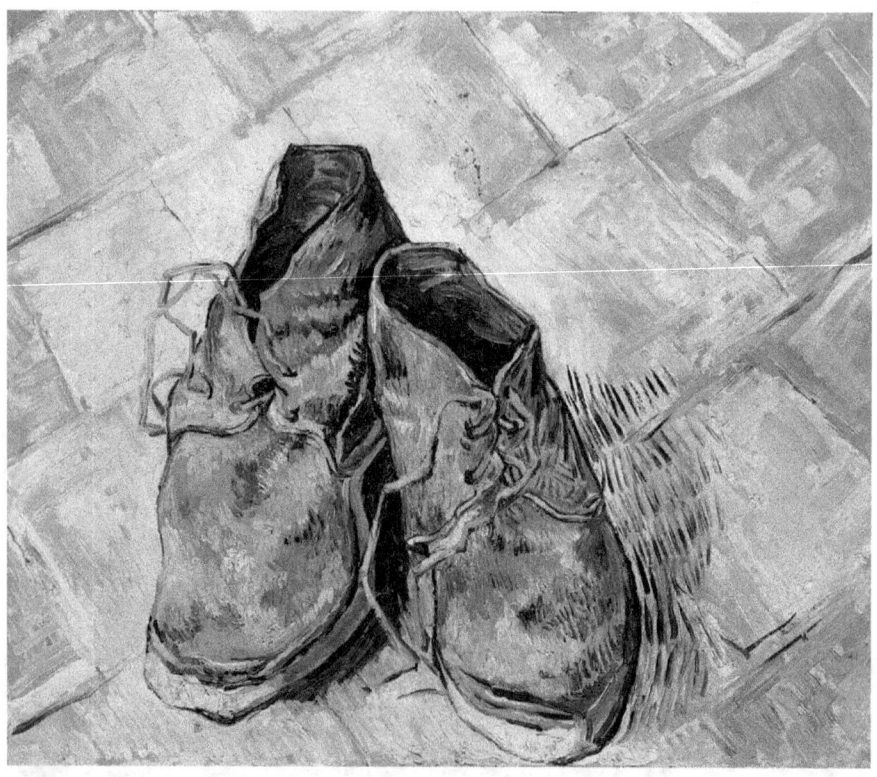

Sit down. Relax. Take your shoes of van Gogh for there are more portraits and landscapes to paint in the morning. Painted in Arles with the red-tile floor of the Yellow House as a backdrop in 1888, this is one of the many shoe and boot portraits Vincent painted throughout the years.

The Brothel (Le Lupanar), 1888

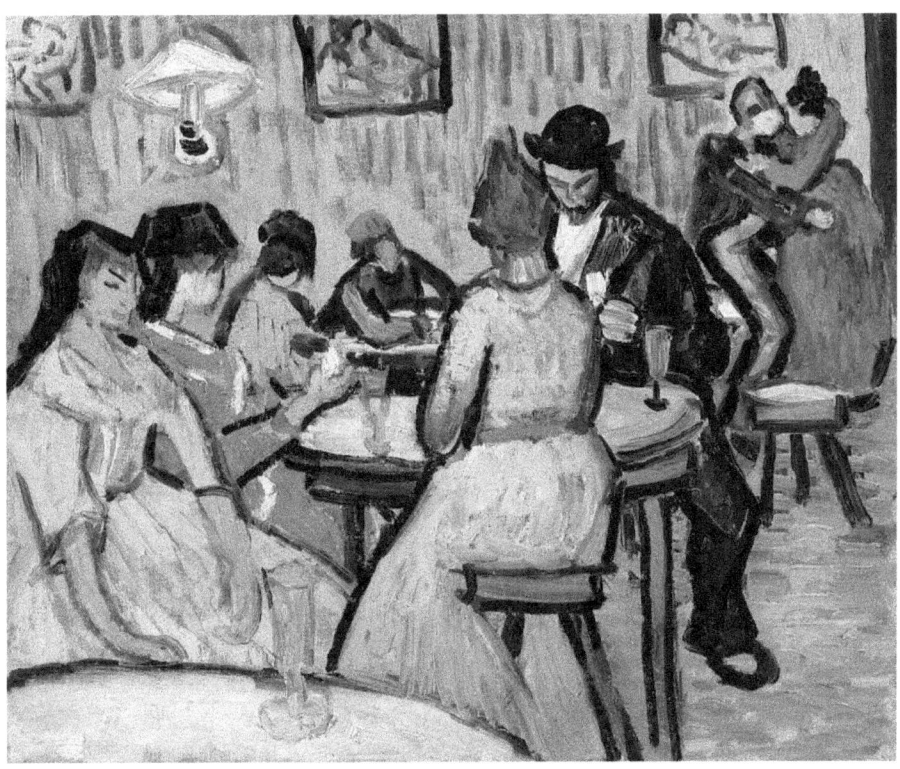

Let me paint a picture for you. A red-haired Vincent van Gogh in his most dapper clothing going brothel hopping with fellow consort and artist Paul Gauguin in the fall of 1888 all throughout Arles, France to look for figural subjects, a.k.a., artist models, they could use as subjects in their paintings in the coming weeks and days. If they were not both so poor the story would be almost unbelievable. This particular portrait was painted by van Gogh from memory after a visit to one of the local colorful brothels. If only one could have been a fly-on-the-wall of that place!

Houses and Figure, 1890

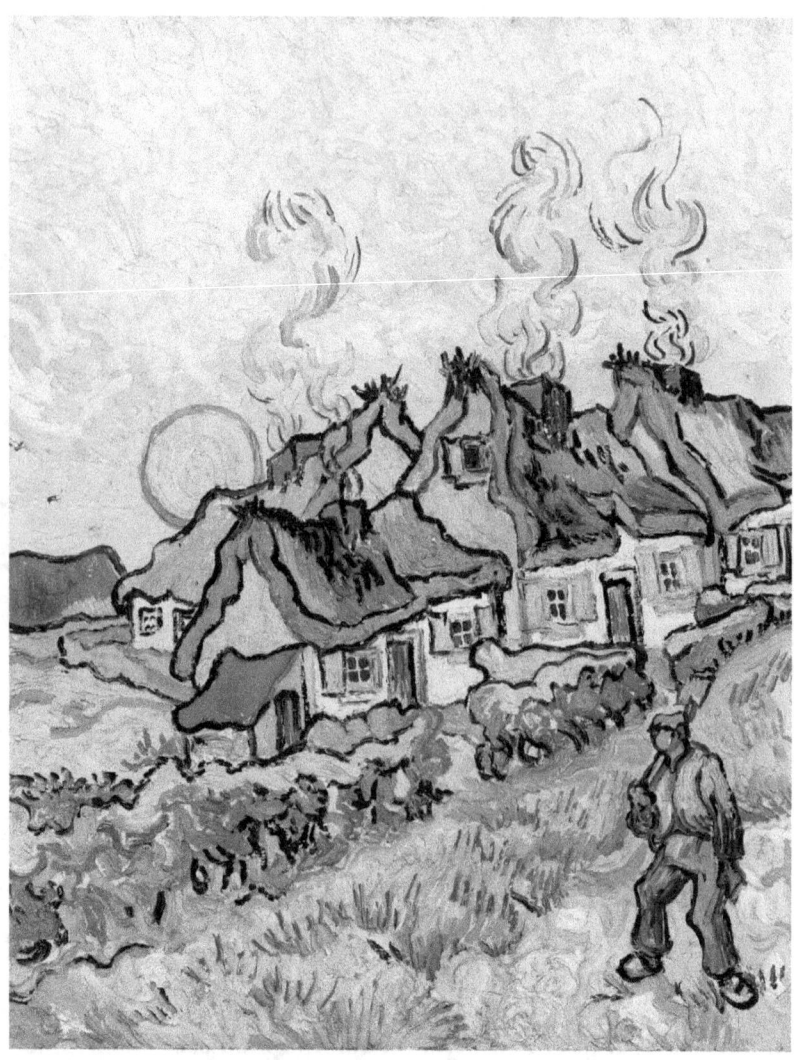

Woodsmoke snakes into pink skies as the sun begins to rise amid thatched roof houses and a man on his way to work sets the stage for us in 1890's *House and Figure*. Painted in Arles while Vincent was interned at the asylum, here he mixes the landscape outside his hospital window with the memory of childhood as there certainly are no Dutch thatched roof houses in France when he set this painting to canvas. In a way we get the best of both worlds here as the mind stretches its muscle through twenty years of computation and remembrance to create a photograph of something that can never exist except right here in this painting.

Cypresses, June 1889

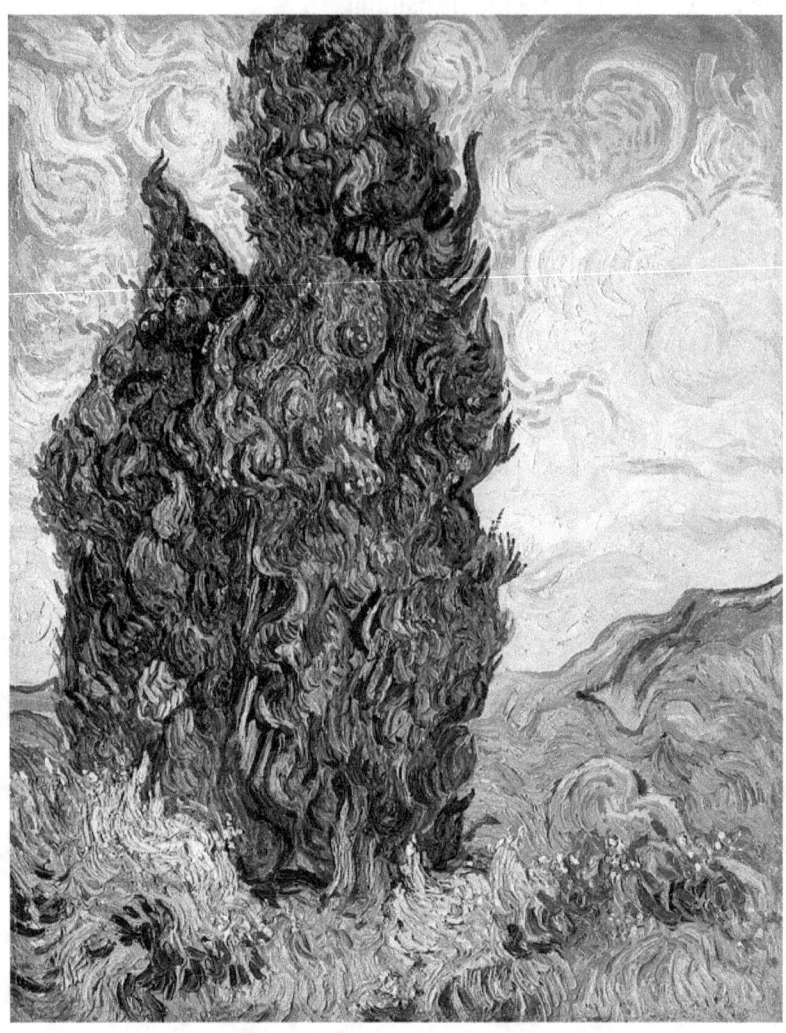

Cypresses, circa 1889, is so ethereal and utterly beautiful it literally almost begs one, the one-percent atheist in almost most all of us, to believe in God. *Heavens to Murgatroyd*, Snagglepuss, is it quite the celestial beauty! This was painted indoors at the asylum from memory. *Cypresses* is on view at the Metropolitan Museum of Art in Manhattan, New York City. Gallery 825. Ten paces from the door. Go see it! Please. Hurry!

Orchard Bordered by Cypresses, 1888

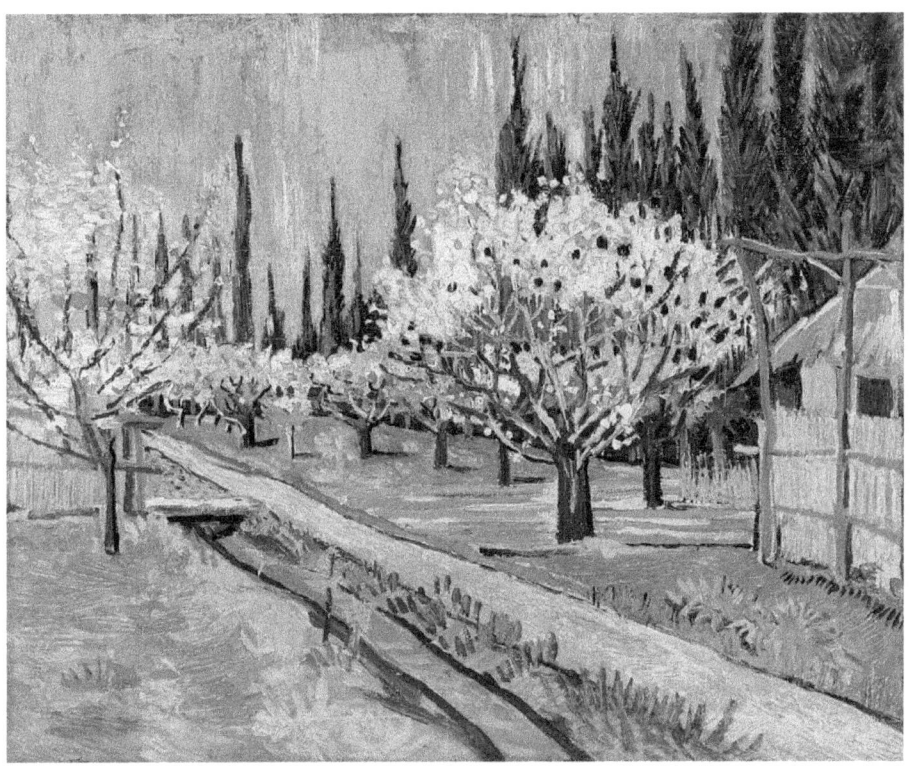

Vincent painted fourteen oil on canvas paintings of fruit trees and Provencal French orchards during the months of April and May of 1888. In the above *Orchard Boarders by Cypresses* this is the first time he has encountered the towering black cypress trees of Southern France and although not his main focus they heighten the silver-blue of the sky to frame in the orchard in a way that no one other artist ever can. I will take all fourteen *monsieur*. And some of the leafy greens, garlic, and leeks. And call me when some of the ripe peaches come in!

Square Saint-Pierre, Paris, 1887

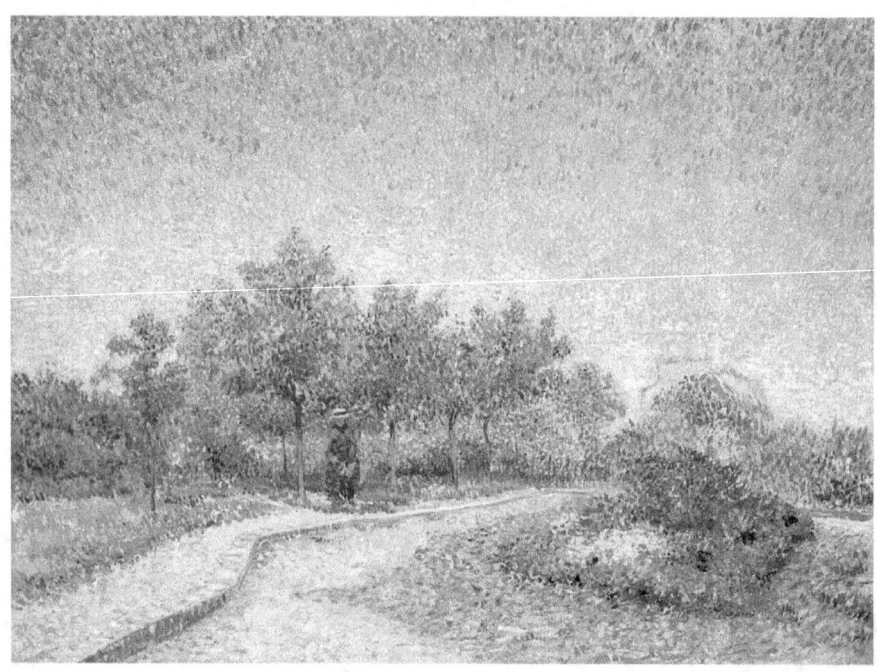

A blue fireworks brushed sky seems to want to fly off into outer space in the gorgeous Square Saint-Pierre, Paris, 1887. How exuberance must have filled the air up in Vincent's lungs after finishing this masterpiece. Surely one will be able to appreciate how good this is, how beautiful, serene, and lovely. Alas, no one did at the time. It is baffling really—how so many people could have been blind all at once. Square Saint-Pierre, Paris resides at the Yale University Art Gallery in New Haven, Connecticut—right down the road from me. No, Rhode Island is not an island off the coast of New York. Damn millennials.

Grapes, Lemons, Pears, and Apples, 1887

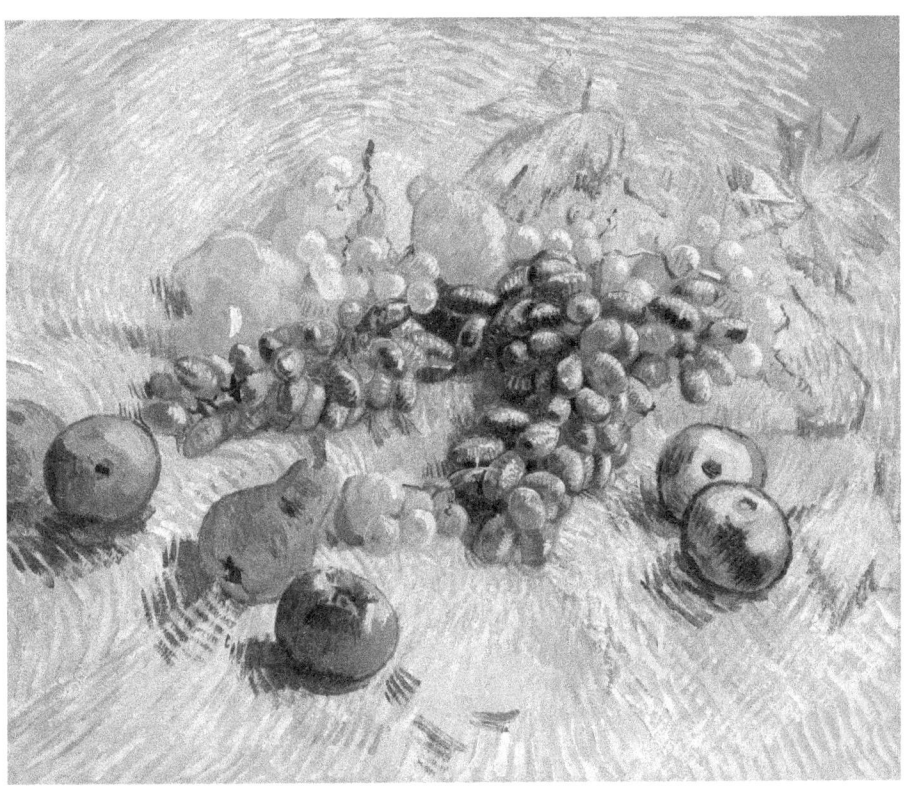

A beautiful still life with fruit circa 1887 it screams that this is a Vincent van Gogh. An elementary school child could tell who painted this yet it still seems fascinating, brilliant, and somehow altogether new. Give me this one for my little wine shack attached to the grape arbor at my tiny vineyard in Tuscany. Then we can grill some beefsteaks with olive oil and branches of rosemary Tuscan style. Of course, some good bubbly Moscato wine as well. And then chocolate cake. You've got to have chocolate cake every day. I believe this was on one of the tablets Moses dropped coming down the mountain. Its true!

The Factory, 1887

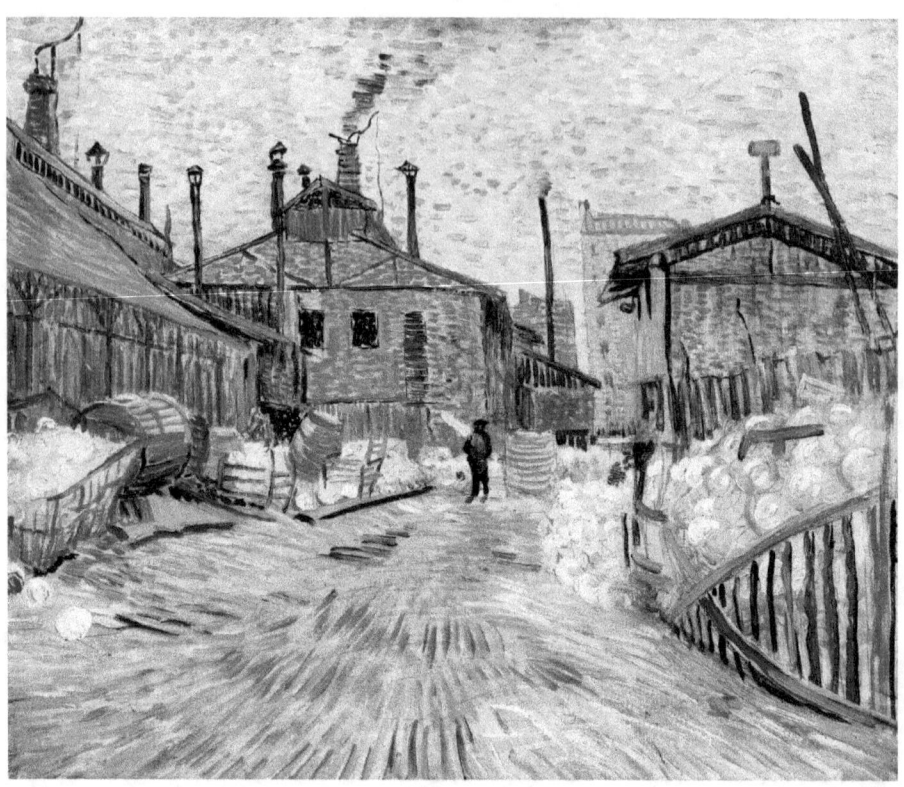

The Factory from 1887 shows where and why van Gogh pursued his artwork so passionately, because who in their right mind would want to work for someone else in this God-forsaken place? Man is dwarfed by everything that is piled up high over him; not to mention the black soot of the smokestacks. This was the open space cubicle setting of its day. Obviously, invented by business owners who hate and distain the very people they employee. All one could have hoped for here was to have been run over by one of the heavy oak barrels.

Peach Trees in Blossom, 1889

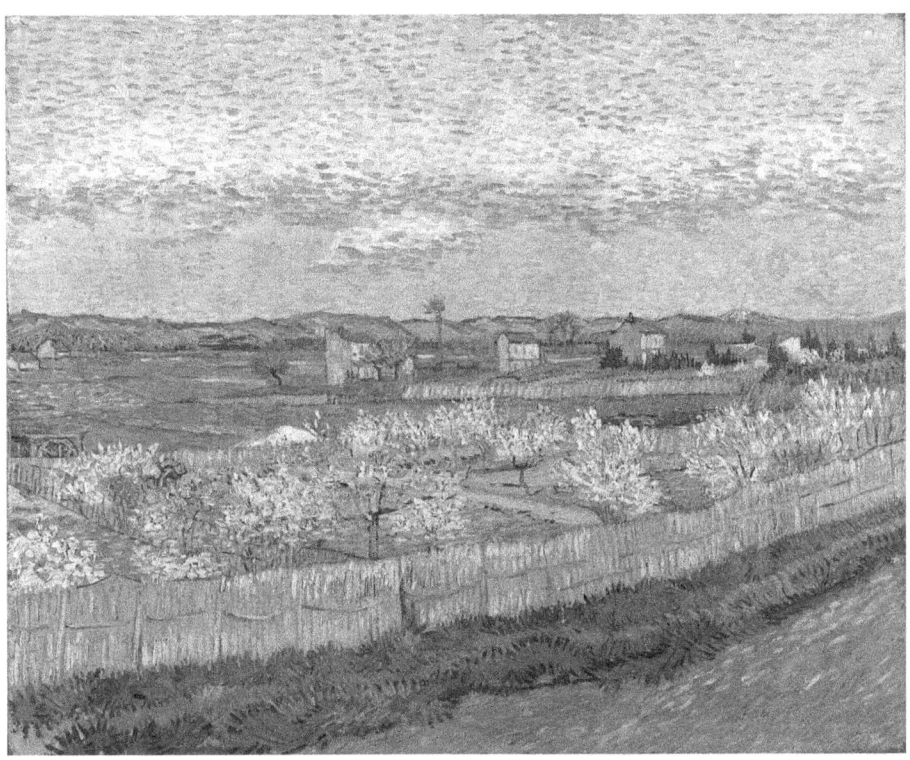

I won't tell you that one of the most beautiful landscapes of agricultural ecology ever painted in 1889 on the outskirts of Arles with the Alpilles mountains in the background and the skies up above dotted in blue and white gemstone was damaged by two illogical climate activists who thought it would be a good idea to glue their hands to a van Gogh painting in some hair-brained scheme to protest oil production and climate change. That would be stupid, because any climate change protester worth their salt would have to know they needed to glue themselves to something like the bronze Charging Bull of Wall Street or to a pair of McDonalds arches or perhaps, maybe to the front doors of ExxonMobil's Global Headquarters, which is at 22777 Springwoods Village Parkway, Spring, TX 77389-1425; Telephone number: 1-972-940-6000. Right?

The masterpiece presently hangs under lock and key inside the Great Room of the Courthald Institute of Art, where two buffy security guards that look a lot like Arnold Schwarzenegger, circa 1973, standby to protect it from climate activists who may have received one too many participation awards in elementary school. Huh, guys? Yeap.

The Berceuse, Woman Rocking a Cradle, 1889

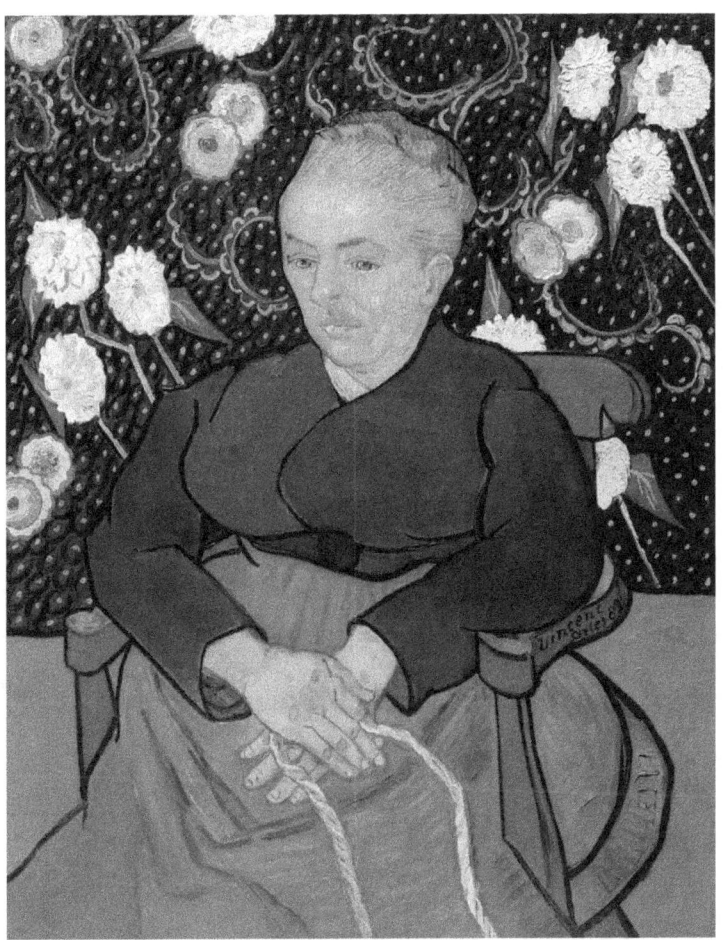

Hey, she may not be a young Rebecca De Mornay, but the sitter for *The Berceuse, Woman Rocking a Cradle*, Augustine Roulin, wife of Vincent's close friend, the postmaster of Arles, Joseph Roulin, well, hey, she does have a certain little bit of *je ne sais quoi* De Mornay. "La Berceuse," means "lullaby, or woman who rocks the cradle." She holds a rope of twine in her hand that obviously is looped onto the sides of a cradle placed gently down upon the floor out of sight. The peonies and dahlia of the wallpaper are almost as beautiful as the real thing. And the blood red wall will look familiar to every parent who has a child and wants to *brain* them with the back of a wooden spoon every-so-often, especially when good company arrives for a Sunday visit.

Le café de nuit (The Night Café), 1888

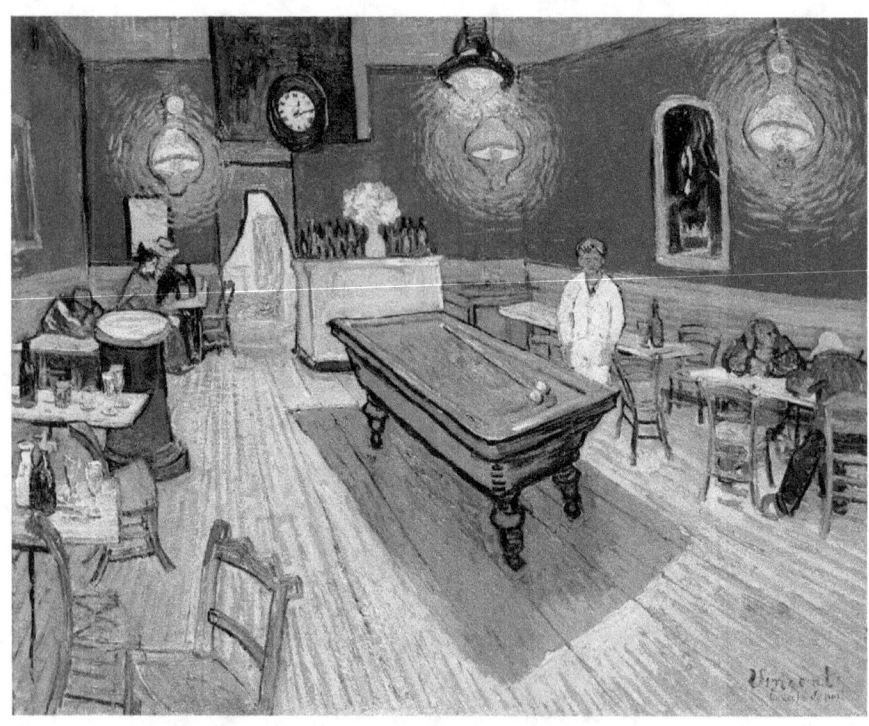

Billiards, a red wall, half-empty wine glasses and carafes and sunken shoulders amid the chairs of the café make for a beautiful, funny, heartbreaking, and lovely portrait that exudes confidence and brevity. I loved this painting and only wish I had known about it before I was 56-years-old, because I think it is one of van Gogh's very best.

"Here's to your death. May I build your coffin myself from the wood of a hundred year old oak tree I plant tomorrow!"

Olive Trees, 1889

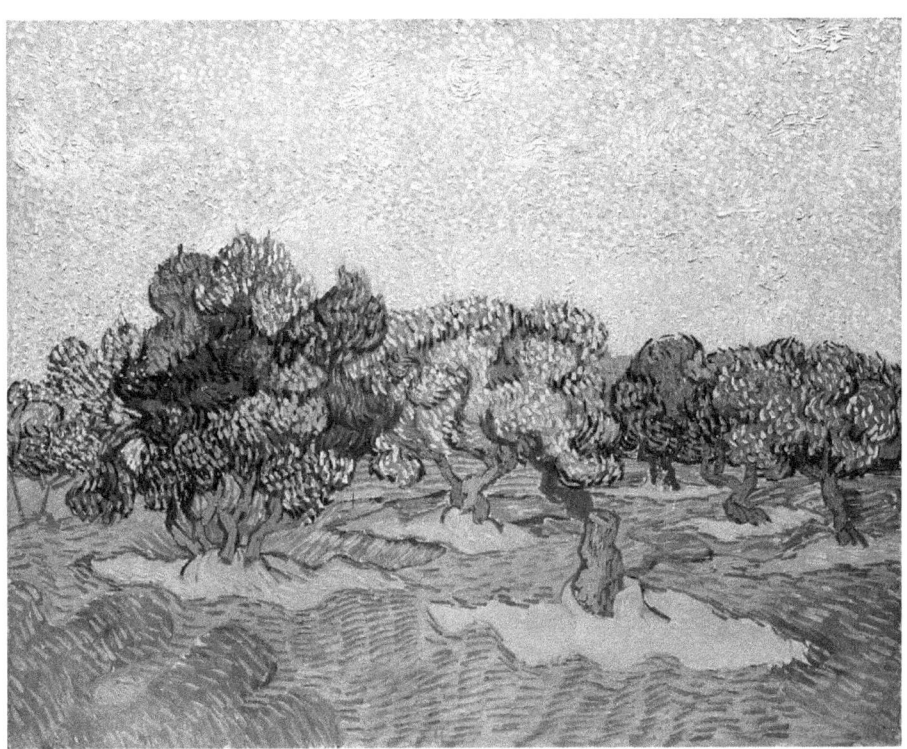

Another in the 15 paintings of the Olive Trees series done outside in Saint-Rémy-de-Provence in 1889 this one has its own unique blend of colorful cheekiness. The sky dotted with pinks and blues and the olive trees usual silver-green is brushed with whites, pinks, greens, and goldish-white to make the viewer linger. A fantastic landscape that is now on display at the Metropolitan Museum of Art, Manhattan, New York City.

The Potato Eaters, 1885

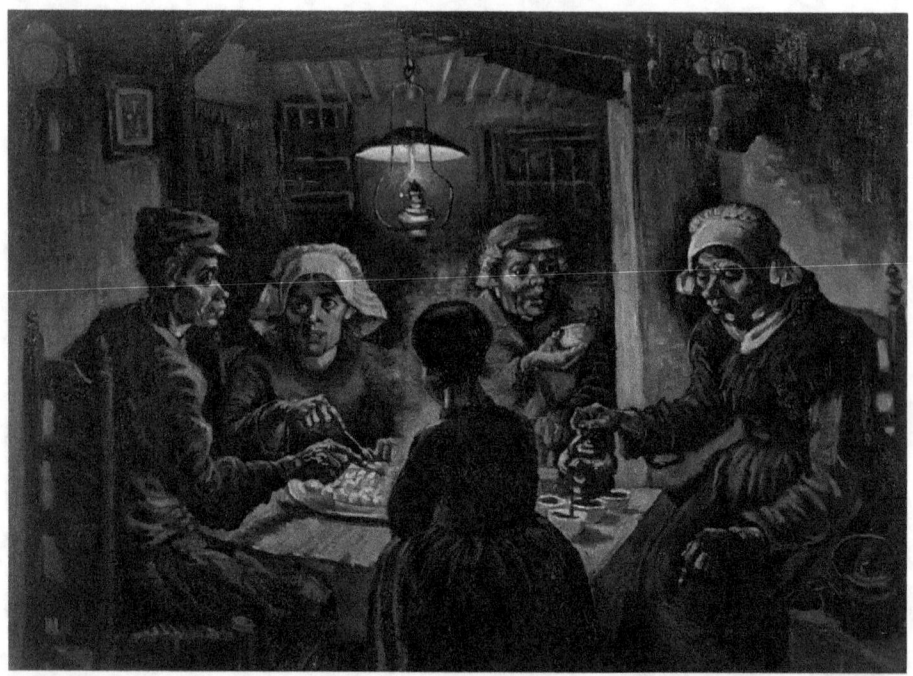

The enigmatic *The Potato Eaters* was one of van Gogh's personal favorite portraits. His brother, Theo, hated it. His Dutch friend and mentor, Anthon van Rappard, hated the marbled look of the work. Van Gogh himself even selected the most ugly peasant models he could find in Nuenen, quite on purpose, so they would look *genuine* and *honest* eating the very potatoes that they hand-picked in the gold-dust light of their barely lit dining room. He said the following in one of his letters to Theo about the models he choose to depict in the painting:

"Anyone who would rather see insipidly pretty peasants can go ahead. For my part, I'm convinced that in the long run it produces better results to paint them in their coarseness than to introduce conventional sweetness.

A peasant girl is more beautiful than a lady — to my mind — in her dusty and patched blue skirt and jacket, which have acquired the most delicate nuances from weather, wind and sun. But — if she puts — a lady's costume on, then the genuineness is lost. A peasant in his suit of fustian in the fields is finer than when he goes to church on Sundays in a sort of gentleman's coat.

And likewise, one would be wrong, to my mind, to give a peasant painting a certain conventional smoothness. If a peasant painting smells of bacon, smoke, potato steam — fine — that's not unhealthy — if a stable smells of manure — very well, that's what a stable's for — if the field has an odor of ripe wheat or potatoes or — of guano and manure — that's really healthy — particularly for city folk. They get something useful out of paintings like this. But a peasant painting mustn't become perfumed."

Vincent went through several iterations before he completed the definitive version of *The Potato Eaters*.

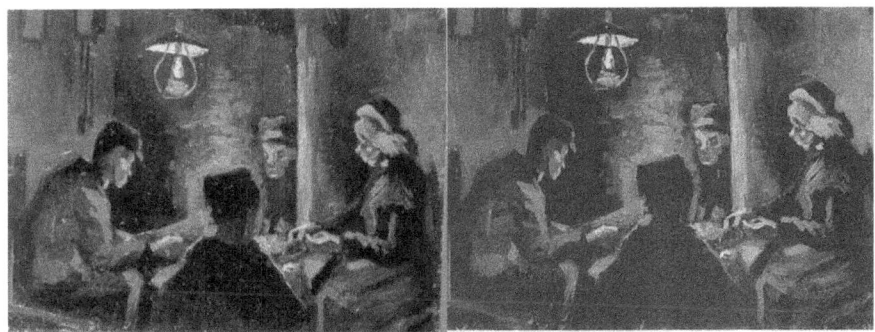

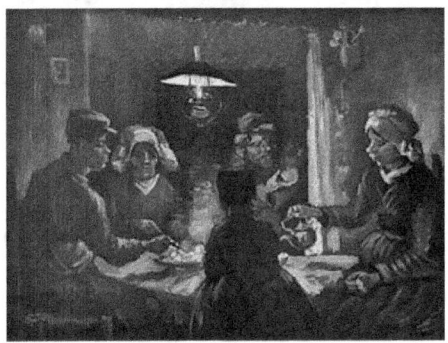

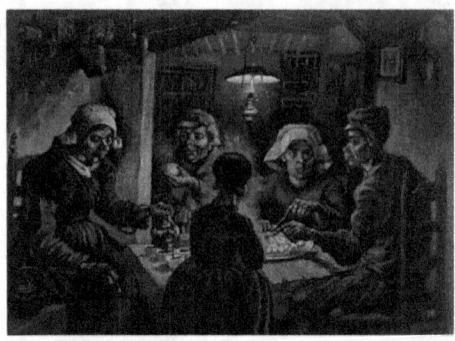

Notice the density of the darkness that he added to definitive
and final version of the painting with a tinge of a gold hue
added for dramatic effect.

So in love was he in the end effect of *The Potato Eaters* that Vincent even had lithographs of the piece made in hopes of capitalizing on its brilliance.

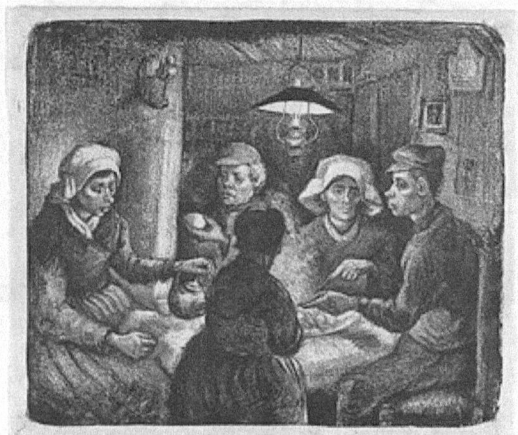

The entire genesis of The Potato Eaters lies, quite frankly, on a much better and more impactful portrait that the great Belgian painter Charles de Groux painted entitled *The Blessing Before Supper* which might have looked like straight out of a scene from Vincent's own teenage household with all his siblings and parents saying grace (maybe that is what this painting spoke to him so much and he so badly wanted to emulate it).

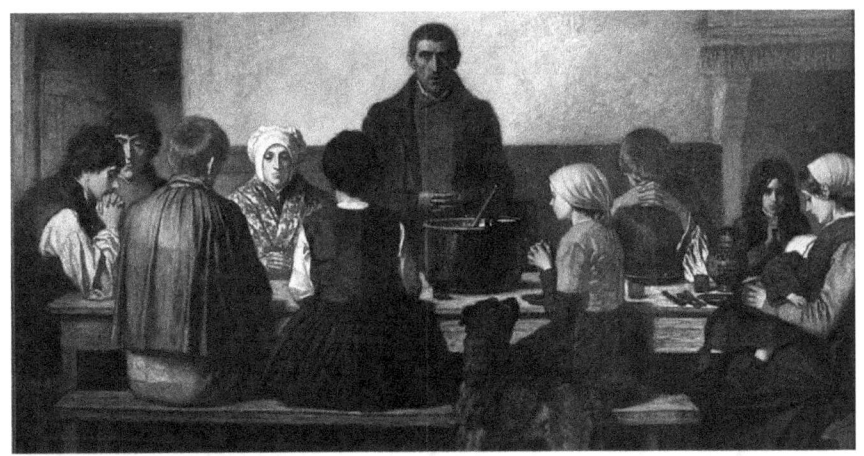

Charles de Groux, 1861, *The Blessing Before Supper*

But let's put the two iconic paintings one over the other. The sense one gets from the de Groux is one of thanks, family, and spiritual religiosity. And in the van Gogh there is not fulfillment like Vincent might have hoped amid the peasants who he wants to be viewed as a thankful poor, but one of depression, exhaustion, defeat, and insecurity. I personally do not think that is what he was aiming for, but he did say to Theo that he wanted the painting to be *honest*. And that it is. He got it right. Even when he was hoping to show the beauty of something that only exists if you don't have to be a party to the all that labor and grief. I sometimes can be accused of being intellectually lazy (when I want to be), so give me the gleams of hope in The Sower any day over *The Potato Eaters*. And who really likes potatoes anyway? The portrait now resides at the Van Gogh Museum in Amsterdam in the Netherlands

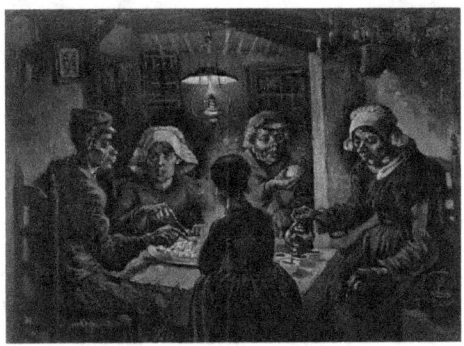

Couple Walking among Olive Trees in a Mountainous Landscape with Crescent Moon, May 1890

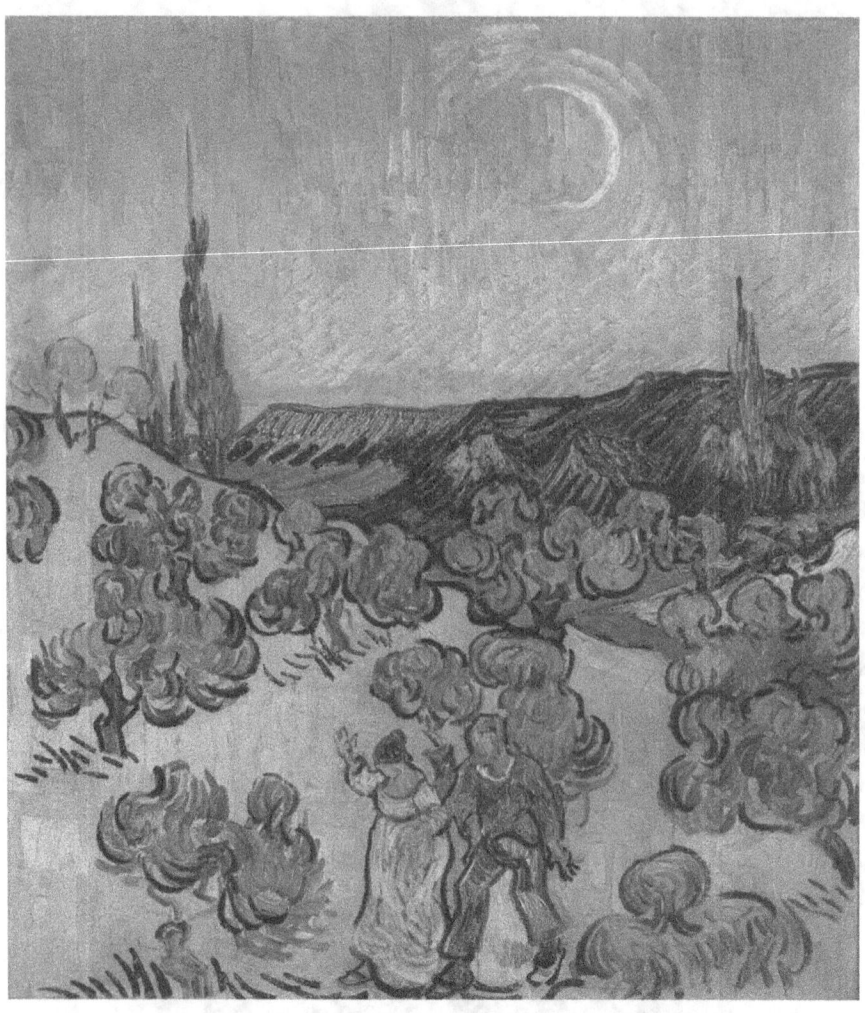

One of the more romantic in the series of Olive Trees painted from May and June 1889 this landscape shows a couple in a delicate balancing act as they walk amid the olive groves under a crescent moon with the blue shouldered mountains off on the horizon as the afterglow of the sunset builds to a crescendo. *Couple Walking among Olive Trees in a Mountainous Landscape with Crescent Moon* now delights visitors at the Museu de Arte de São Paulo in São Paulo, Brazil.

Green Wheat Fields, Auvers, 1890

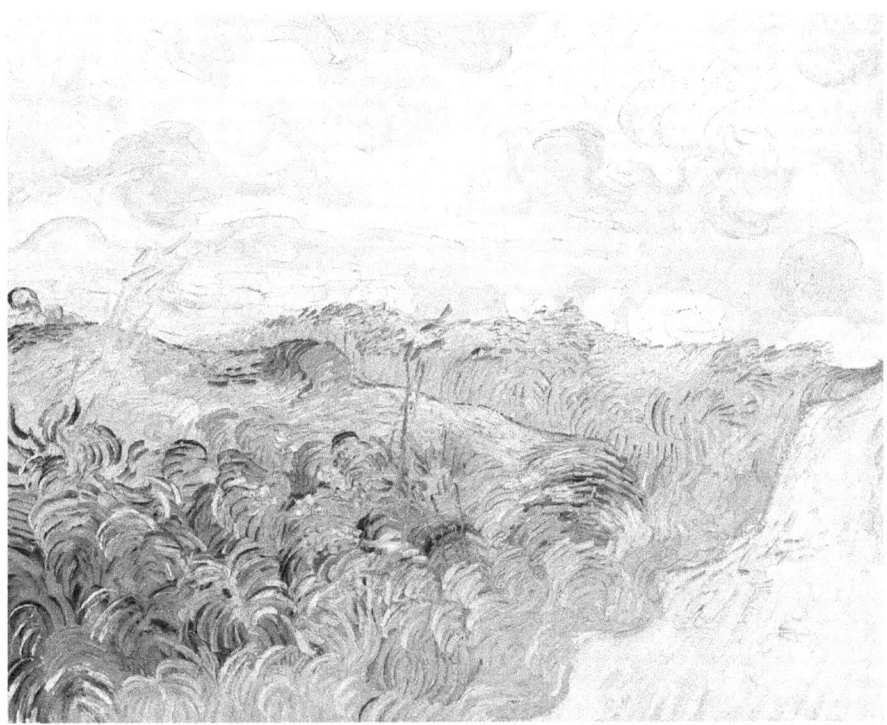

A swirling energetic sky full of cumulous clouds and bustling tourmaline sky screams across the canvas of Green Wheat Fields painted in Auvers in 1890. The spring wheat has just flushed in full grown before it will be cultivated and reaped into giant heaps of golden haystacks. The weather and flora and fauna almost look tropical in essence, which might have delighted Paul Gauguin to no end. You can find this landscape located at the National Gallery of Art in Washington DC.

Houses at Auvers, 1890

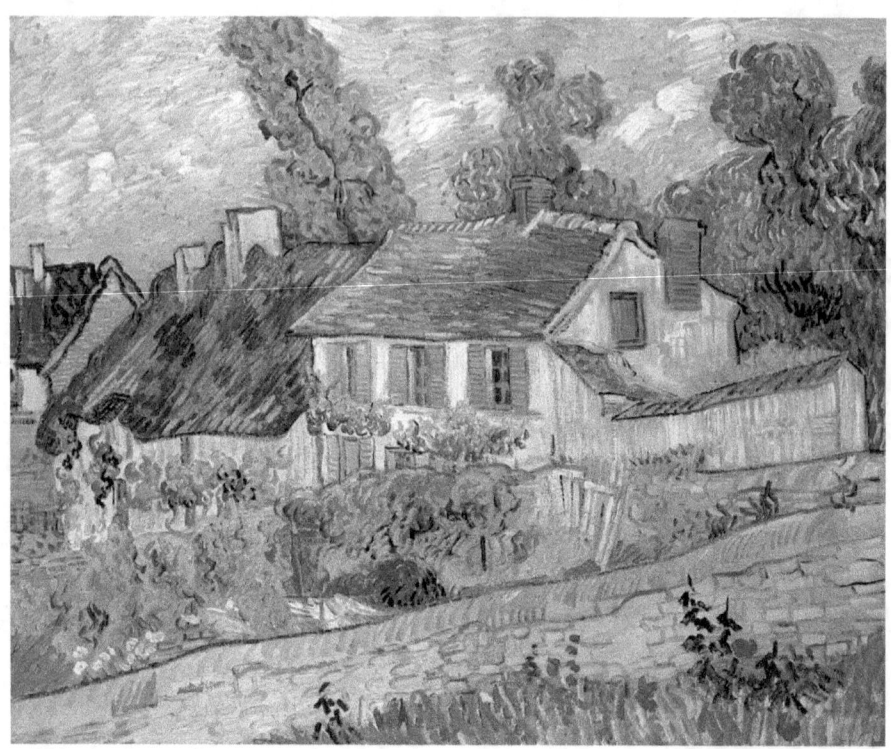

Vincent van Gogh can make even a cloudy day in the French countryside of Auvers-sur-Oise look beautiful. Teal shutters looked smacked open from the sunny day beforehand against the façade of the nearby cottage walls. The roadside poppy is still stiffened upward when it bent toward yesterday's sun, the garden flowers and vegetables still looking spry, and the gusty wind in the trees that blow westward are a good omen for calm at sunset, which is always one of the most beautiful times of any summer day. Houses at Auvers calmly rests now at the Toledo Museum of Art in Toledo, Ohio.

Imperial Fritillaries in a Copper Vase, 1887

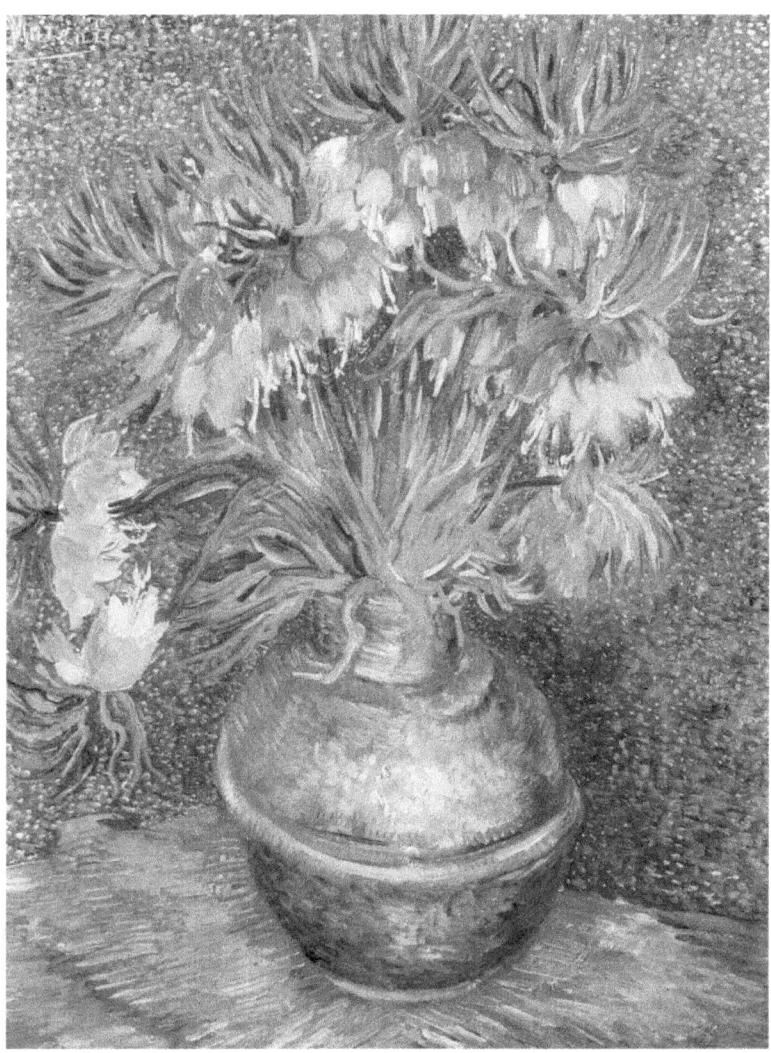

Imperial Fritillaries in a Copper Vase, circa 1887 is a cheery still life with the most beautiful orange blossoms with beautiful white pistils drooping downward with an almost water lily pond backdrop. The copper-orange table is full of dashed brushstrokes that act almost as a mirror to the imperial fritillaries. The still life can be located at the Musée d'Orsay in Paris, France.

Self-Portrait with Dark Felt Hat at the Easel, 1886

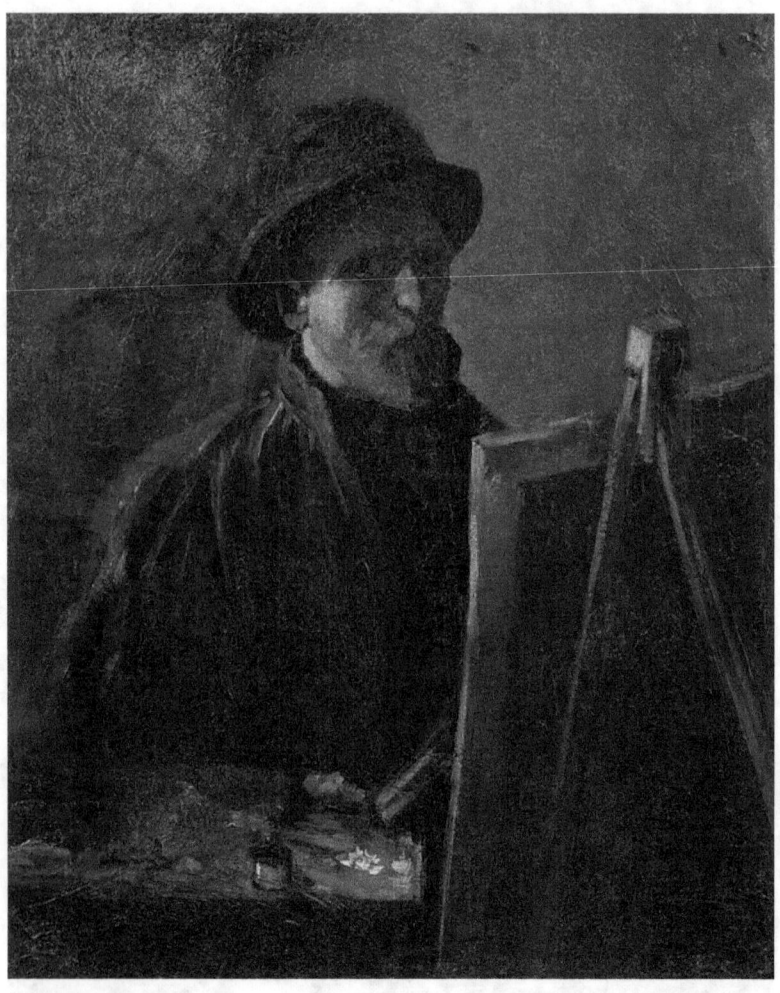

This paintings was done in Paris during the springtime of 1886 and is noted for being one the first self-portraits that van Gogh painted of himself. The dark tones and vivid bursts of light hark back to perhaps a Rembrandt and is much different than his later styles, but nonetheless a flawless pearl of beauty. Notice the luxurious unmixed primary colors that sit scraped together pyramid-like atop the painter's palette, the small jar of turpentine, the two paint brushes at the ready for van Gogh's thumb that pokes into view in the crescent edge of the palette near the artist's belly: little details at their brightest. This self-portrait is on view at the Van Gogh Museum in Amsterdam in the Netherlands.

Olive Trees with the Alpilles in the Background, 1889

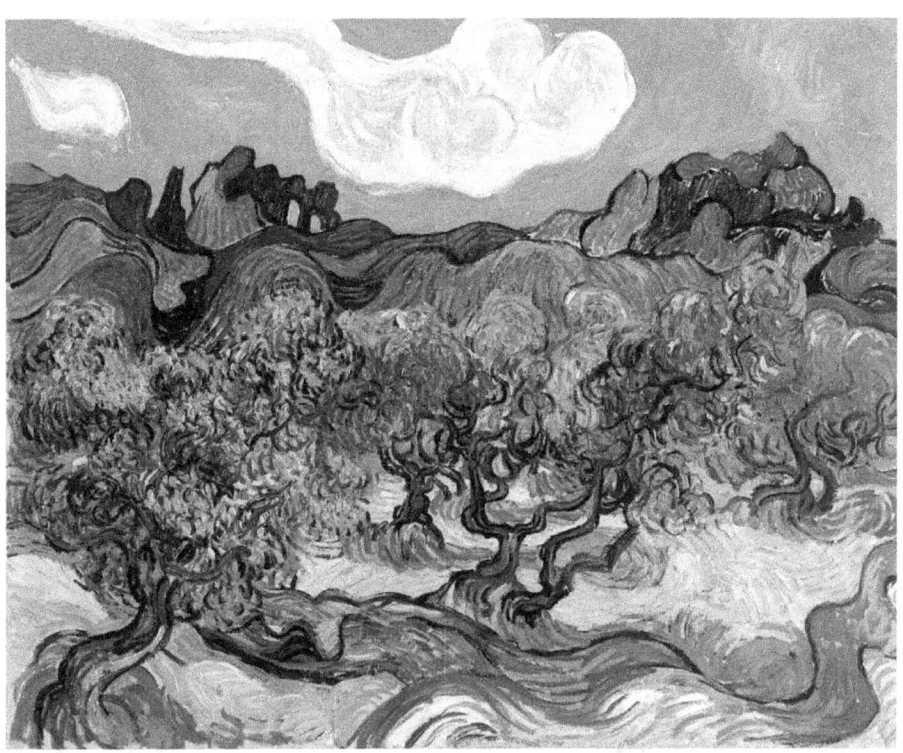

An angry fist-like cloud, as though blown in from an angel of Botticelli up above the blue Alpilles, moves northward across a windblown, tossed about olive grove that looks transported across space and time from very foot of the Mount of Olives of Jerusalem; or perhaps it is the Garden of Gethsemane itself. There is something truly spiritual about this particular Olive Trees series landscape that is different from all its other brothers and sisters. A single teardrop cloud in the left-hand corner. The way the dolomite-like peaks want to become one with the air and the sky. The restless ground. The olive trees readying themselves for blissful olives left to right. This is on display at the Museum of Modern Art in Manhattan, New York City. Definitely worth the price of admission.

Peasant Woman Cooking by a Fireplace, 1885

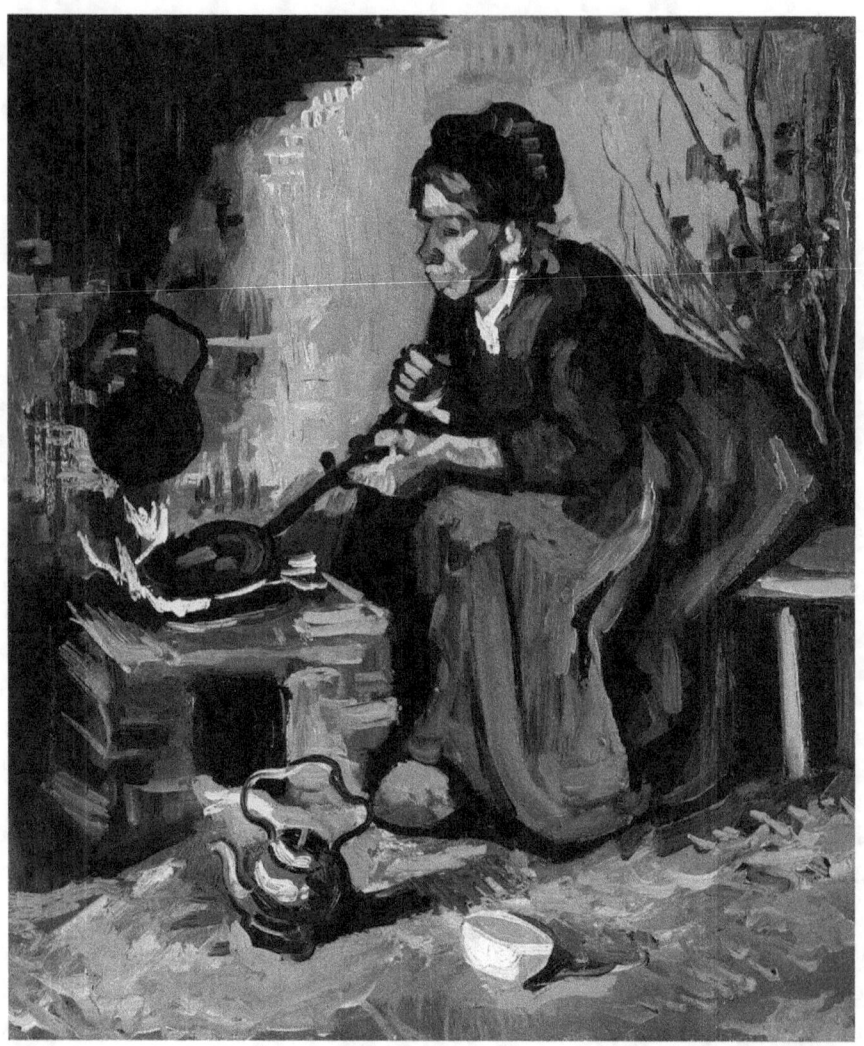

A very early work from Nuenen, Holland in 1885, one can almost envision Vincent painting his subject model just after dark at dinnertime, finishing his portrait, and then sharing a bit of pigeon, bacon, potato or vegetable stew with her afterward and laughing about the antics of their idiots neighbors from earlier in the day. This work is also on display at the Museum of Modern Art in Manhattan, New York City. Definitely worth the price of admission.

Memory of the Garden at Etten (Ladies of Arles), November 1888

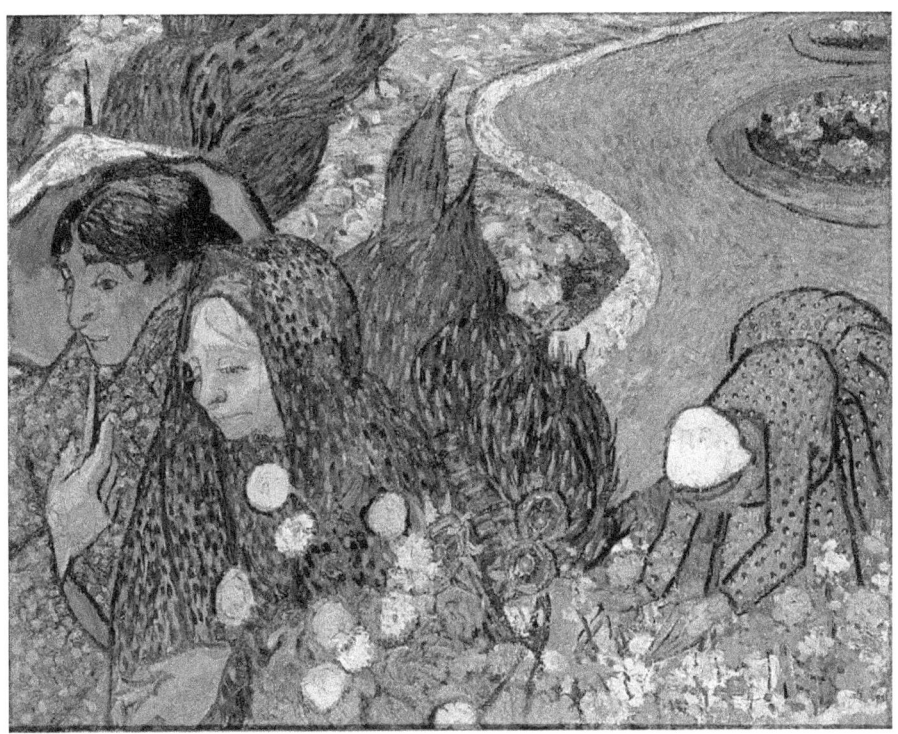

Memory of the Garden at Etten is an intimate portrait of van Gogh's mother Anna Cornelia van Gogh and his younger sister Willemina (Wil) van Gogh to whom he was quite close. In a letter that he penned in response to one of Wil's own letters the older van Gogh wrote to his sister about the above portrait of the garden at their family home: [It's] "you and mother, [in the garden, and you depicted as] "a figure like those in Dickens' novels." Wil carries a red parasol while wearing the red, blue, and green of a plaid shawl while Mother Anna Cornelia is dressed in same only her plaid is shaded blue and red. It is a magical and beautiful painting, but you may have to put long johns and your military hat on if you would like to see it in person, because it resides in the Hermitage Museum in St. Petersburg, Russia. *Blimey rats!*

Willemina (Wil) and Ana van Gogh

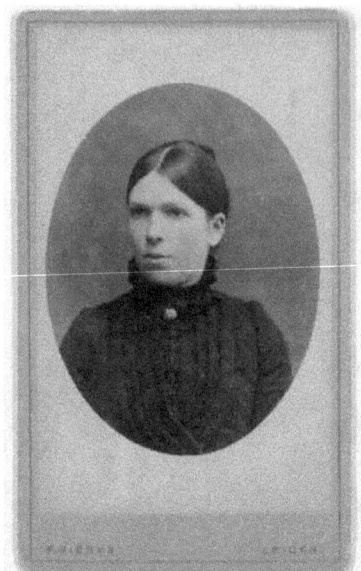

Willemina (Wil) van Gogh, circa 1880

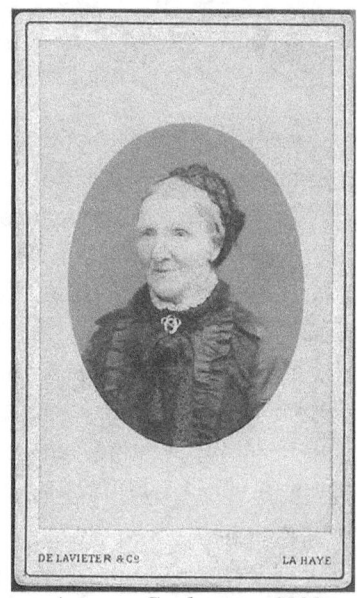

Ana van Gogh, circa 1888

Allotment with Sunflower, July 1887

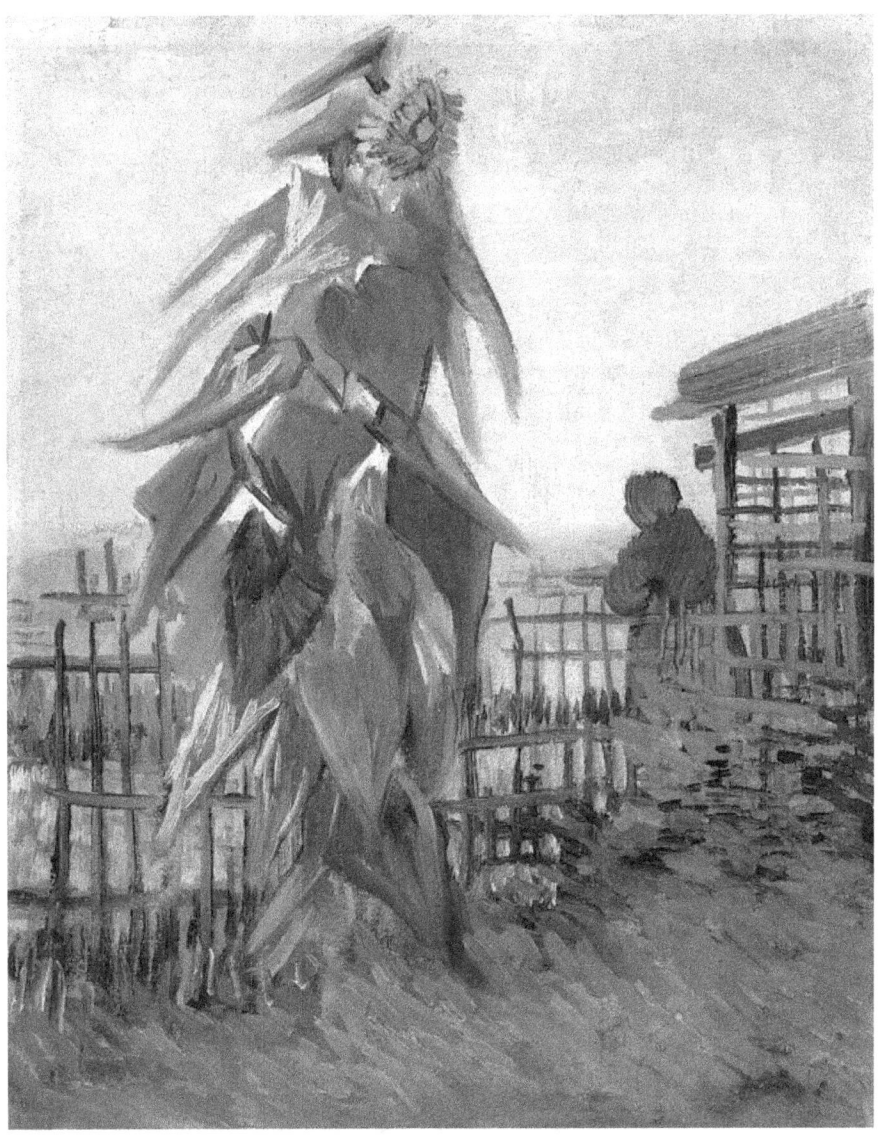

Obviously, they did not have pesky squirrels to contend with in Paris atop Montmartre where his portrait of a giant sunflower was painted in July of 1887. Vincent van Gogh loved sunflowers, who doesn't, and this beauty caught his gaze and he immortalized it forever with its big yellow thunderhead and elephantine leaves. You have to have at least one peasant in a "peasant," painting and there she is overlooking the smokestacks of the factories of the Clichy district of 1887 Paris. Allotment with Sunflower is on display in all her glory at the Van Gogh Museum in Amsterdam in the Netherlands.

Blossoming Almond Branch in a Glass with a Book, 1888

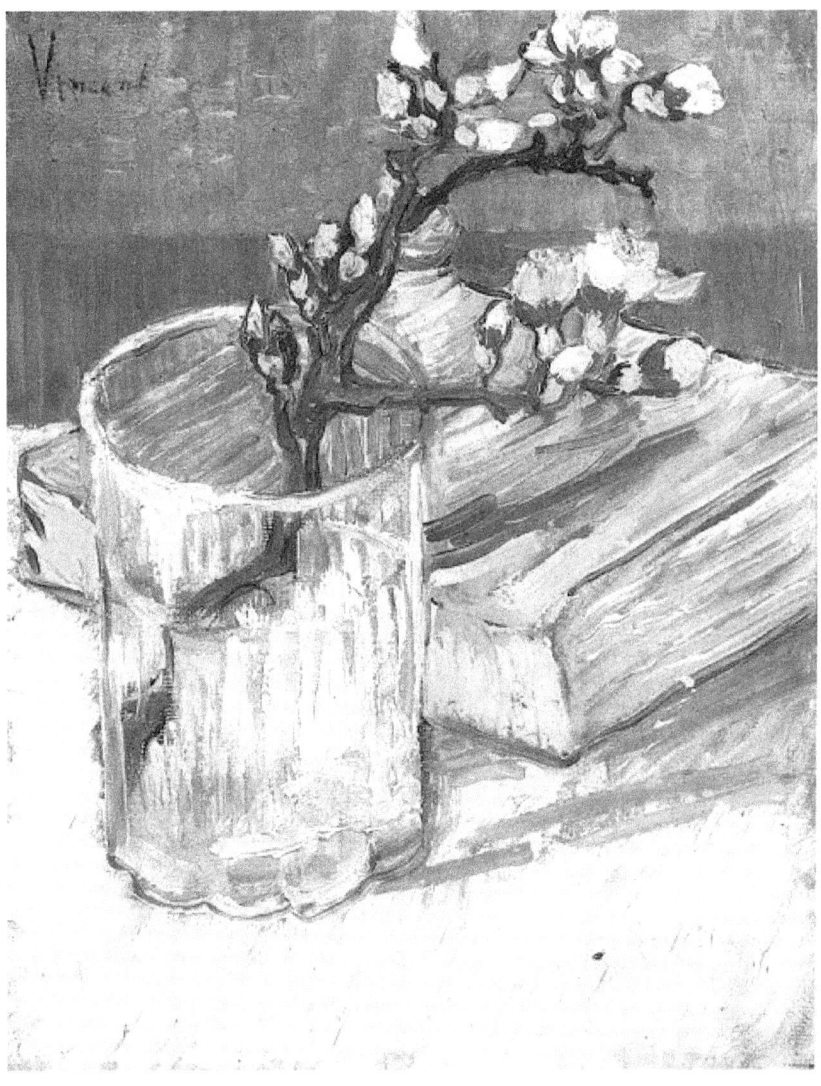

A relatively obscure and rather unknown Arles portrait of Vincent van Gogh is *Blossoming Almond Branch in a Glass with a Book*. Three objects and a table yet so devastatingly beautiful. I love how the rose-pink of the leather bound book jacket with its garish silver-green gilt pages match the nascent pinkish-white hue of the almond blossoms almost to a T. This is one of my favorites of van Gogh's works, but you will have to put get your deerstalker cap and Inverness cape on along and a Sherlock Holmes magnifying glass, because this pinkish hued portrait lives in a private collection at an undisclosed location.

The Mulberry Tree, October 1889

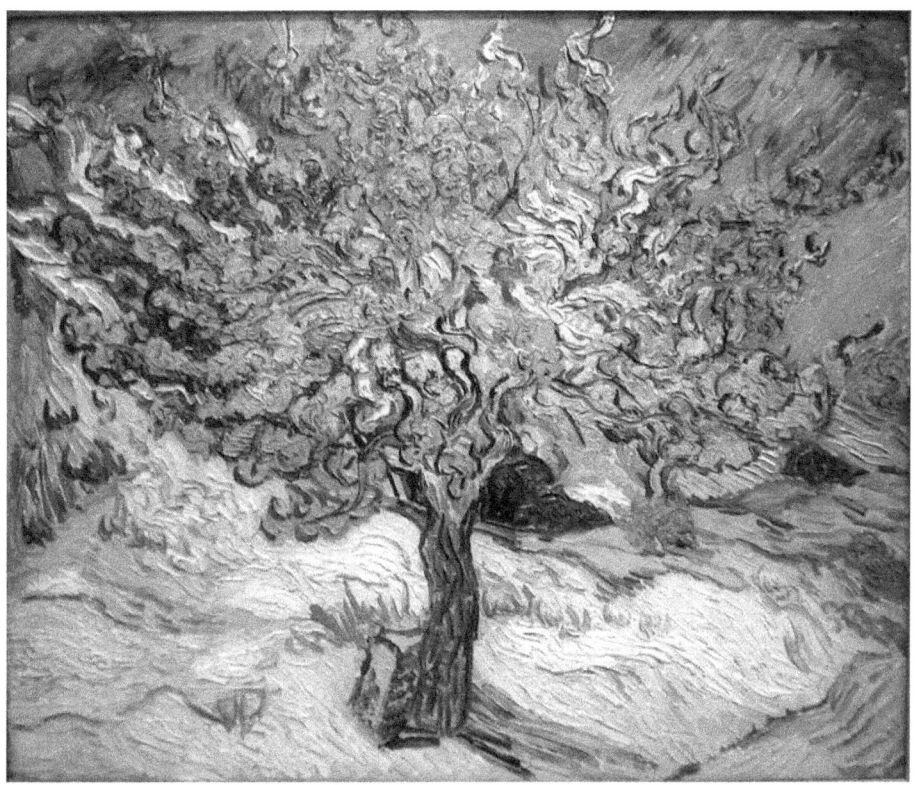

The subject matter of this portrait is a gorgeous mulberry tree that sat within the garden walls of the Saint Paul Asylum in Saint-Remy, France. Earless by this time while fighting bouts of on and off again paranoia van Gogh painted this masterpiece while having the realization that he was not at all an oddity as he witnessed all the other men and women at the asylum who suffered from a similar state of mental illness, which at the time was looked down upon by society as though the suffer was somehow at fault. Thank goodness much of the civilized world has come a long way. To remind the world that those of us who suffer from mental illness, depression, and anxiety he gifted us a golden-lit mulberry tree set admi a sapphire blue sky as a sign of the humanity that exists in everyone no matter the condition their mind may be in on any given day. And amen to that.

VINCENT VAN GOGH'S DESTROYED BY FIRE

Donkey Cart with Boy and Scheveningen Woman, 1882

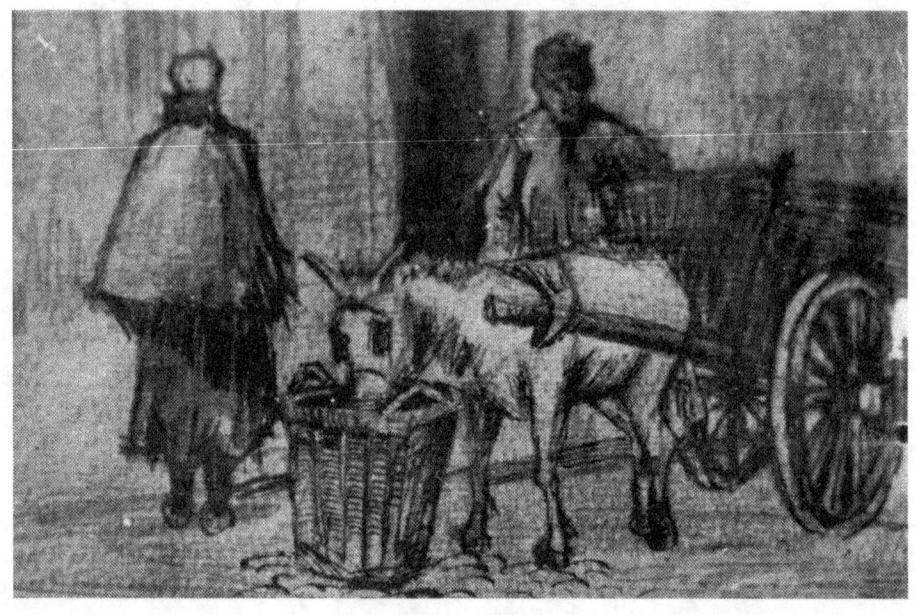

Destroyed by fire in Rotterdam during the Second World War.

Windmill on Montmartre, 1886

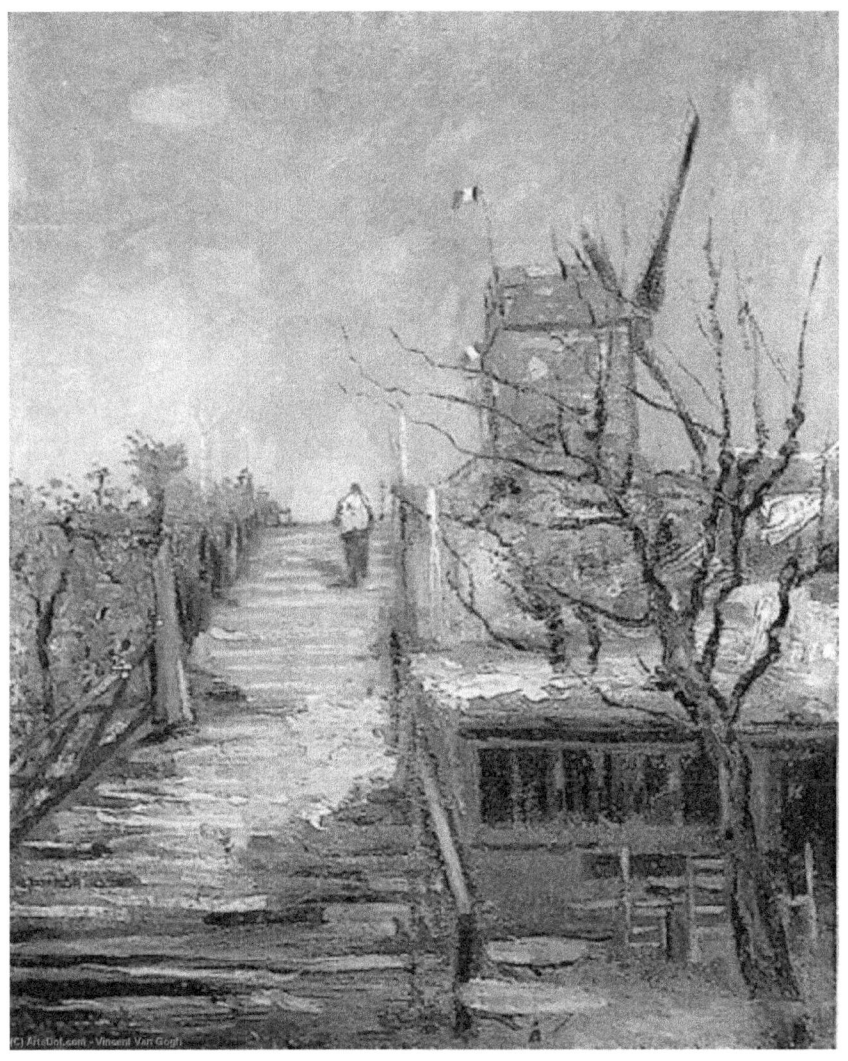

Destroyed by fire in 1967.

The Parsonage Garden at Nuenen with Pond and Figures, 1886

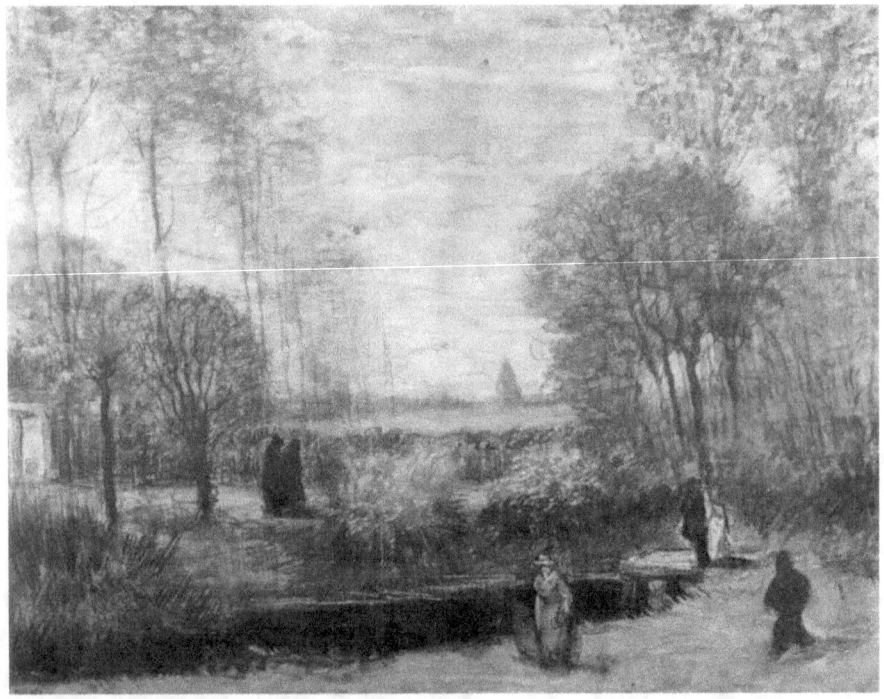

Destroyed by fire in Rotterdam during the Second World War.

Still Life: Vase with Six Sunflowers, 1888

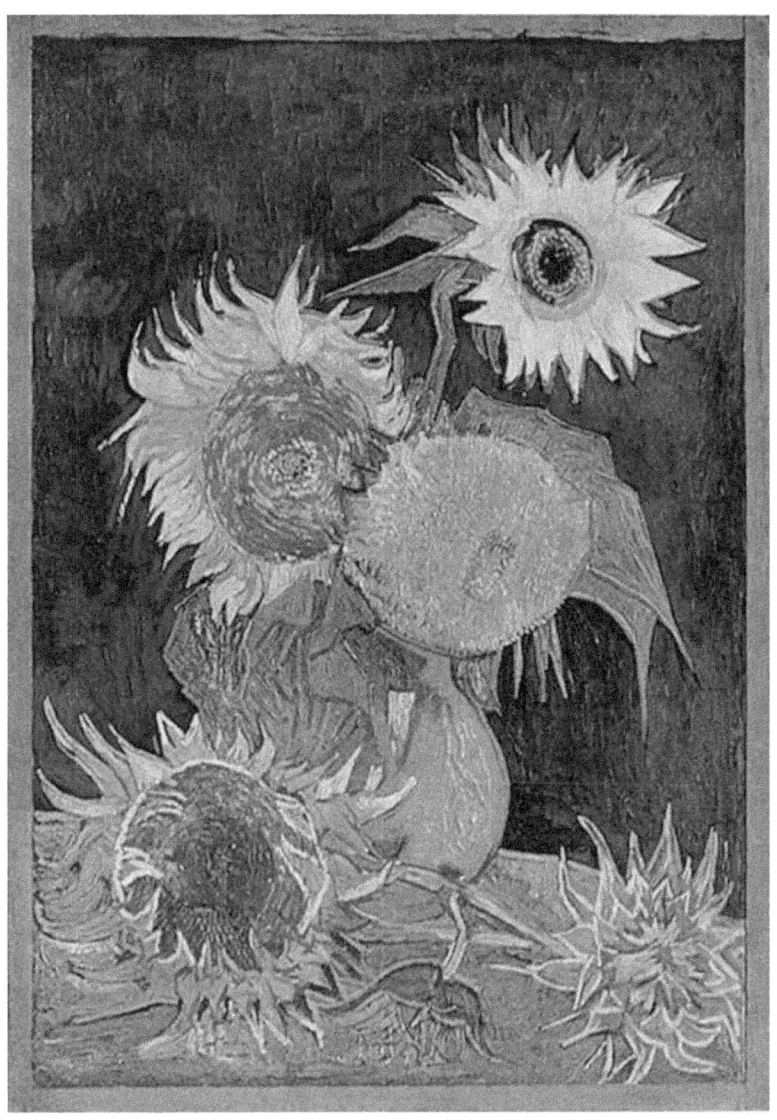

Destroyed by fire in the Second World War.

The Park at Arles with the Entrance Seen through the Trees, 1888

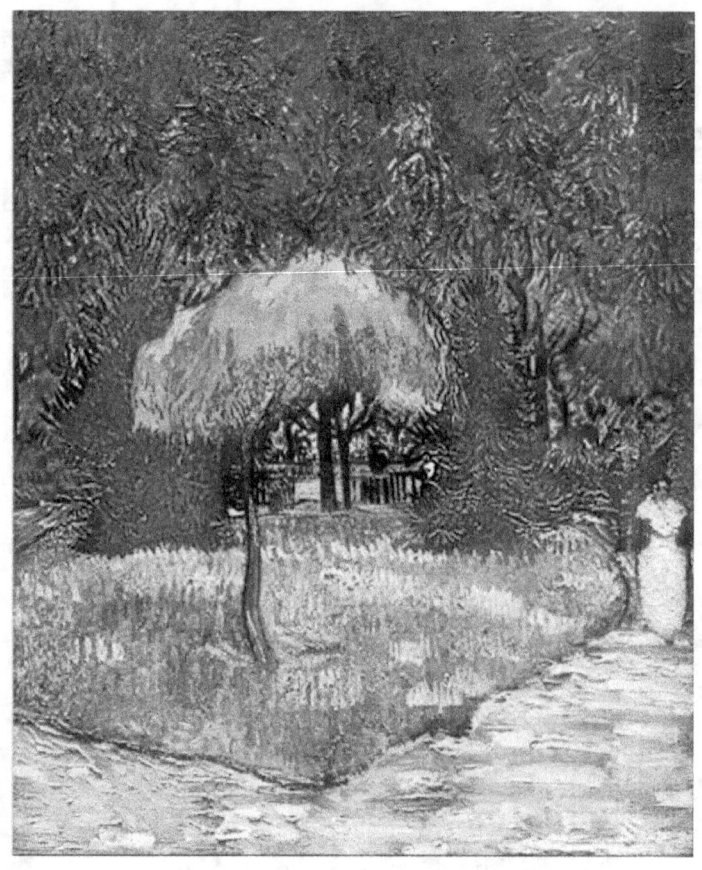

Destroyed by fire in the Second World War.

The painter on the way to Tarascon, July 1888

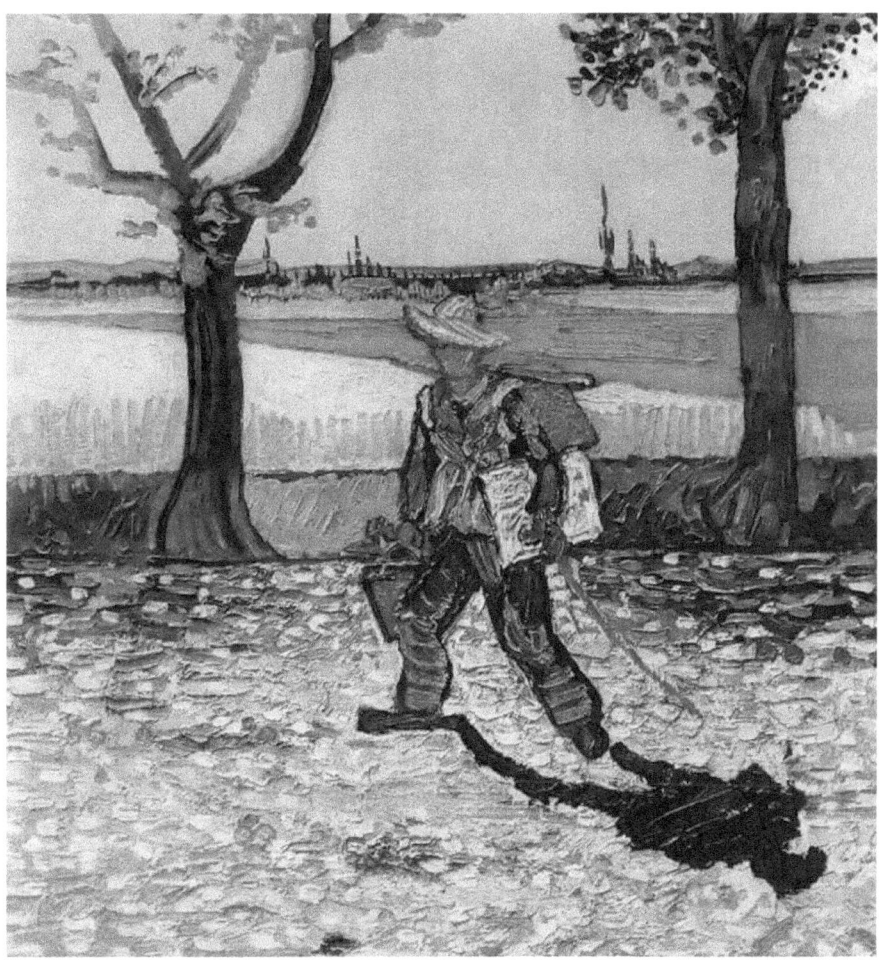

Destroyed by fire in the Second World War; Magdeburg, Germany.

ABOUT THE AUTHOR

A 10-time Pushcart Prize nominee, Jéanpaul Ferro's work has appeared on NPR, Columbia Review, Emerson Review, Connecticut Review, Portland Monthly, Arts & Understanding Magazine, Contemporary American Voices, Saltsburg Review, Hawaii Review, and others. He is also the author of All The Good Promises (Plowman Press, 1994), Becoming X (BlazeVox Books, 2008), You Know Too Much About Flying Saucers (Thumbscrew Press, 2009), Hemispheres (Maverick Duck Press, 2009) Essendo Morti – Being Dead (Goldfish Press, 2009), nominated for the 2010 Griffin Prize in Poetry; and It Rains Diamonds on Saturn (Cyber Press, 2020). He was born in Scituate, Rhode Island in 1967.

NOVELS BY JÉANPAUL FERRO

Torchlight Parade
The Knife of Never Letting Go
The 12 Coins
Suicide Six
Midnight City
The Devil and the Blacksmith
The Final Farewell

NON-FICTION EDITED BY JÉANPAUL FERRO

The Unforgettable Fire: John Brown and the Raid on Harpers Ferry
by W. E. B. Du Bois
Ravished Armenia: The Brutal Truth About The Armenian Genocide
by Aurora Mardiganian